YOUR TOTAL SOLUTION FOR READING

GRADE 1

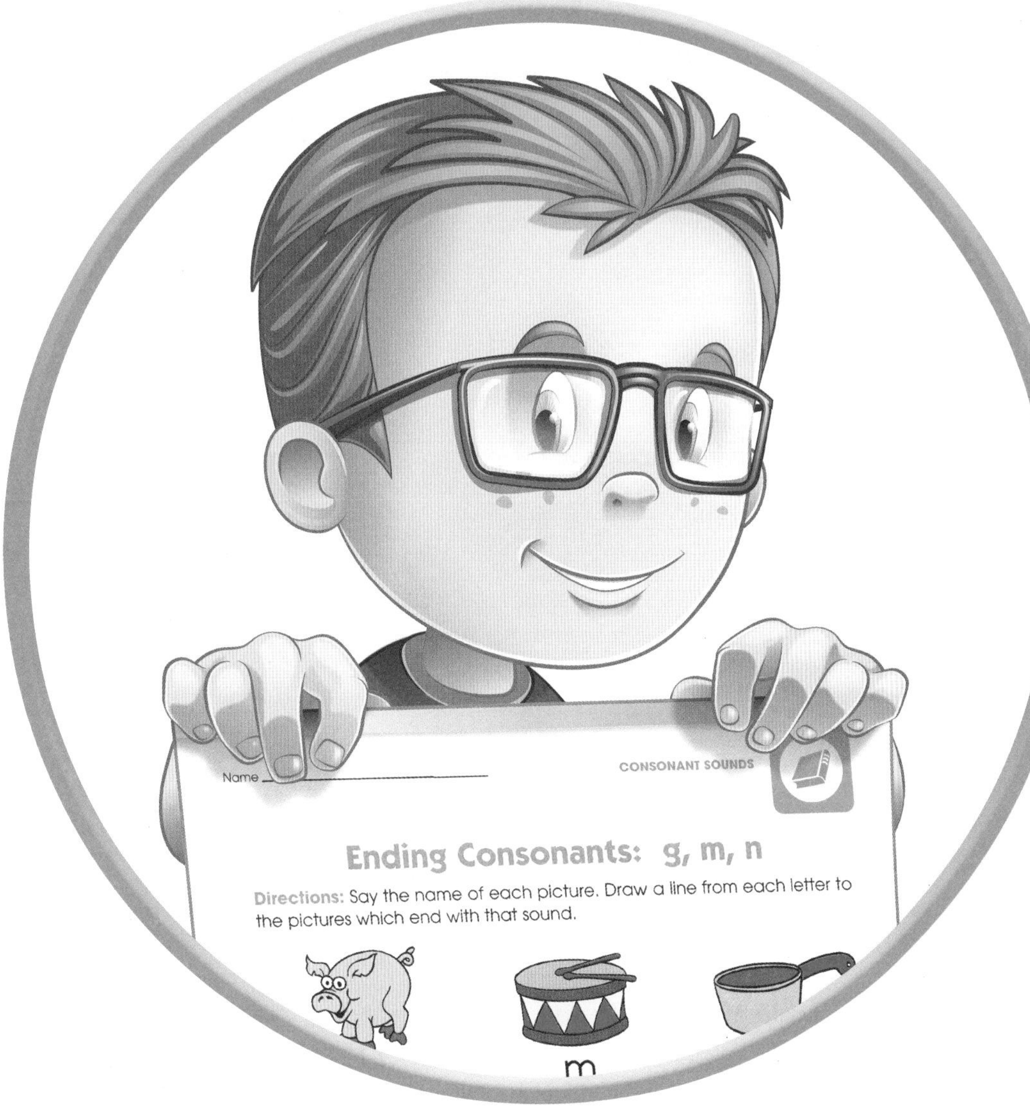

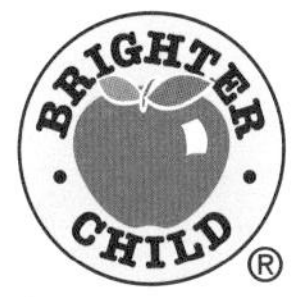

An imprint of Carson-Dellosa Publishing LLC
P.O. Box 35665
Greensboro, NC 27425 USA

Brighter Child®
An imprint of Carson-Dellosa Publishing, LLC
P.O. Box 35665
Greensboro, NC 27425-5665

carsondellosa.com

ISBN 978-1-4838-0714-0

01-097147811

Table of Contents

Name ______________________

Writing the Alphabet

Directions: Trace the letters **Aa-Mm**. Then, practice writing them on the lines below.

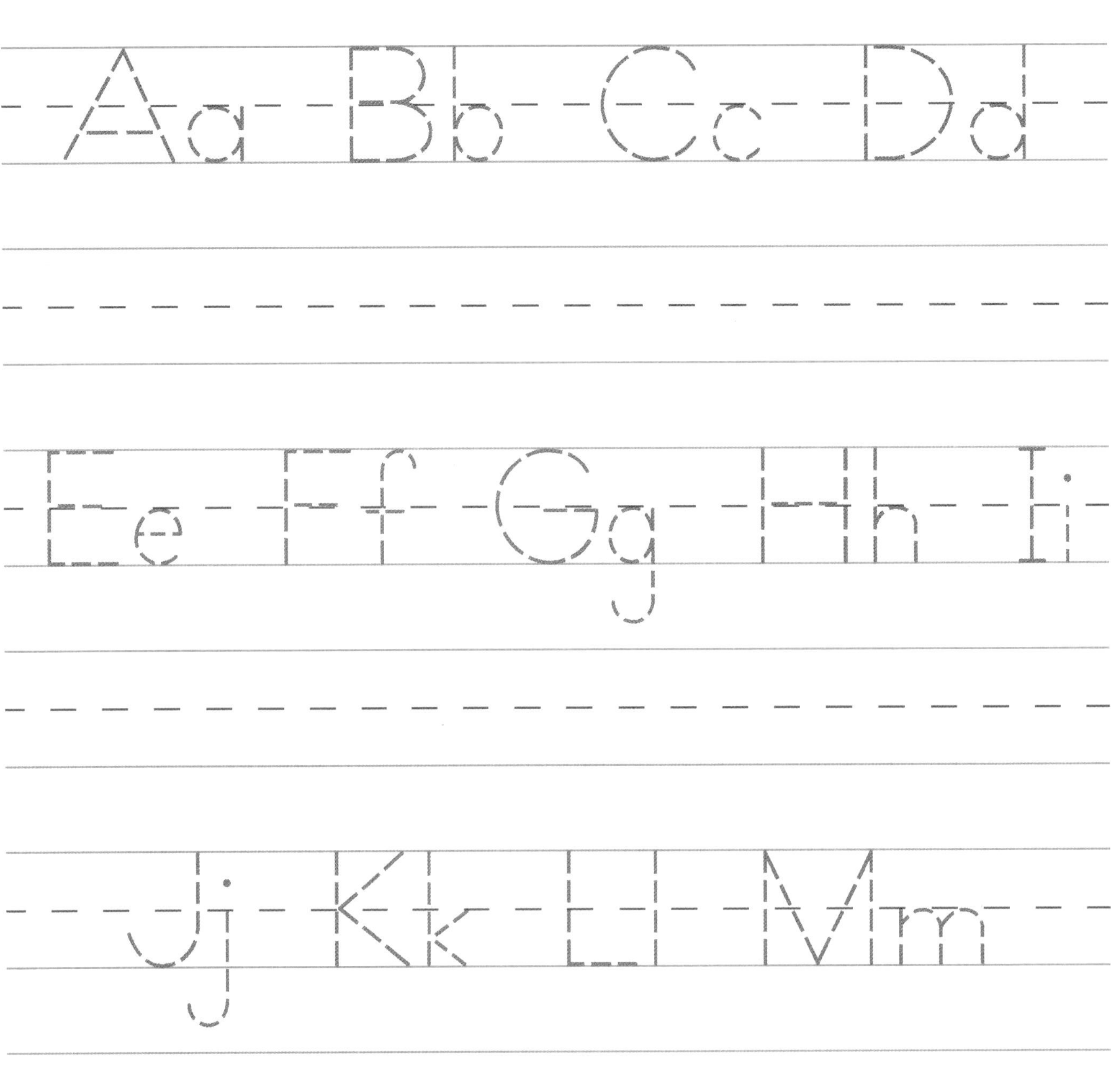

Name ____________________

Writing the Alphabet

Directions: Trace the letters **Nn-Zz**. Then, practice writing them on the lines below.

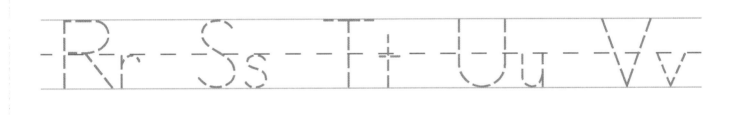

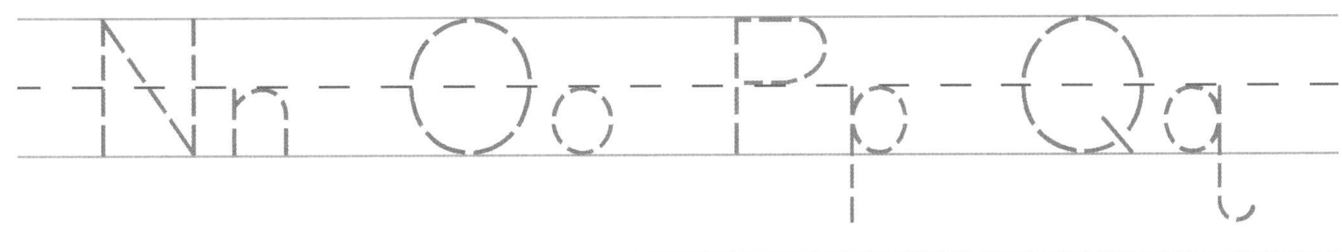

Nn Oo Pp Qq

Rr Ss Tt Uu Vv

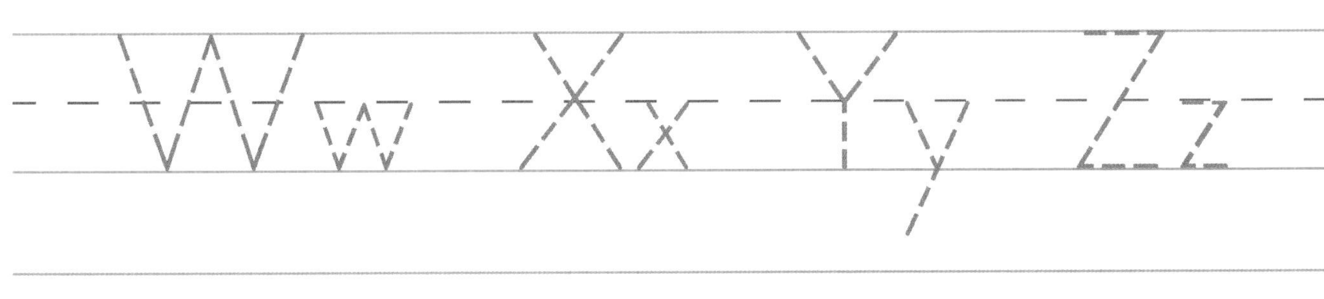

Ww Xx Yy Zz

Name ______________________

Write and Hear Mm

M and **m** are letter partners.

Map begins with the sound of **Mm**.

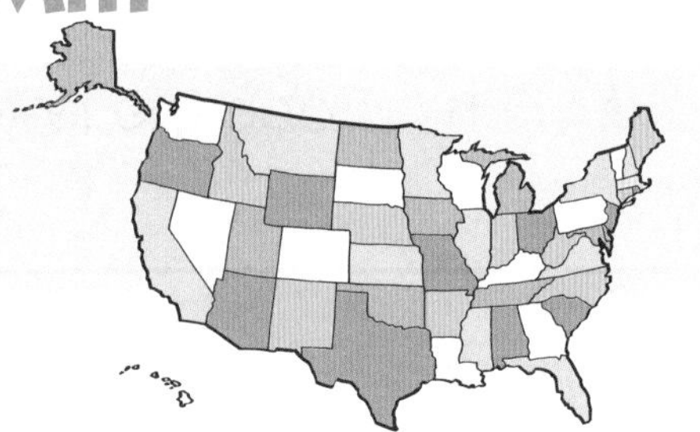

Directions: Trace the letter. Write it on the line.

M _

m _

Directions: Color the pictures whose names begin with the sound of **m**.

Name ______________________

Write and Hear Ss

S and **s** are letter partners.

Sock begins with the sound of **Ss**.

Directions: Trace the letter. Write it on the line.

S

s

Directions: Circle the socks with pictures whose names begin with the sound of **s**.

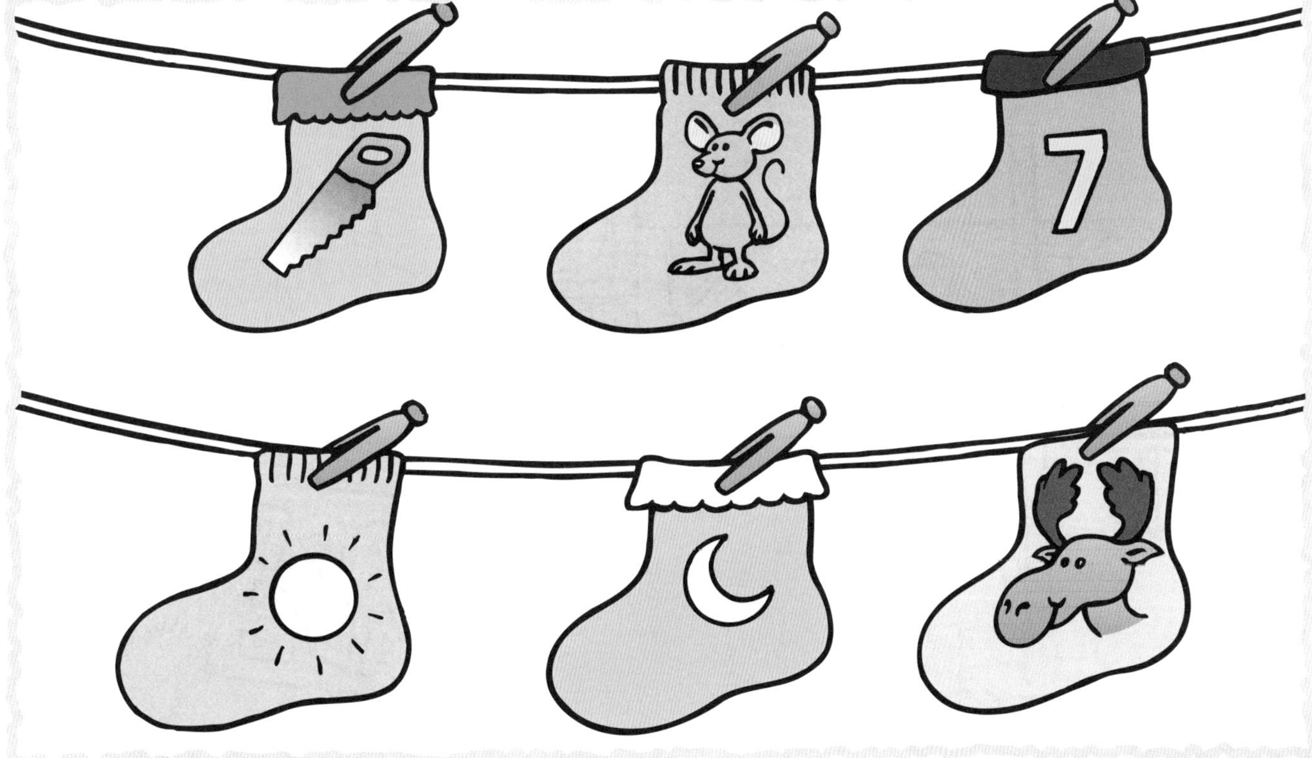

Name ______________________

Write and Hear Tt

T and **t** are letter partners.

Tiger begins with the sound of **Tt**.

Directions: Trace the letter. Write it on the line.

T

t

Directions: Color the pictures whose names begin with the sound of **t**.

Name ______________________

Write and Hear Hh

H and **h** are letter partners.

Hat begins with the sound of **Hh**.

Directions: Trace the letter. Write it on the line.

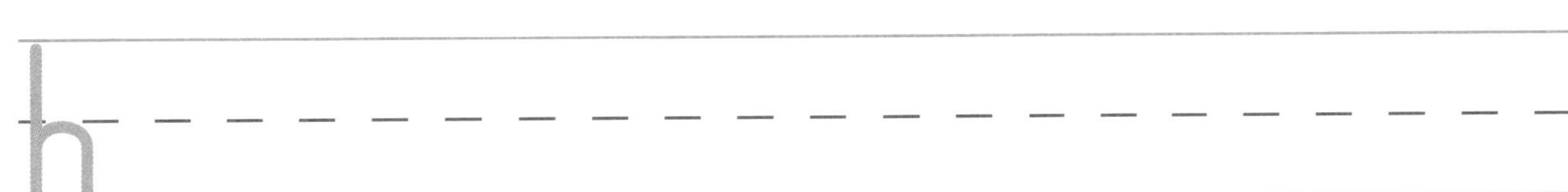

Directions: Play Tic-Tac-Toe. Find three pictures in a row whose names begin with the sound of **h**. Draw a line through them.

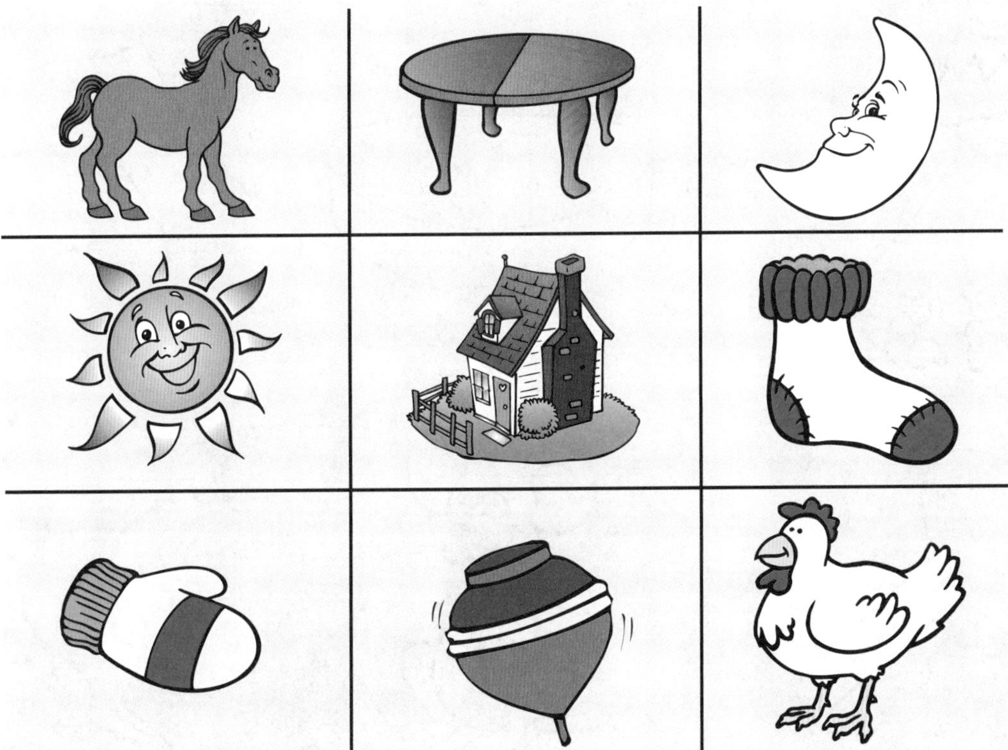

Name ______________________________

Write and Hear Kk

K and **k** are letter partners.

Kitten begins with the sound of **Kk**.

Directions: Trace the letter. Write it on the line.

K

k

Directions: Color the pictures whose names begin with the sound of **k**.

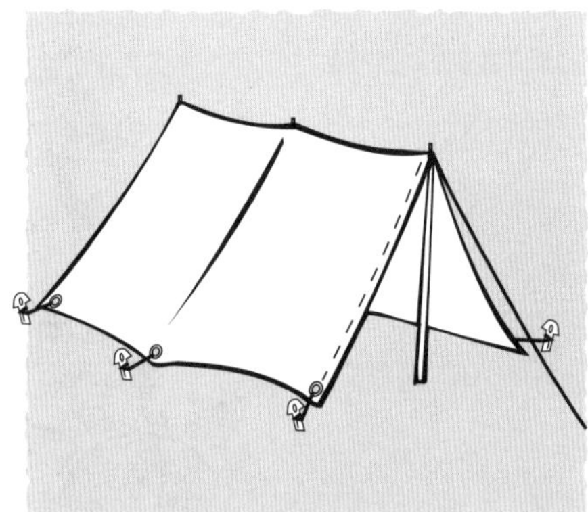

Name ______________________________

Write and Hear Bb

B and **b** are letter partners.

Ball begins with the sound of **Bb**.

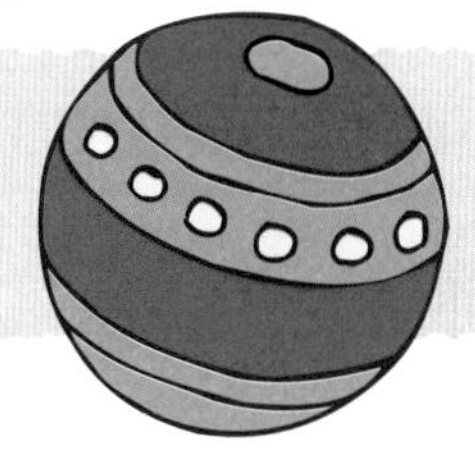

Directions: Trace the letter. Write it on the line.

B

b

Directions: Color the bow if the name of the picture on the box begins with the sound of **b**.

Name ______________________

Write and Hear Ff

F and **f** are letter partners.

Fox begins with the sound of **Ff**.

Directions: Trace the letter. Write it on the line.

F _

f _

Directions: Help the farmer find the fox. Draw a line through the pictures whose names begin with the sound of **f**.

Name ______________________________

Write and Hear Gg

G and **g** are letter partners.

Goat begins with the sound of **Gg**.

Directions: Trace the letter. Write it on the line.

G

g

Directions: Write **g** if the name of the picture begins with the sound of **g**.

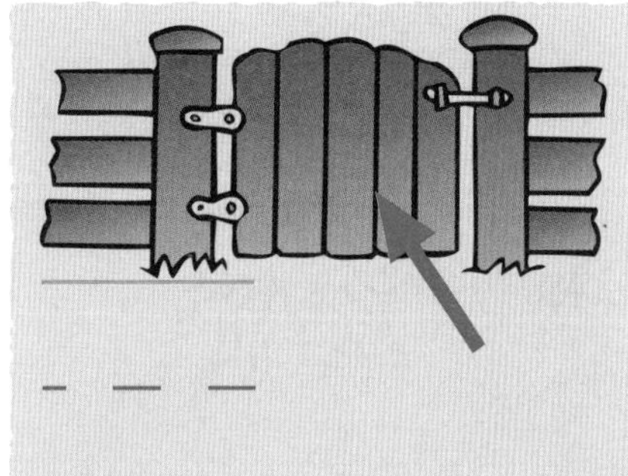

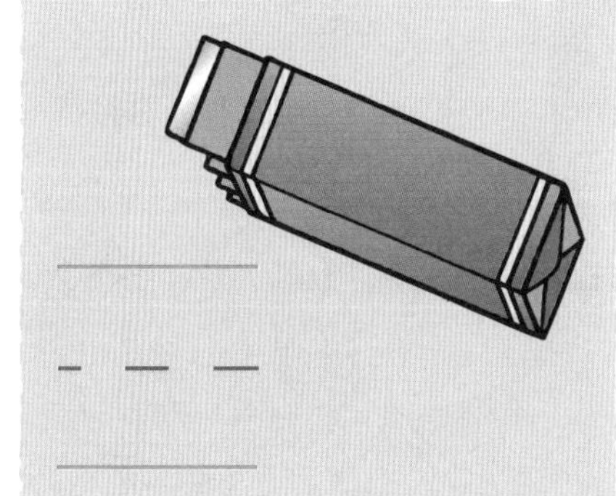

Name ______________________________

Write and Hear Ll

L and **l** are letter partners.

Leaf begins with the sound of **Ll**.

Directions: Trace the letter. Write it on the line.

L

l

Directions: Color the leaves with pictures whose names begin with the sound of **l**.

Name ____________________

Write and Hear Nn

N and **n** are letter partners.

Nest begins with the sound of **Nn**.

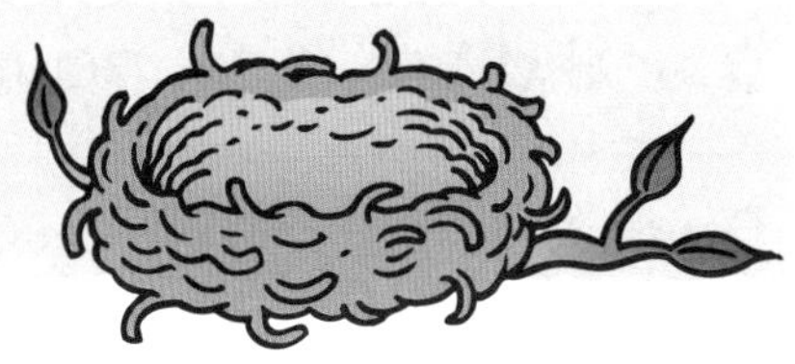

Directions: Trace the letter. Write it on the line.

N

n

Directions: Color the pictures whose names begin with the sound of **n**.

Name ____________________

Write and Hear Dd

D and **d** are letter partners.

Desk begins with the sound of **Dd**.

Directions: Trace the letter. Write it on the line.

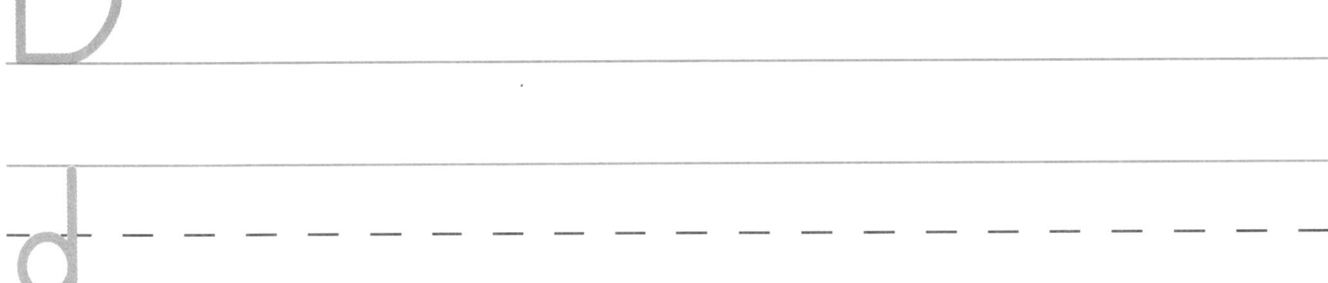

Directions: Color the pictures whose names begin with the sound of **d**.

Name ________________________________

Write and Hear Ww

W and **w** are letter partners.

Window begins with the sound of **Ww**.

Directions: Trace the letter. Write it on the line.

W

w

Directions: Color the curtains if the name of the picture begins with the sound of **w**.

Name ____________________

Write and Hear Cc

C and **c** are letter partners.

Cap begins with the sound of **Cc**.

Directions: Trace the letter. Write it on the line.

C

c

Directions: Play Tic-Tac-Toe. Find three pictures in a row whose names begin with the sound of **c**. Draw a line through them.

10		

Name ______________________

Write and Hear Jj

J and **j** are letter partners.

Jacket begins with the sound of **Jj**.

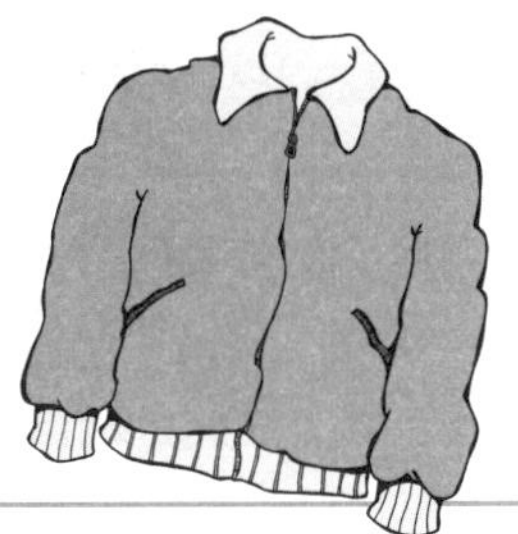

Directions: Trace the letter. Write it on the line.

J

j

Directions: Color the jack-in-the-box if the name of its picture begins with the sound of **j**.

Name ________________________

Write and Hear Rr

R and **r** are letter partners.

Ring begins with the sound of **Rr**.

Directions: Trace the letter. Write it on the line.

R

r

Directions: Write **r** on the line if the name of the picture begins with the sound of **r**.

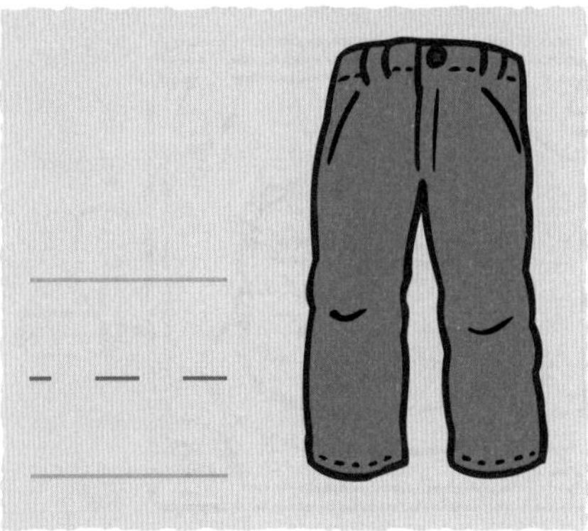

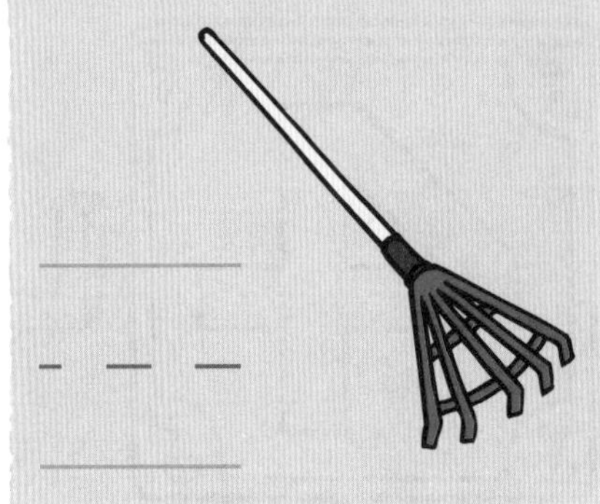

Name ____________________

Write and Hear Pp

P and **p** are letter partners.

Pen begins with the sound of **Pp**.

Directions: Trace the letter. Write it on the line.

P

p

Directions: Color the pictures whose names begin with the sound of **p**.

Name ____________________

Write and Hear Vv

V and **v** are letter partners.

Vase begins with the sound of **Vv**.

Directions: Trace the letter. Write it on the line.

V

v

Directions: Trace the vases with pictures whose names begin with the sound of **v**. Use a crayon.

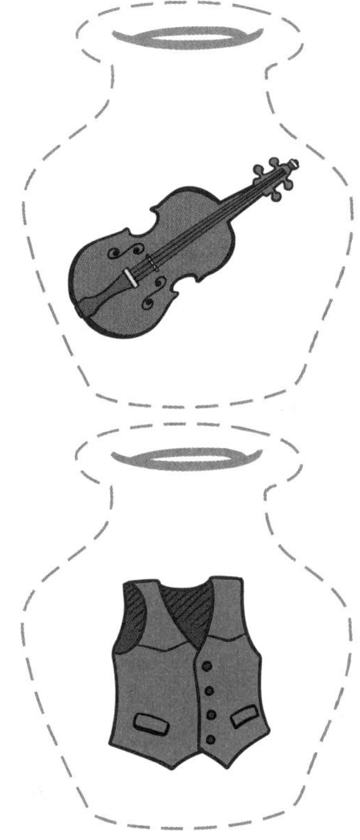

Name ____________________

Write and Hear Yy

Y and **y** are letter partners.

Yellow begins with the sound of **Yy**.

Directions: Trace the letter. Write it on the line.

Y

y

Directions: Play Tic-Tac-Toe. Find three pictures in a row whose names begin with the sound of **y**. Draw a line through them.

Name ______________________

Write and Hear Zz

Z and **z** are letter partners.

Zero begins with the sound of **Zz**.

Directions: Trace the letter. Write it on the line.

Z

z

Directions: Help the zebra find the zoo. Connect all the pictures whose names begin with the sound of **z** from the zebra to the zoo.

Name ________________________

Write and Hear Qq

Q and **q** are letter partners.

Queen begins with the sound of **Qq**.

Directions: Trace the letter. Write it on the line.

Q

q

Directions: Write **q** on the line if the name in the picture begins with the sound of **q**.

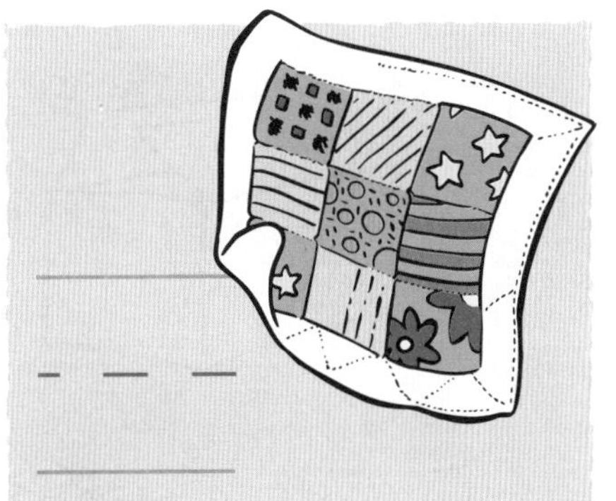

Name ____________________

Write and Hear Xx

X and **x** are letter partners.

Box ends with the sound of **Xx**.

Directions: Trace the letter. Write it on the line.

X

x

Directions: Look at the letter at the end of the row. Then, color the pictures whose names end with the sound of that letter. Circle the pictures whose names **end** with **x**.

Name ______________________________

How Do I Begin?

Directions: Say the name of each picture. Write the beginning sound for each picture.

_____ at

_____ oat

_____ ite

_____ am

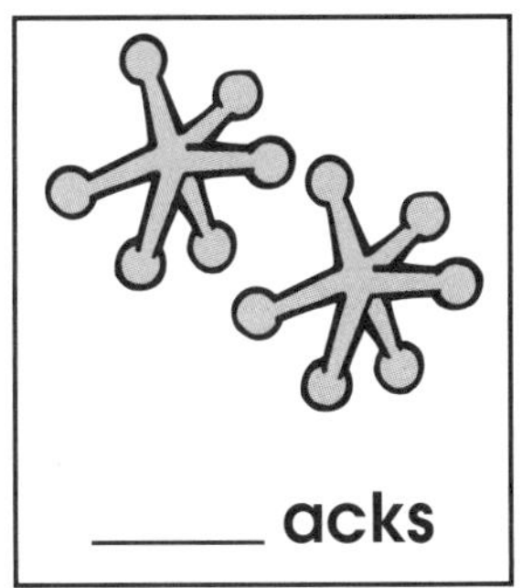

_____ acks

_____ ate

_____ ey

_____ appy

Directions: Write each word next to its beginning sound.

g _ _ _ _ _ _ _ _ _

g _ _ _ _ _ _ _ _ _

h _ _ _ _ _ _ _ _ _

h _ _ _ _ _ _ _ _ _

j _ _ _ _ _ _ _ _ _

j _ _ _ _ _ _ _ _ _

k _ _ _ _ _ _ _ _ _

k _ _ _ _ _ _ _ _ _

Name ______________________

Beginning Consonants: Bb, Cc, Dd, Ff

Beginning consonants are the sounds that come at the beginning of words. Consonants are the letters **b**, **c**, **d**, **f**, **g**, **h**, **j**, **k**, **l**, **m**, **n**, **p**, **q**, **r**, **s**, **t**, **v**, **w**, **x**, **y**, and **z**.

Directions: Say the name of each letter. Say the sound each letter makes. Circle the letters that make the beginning sound for each picture.

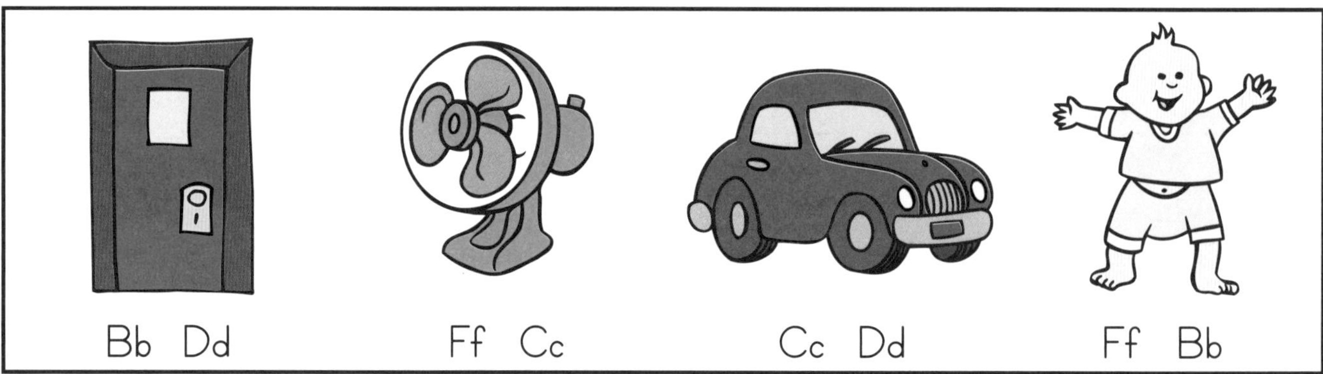

Name ______________________

Beginning Consonants: Gg, Hh, Jj, Kk

Directions: Say the name of each letter. Say the sound each letter makes. Trace the letter pair that makes the beginning sound in each picture.

Gg Hh Jj Kk

Kk Hh

Gg Kk

Gg Hh

Jj Gg

Name ___________________________

Beginning Consonants: Ll, Mm, Nn, Pp

Directions: Say the name of each letter. Say the sound each letter makes. Trace the letters. Then, draw a line from each letter pair to the picture which begins with that sound.

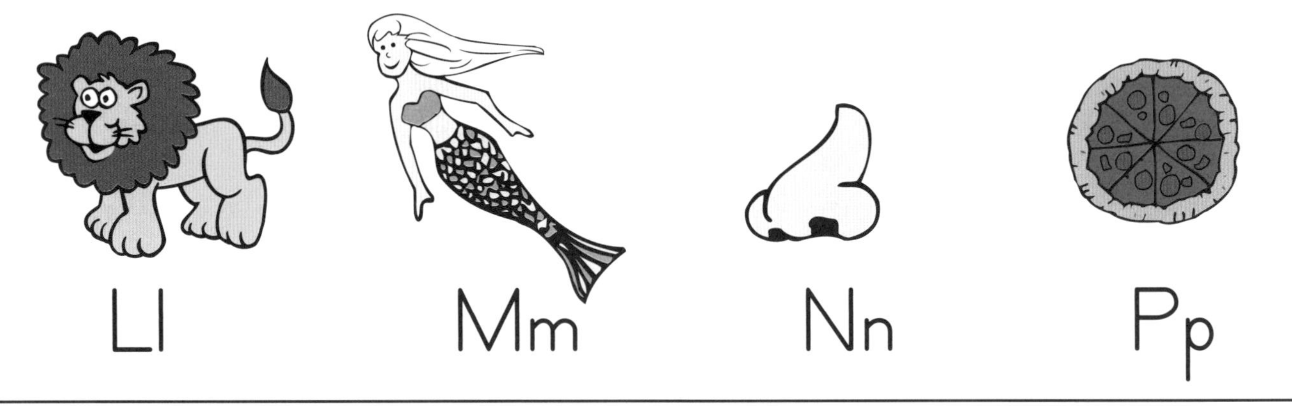

Ll

Mm

Nn

Pp

Name ______________________________

Beginning Consonants: Qq, Rr, Ss, Tt

Directions: Say the name of each letter. Say the sound each letter makes. Trace the letter pair in the boxes. Then, color the picture which begins with that sound.

Qq  Rr  Ss  Tt

Tt

Qq

Rr

Ss

Name ______________________

Beginning Consonants: Vv, Ww, Xx, Yy, Zz

Directions: Say the name of each letter. Say the sound each letter makes. Trace the letters. Then, draw a line from each letter pair to the picture which begins with that sound.

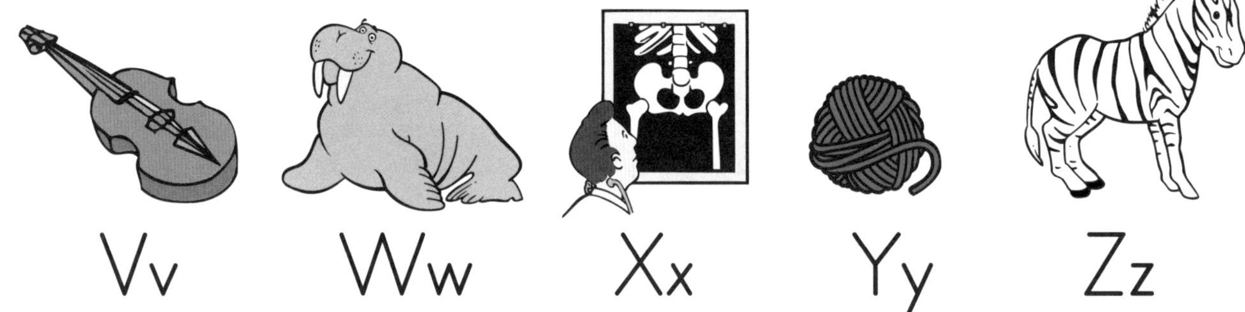

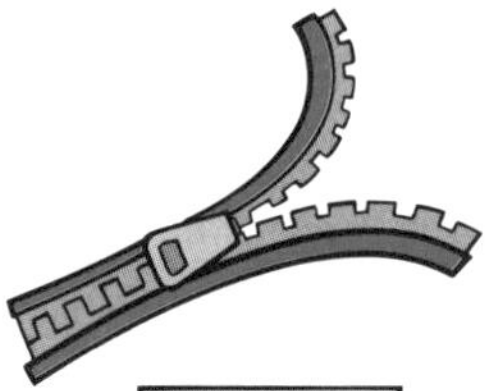

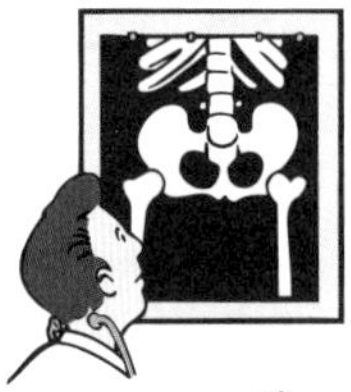

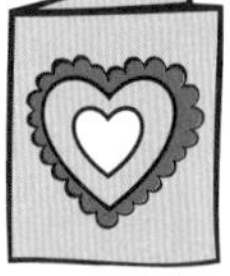

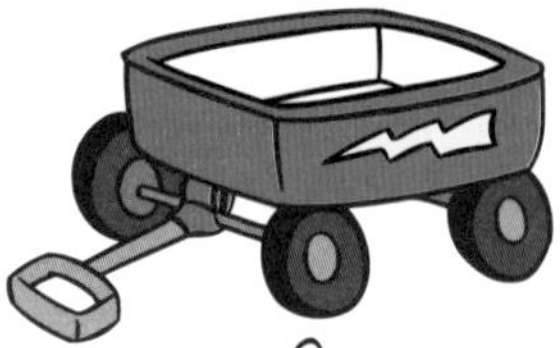

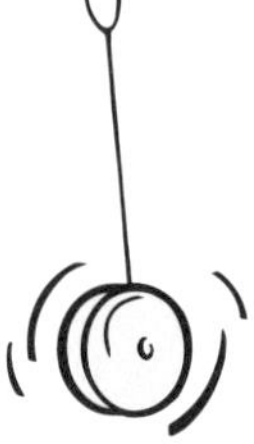

Vv

Ww

Xx

Yy

Zz

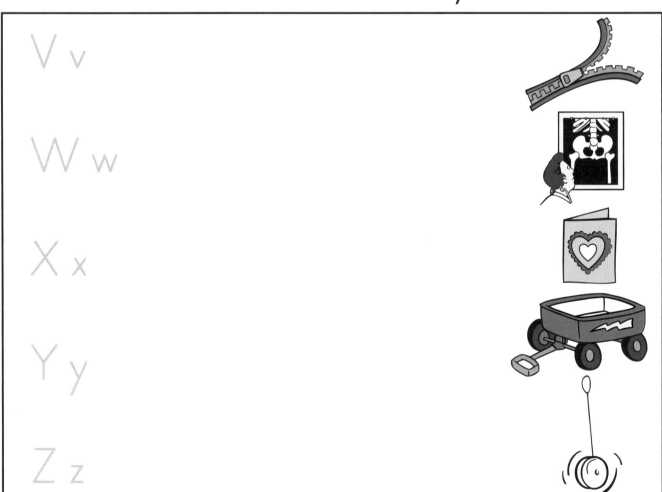

Name ________________________

How Do I Begin Again?

Directions: Say each letter sound. Color the pictures in each row that begin with that sound.

b

c

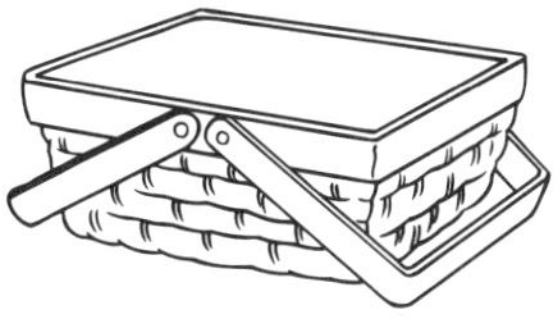

d

f

Directions: Say the name of each picture. Write the beginning sound for each picture.

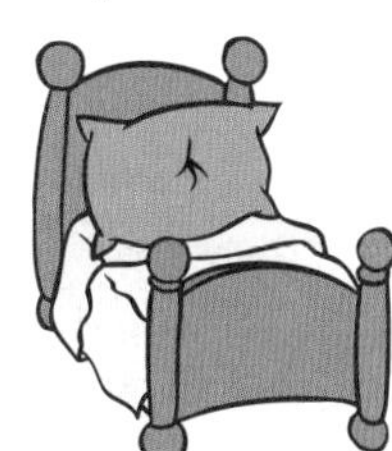

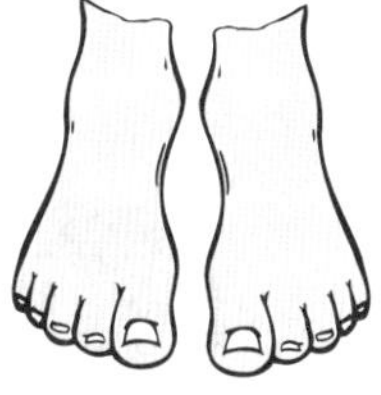

_____ **ed** _____ **og** _____ **eet** _____ **up**

Name ______________________________

Review: Beginning Consonants

Directions: Say each picture name. Circle the letter that stands for the beginning sound.

p m n

v t s

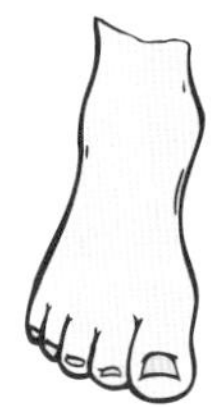

f g p

s c p

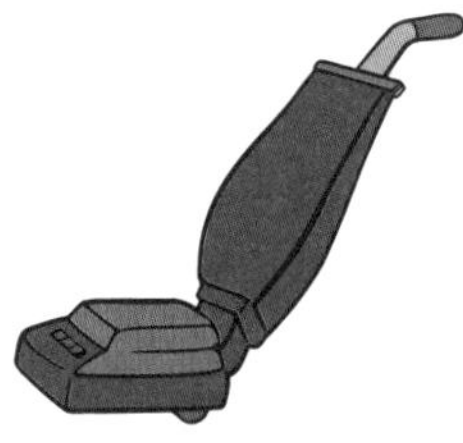

m g v

g p n

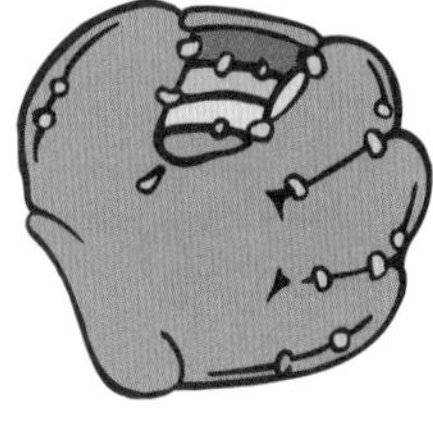

m p n

t g p

s l c

g l c

p b f

v l t

Name ______________________

Review

Directions: Write the letter that makes the beginning sound for each picture.

___ar

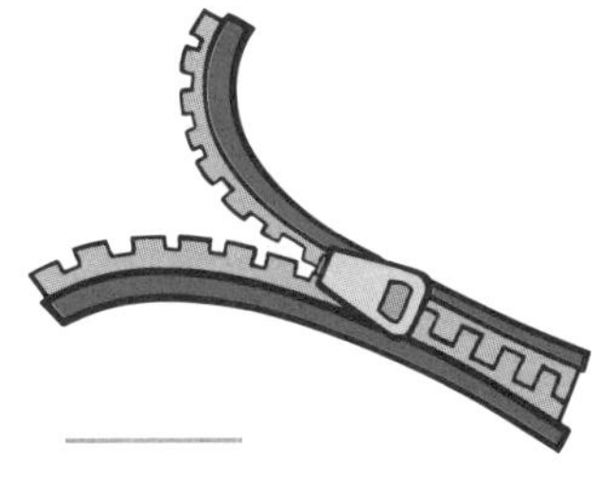

___ipper

___ite

___etter

___oat

___ose

___un

___ouse

___urtle

___lasses

___ar

___og

Name ___________________________

Ending Consonants: b, d, f

Directions: Say the name of each picture. Then, write the letter that makes the ending sound for each picture.

______	______	______
______	______	______
______	______	______
______	______	______

Ending Consonants: g, m, n

Directions: Say the name of each picture. Draw a line from each letter to the pictures which end with that sound.

g

m

n

g

m

n

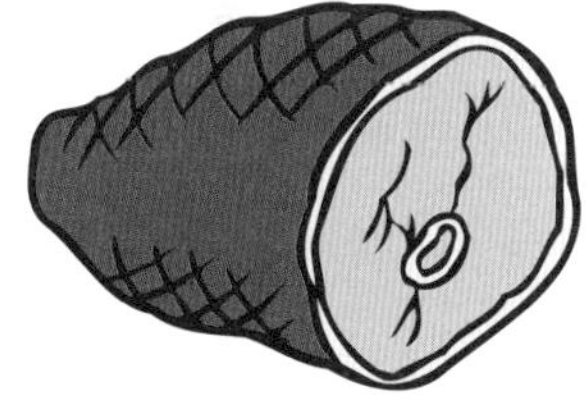

Name ____________________

Ending Consonants: k, l, p

Directions: Trace the letters in each row. Say the name of each picture. Then, color the pictures in each row which end with that sound.

k

l

p

Name ____________________

Ending Consonants: r, s, t, x

Directions: Say the name of each picture. Then, circle the ending sound for each picture.

r s t x

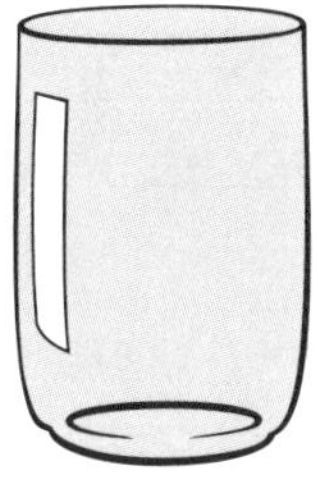

r s t x

r s t x

r s t x

r s t x

r s t x

r s t x

r s t x

Name ______________________

How Does It End?

Ending consonants are the sounds that come at the end of words.

Directions: Write a letter from the box to complete each word.

m	k	b	n	p	r	l	d	g

dru ___

sta ___

be ___

tai ___

bi ___

lo ___

fa ___

mo ___

boo ___

And Finally...

Directions: Say each picture name. Write the ending sound for each picture.

tu ___

pai ___

pa ___

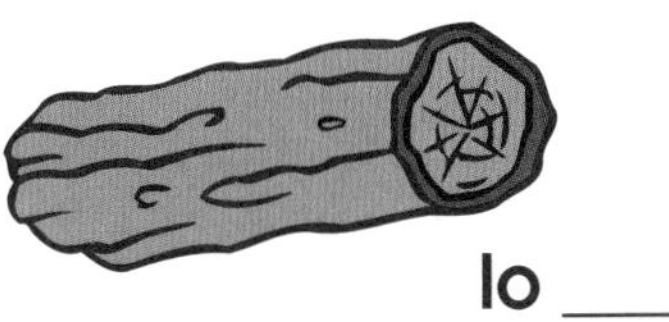

lo ___

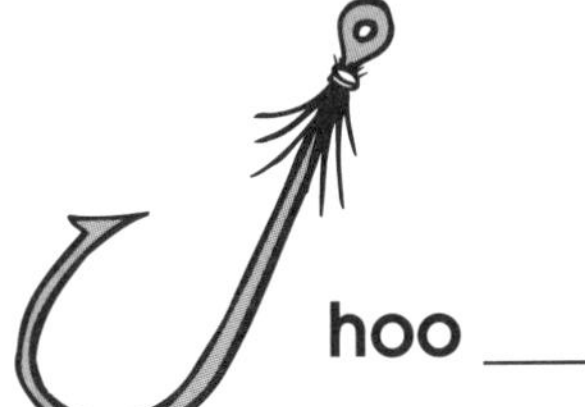

hoo ___

mu ___

boo ___

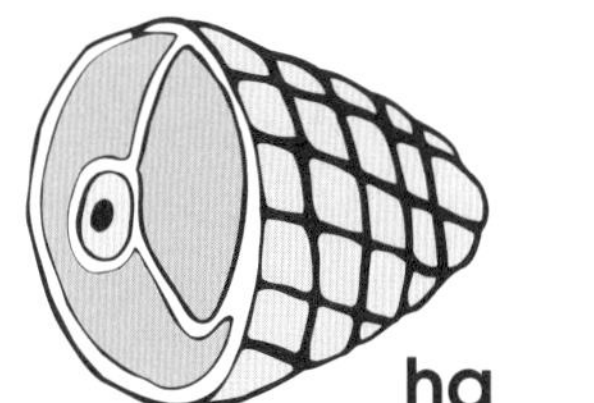

ha ___

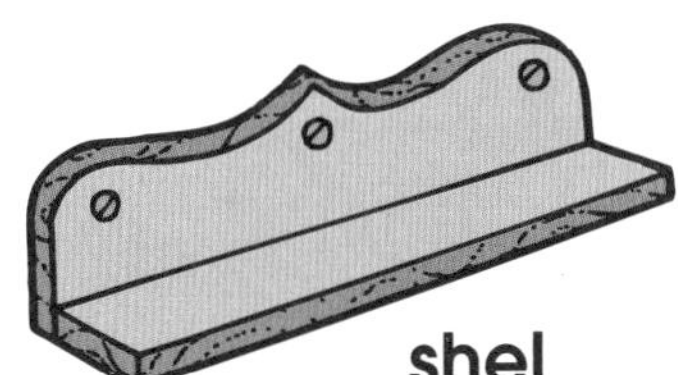

shel ___

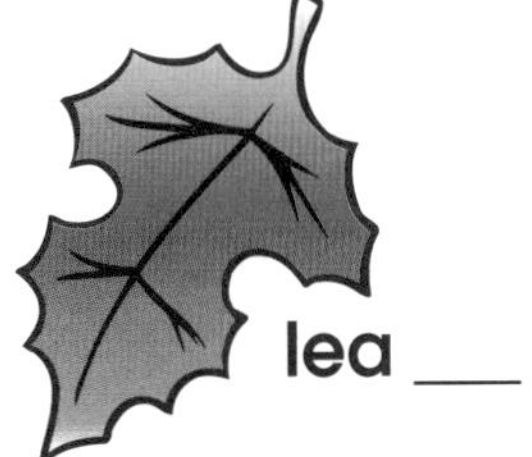

lea ___

cra ___

li ___

gir ___

bea ___

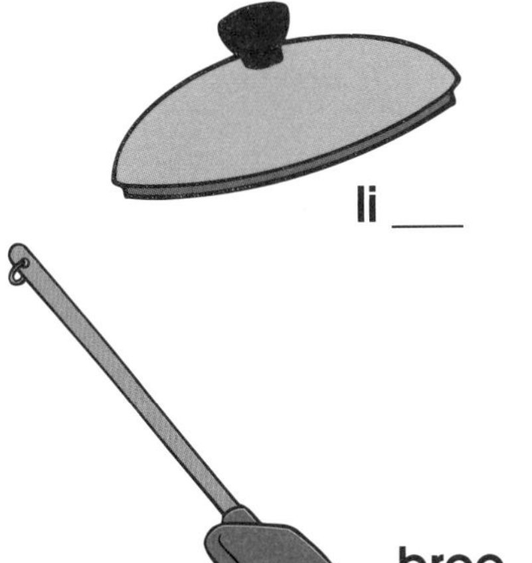

broo ___

Name ____________________

Consonant Review

Directions: One letter is missing in each word. Write the missing letter on the line.

_og
bo_
_un

he_
tu_ip
_op

lo_
lea_
wa_on

Name ______________________________

Consonant Review

Directions: Write all the missing consonants.

_ a _

_ o _

_ i _

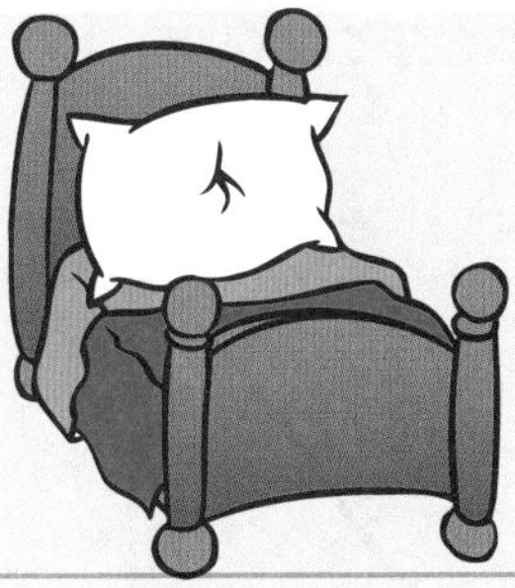

_ e _

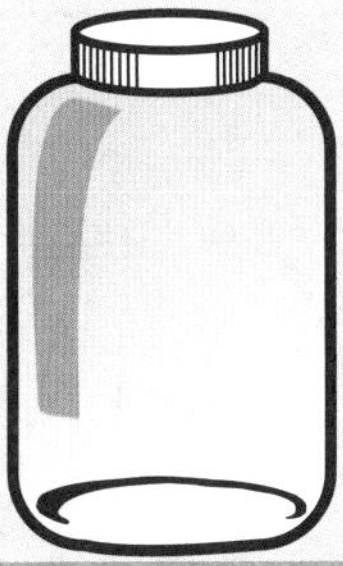

_ a _

_ a _ e _

_ oa _

_ a _

_ a _

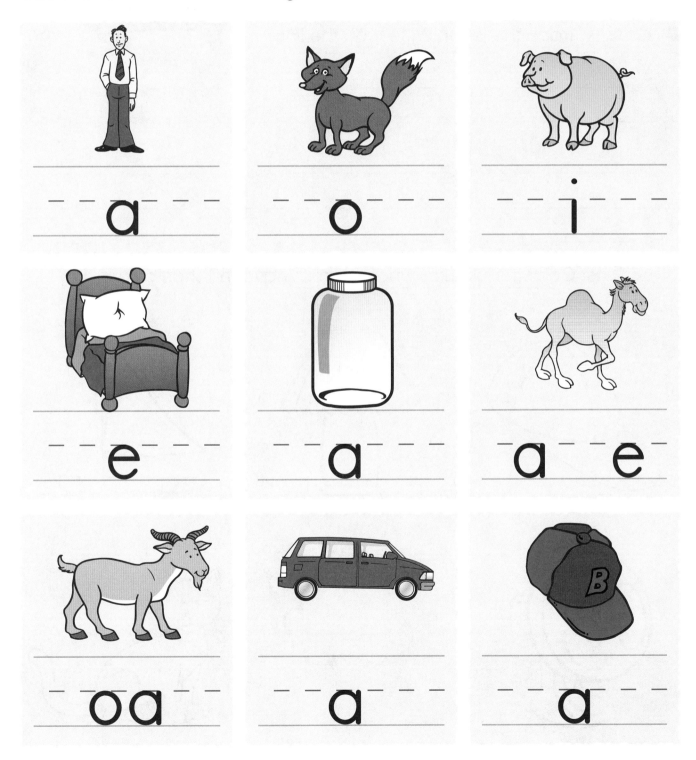

Name ______________________

Meet Short a

Listen for the sound of short **a** in **van**.

Directions: Trace the letter. Write it on the line.

v**a**n

A

a

Directions: Color the pictures whose names have the short **a** sound.

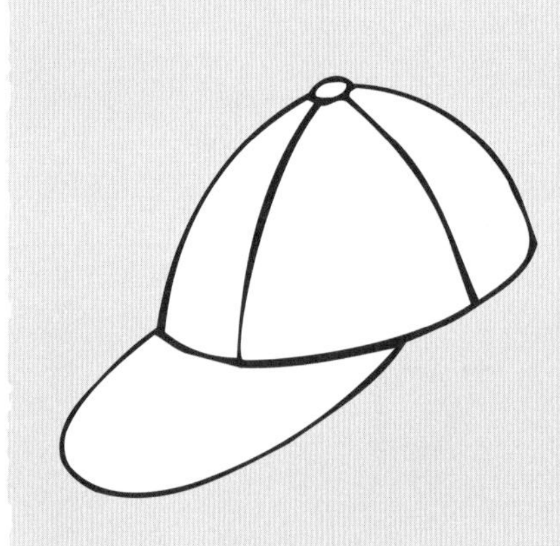

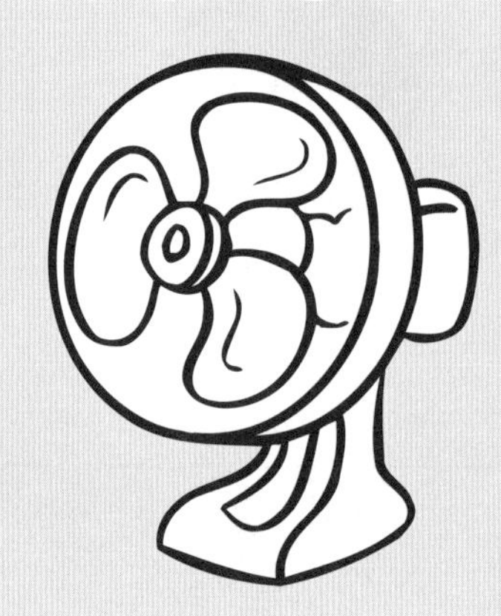

Name ______________________________

Short a Maze

Directions: Help the cat get to the bag. Connect all the pictures whose names have the short **a** sound from the cat to the bag.

Name ____________________

Meet Short i

Listen for the sound of short **i** in **pig**.

pig

Directions: Trace the letter. Write it on the line.

I

i

Directions: Say the name of each picture. Color the trim on the bib if the name has the short **i** sound.

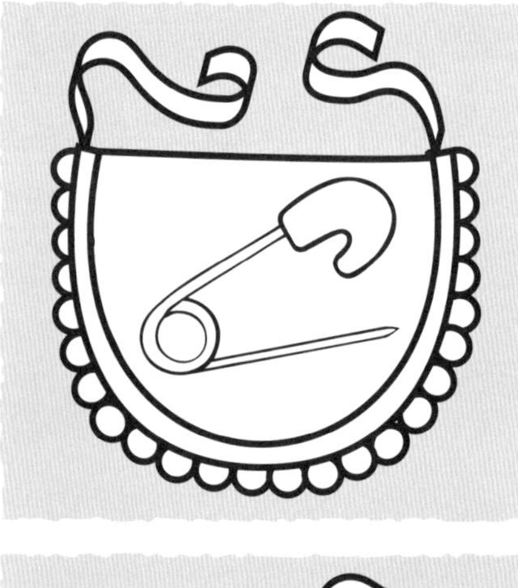

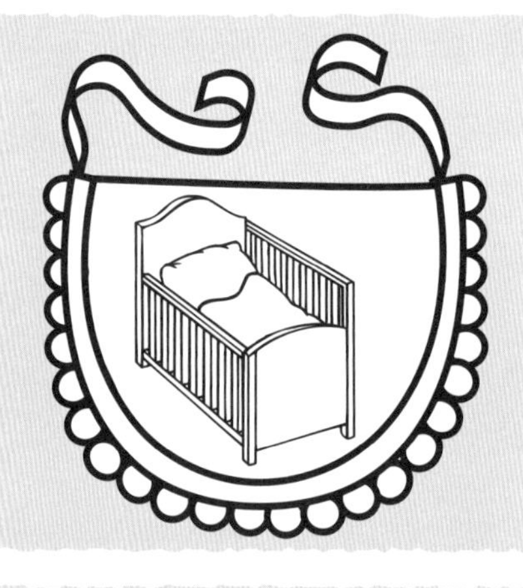

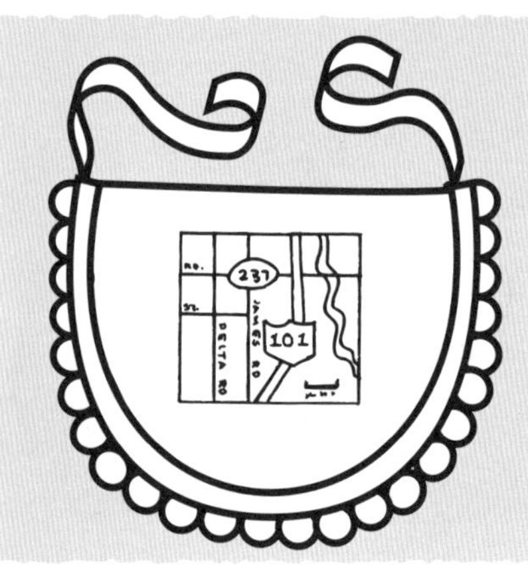

Name ____________________

Read and Color Short i

Directions: Say the name of each picture. Color the pictures whose names have the short **i** sound. The words in the box will give you hints.

milk	**crib**	**bib**
pig	**kitten**	**fish**

Name ______________________

Meet Short u

Listen for the sound of short **u** in **bug**.

Directions: Trace the letter. Write it on the line.

U

u

Directions: Say the name of each picture. Color the sun yellow if you hear the short **u** sound in the name.

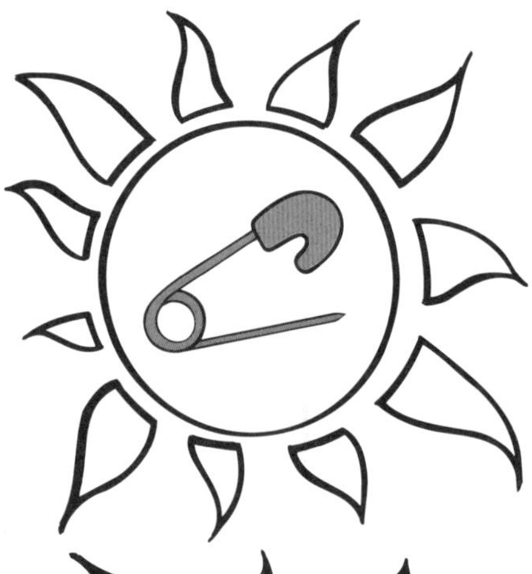

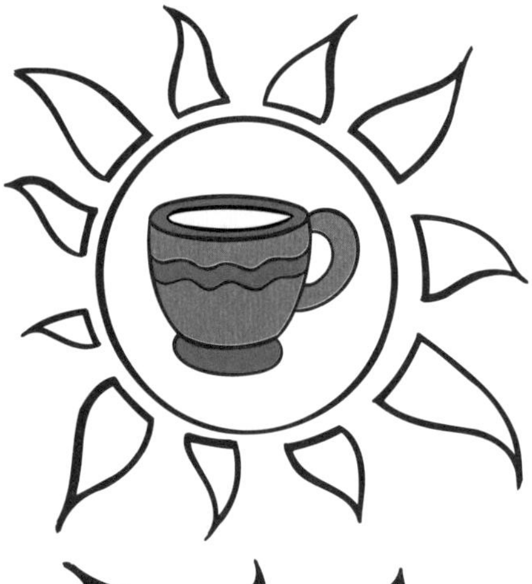

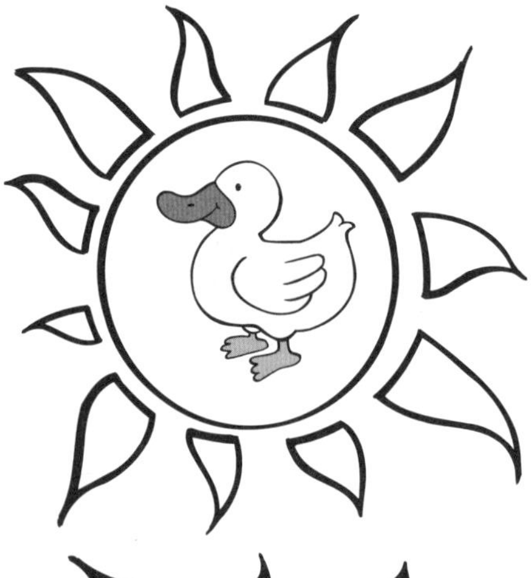

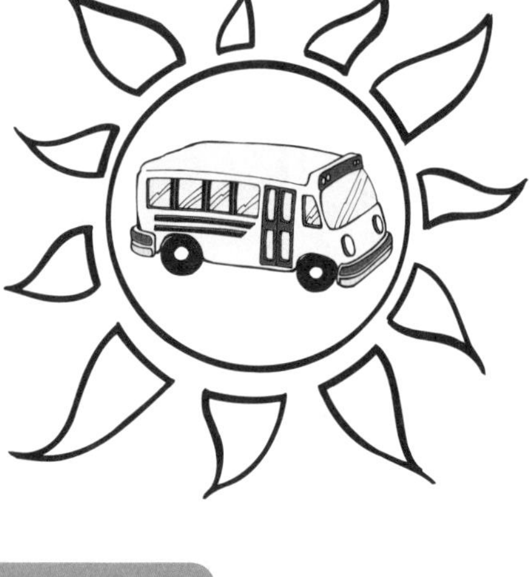

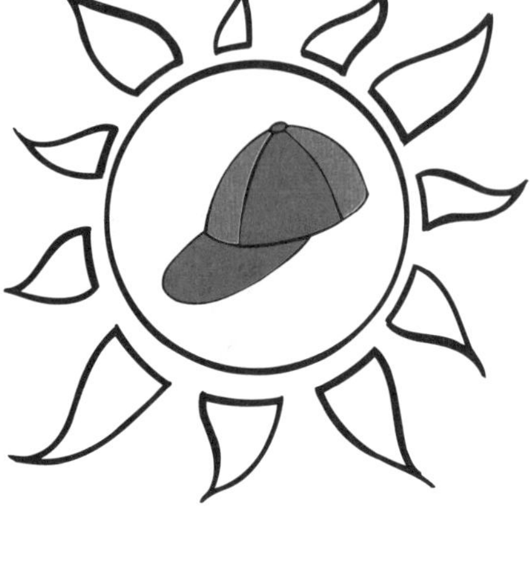

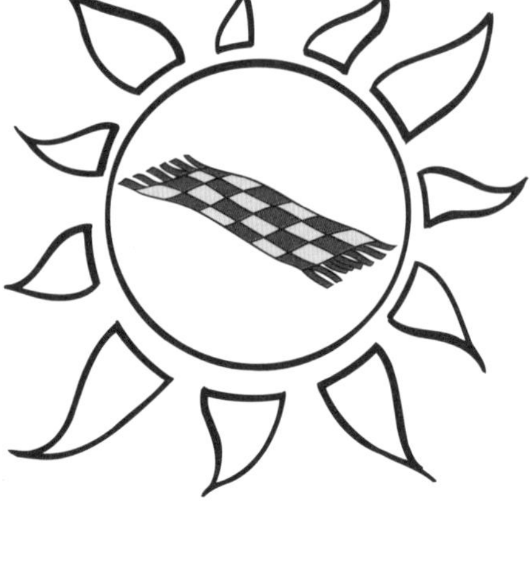

Name ________________________________

Short u Tic-Tac-Toe

Directions: Color the pictures whose names have the short **u** sound. Then, play Tic-Tac-Toe. Draw a line through three colored pictures in a row.

	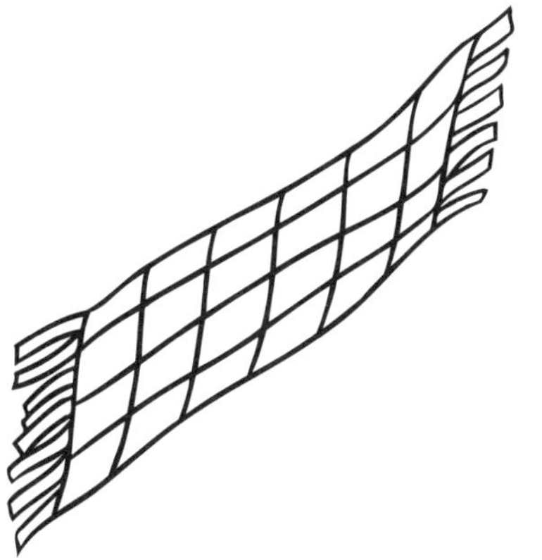	

Name ____________________

Meet Short o

Listen for the sound of short **o** in **fox**.

Directions: Trace the letter. Write it on the line.

Directions: Say the name of each picture. Write **o** under the picture if the name has the short **o** sound.

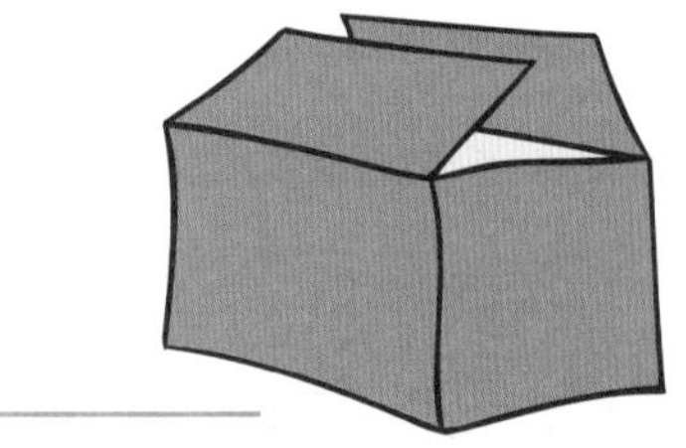

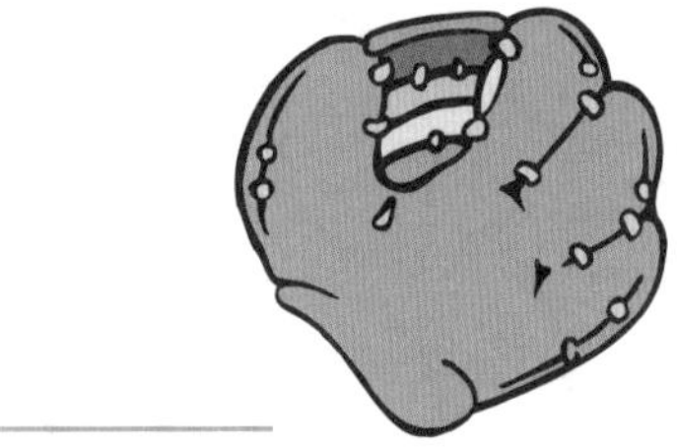

Name ______________________________ **VOWEL SOUNDS**

Find Short o Words

Directions: Draw a line under each picture whose name has the short **o** sound.

Directions: The words that match the underlined pictures above are hidden in this puzzle. Circle the words. They may go **across** or **down**.

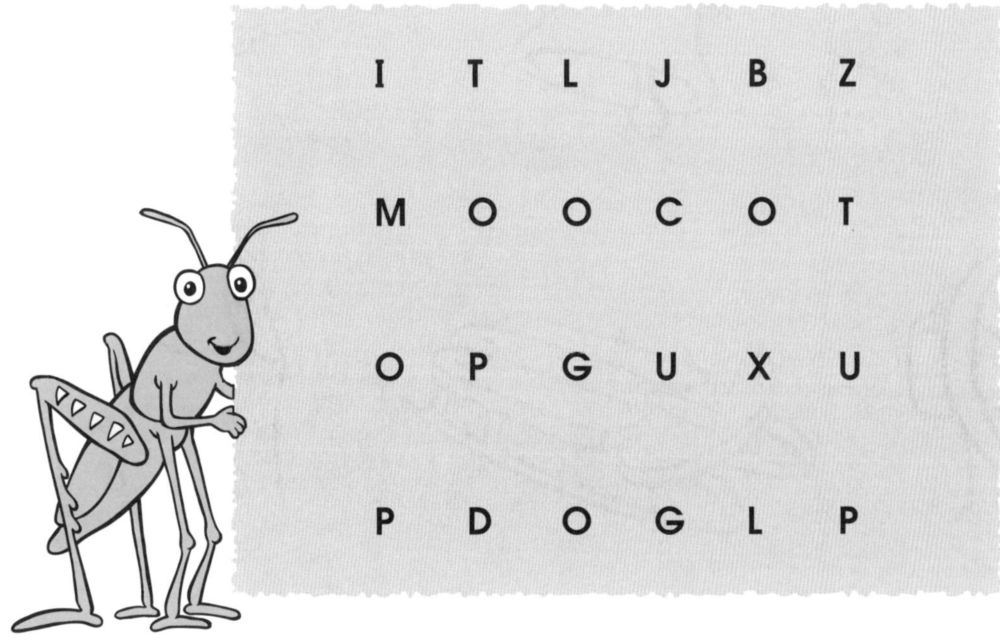

I	T	L	J	B	Z
M	O	O	C	O	T
O	P	G	U	X	U
P	D	O	G	L	P

Name ____________________

Meet Short e

Listen for the sound of short **e** in **hen**.

h**e**n

Directions: Trace the letter. Write it on the line.

E

e

Directions: Color the pictures whose names have the short **e** sound.

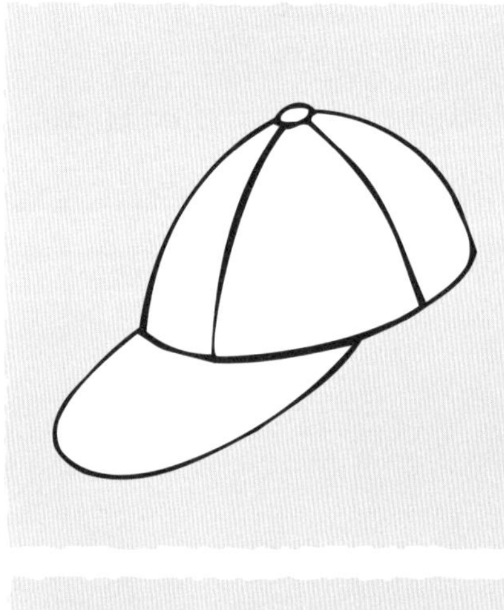

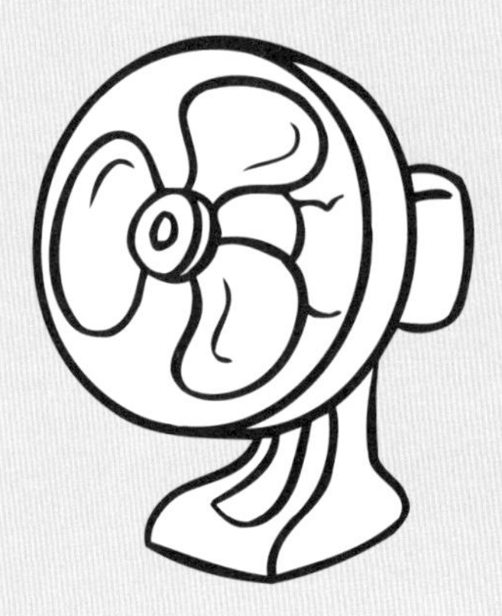

Name ____________________

A Matching Game

Directions: Draw a line to connect each picture with its matching short **e** word.

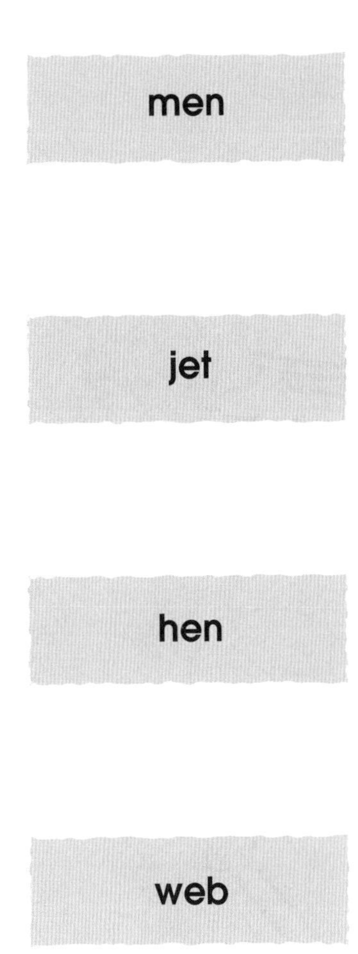

Name ____________________

Meet Long a

Listen for the sound of long **a** in **cake**. Look for **a**_**e**.

Directions: Color the pictures whose names have the long **a** sound.

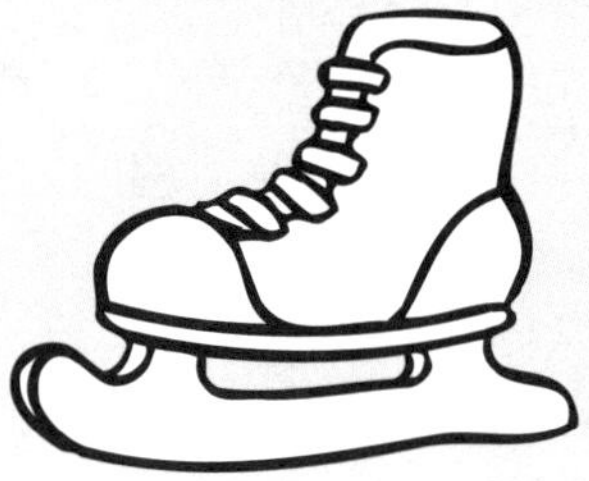

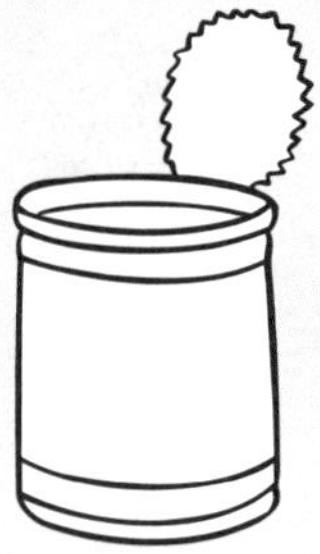

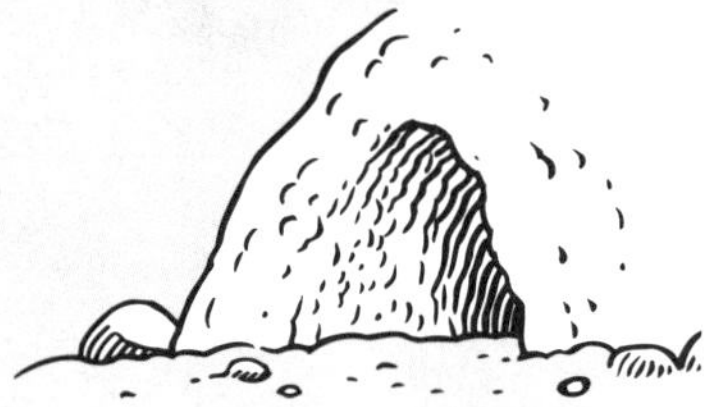

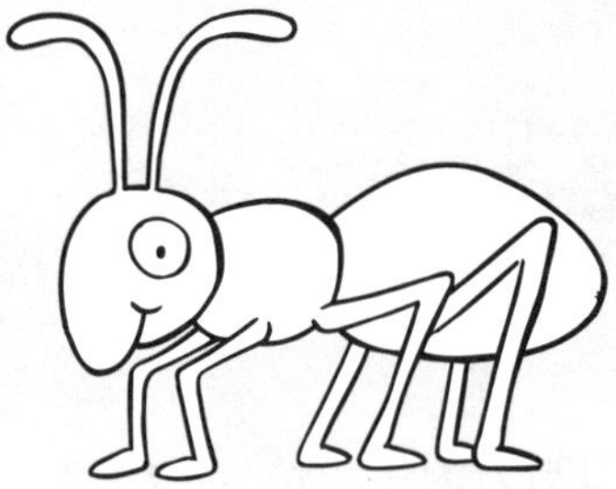

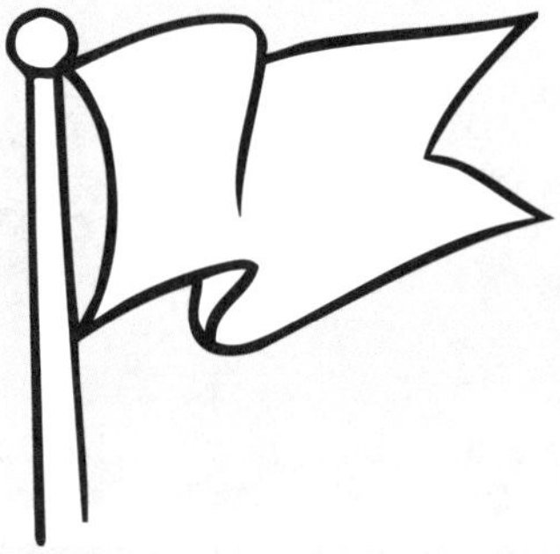

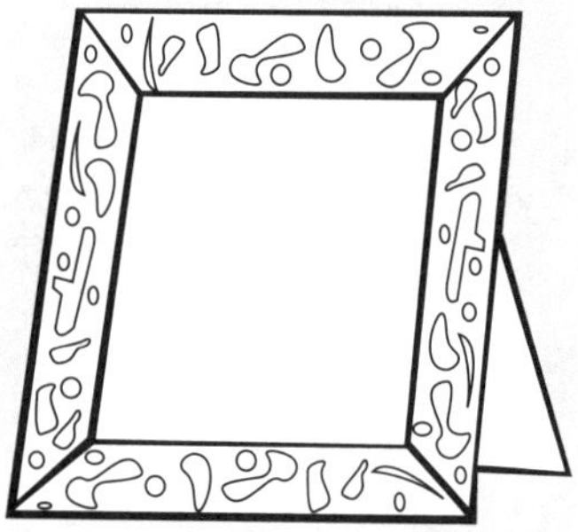

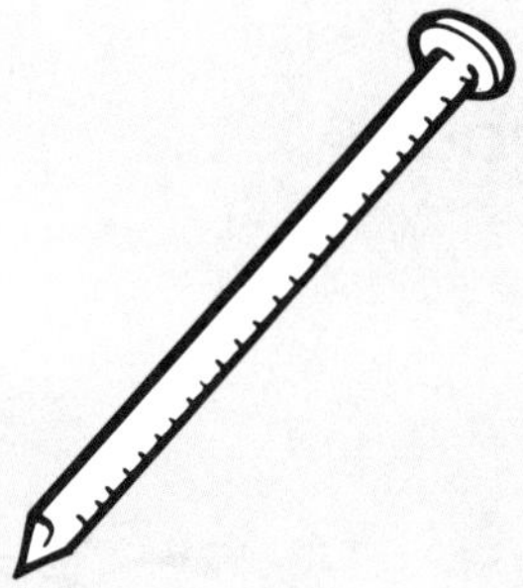

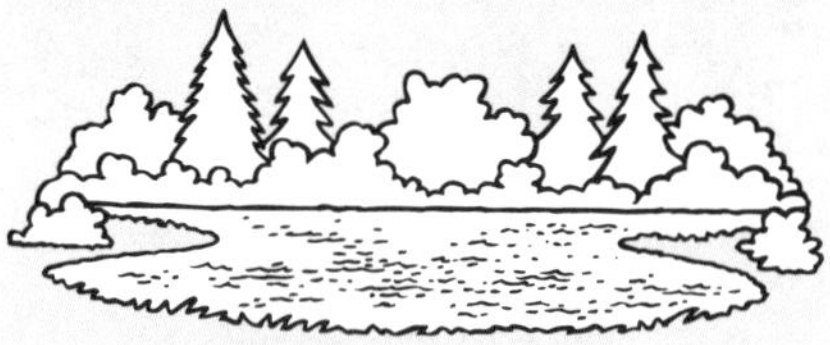

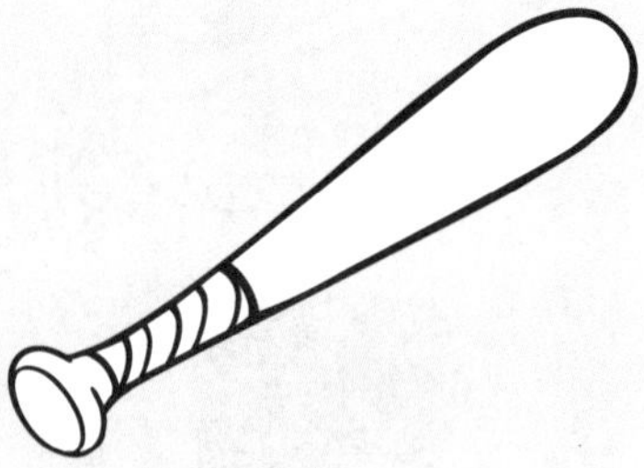

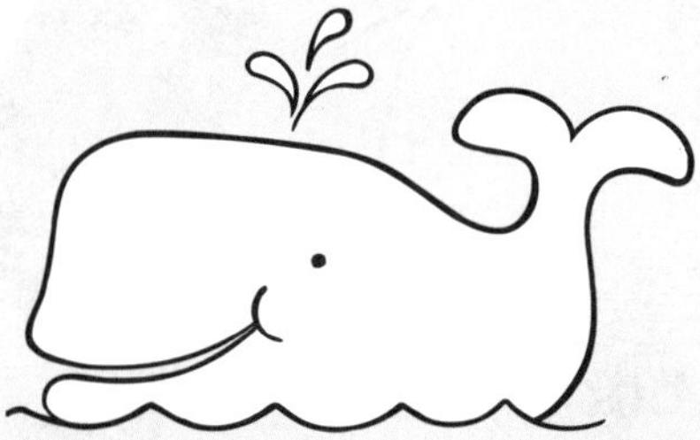

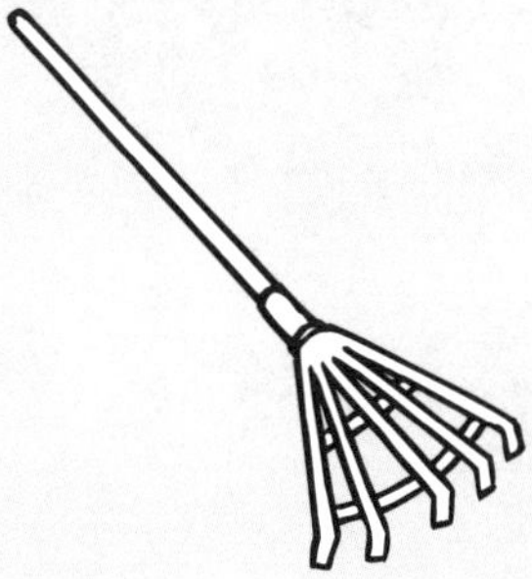

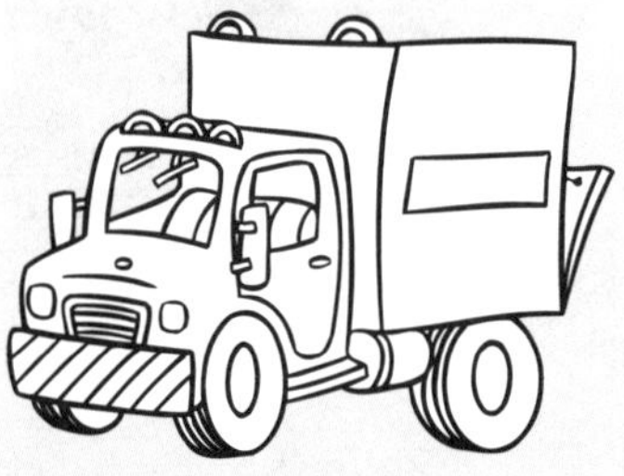

Meet Long i

Listen for the sound of long **i** in **bike**. Look for **i_e**.

bi**k**e

Directions: Fill in the circle beside the name of the picture.

○ dim
○ date
○ dime

○ five
○ fix
○ fame

○ kite
○ cat
○ kit

○ pane
○ pin
○ pine

○ tin
○ tire
○ tale

○ red
○ ride
○ rid

○ hive
○ hid
○ had

○ nip
○ name
○ nine

○ fame
○ fire
○ fin

Name ______________________

Meet Long u

Listen for the sound of long **u** in **mule**. The letters **u__e** and **ue** usually stand for the long **u** sound.

m**ule**

Directions: Circle the pictures whose names have the long **u** sound.

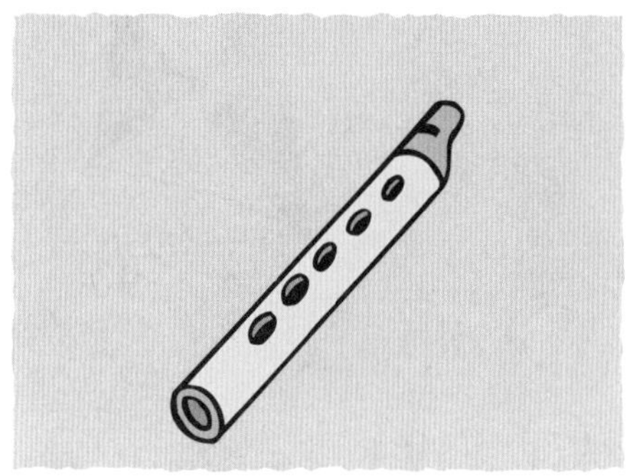

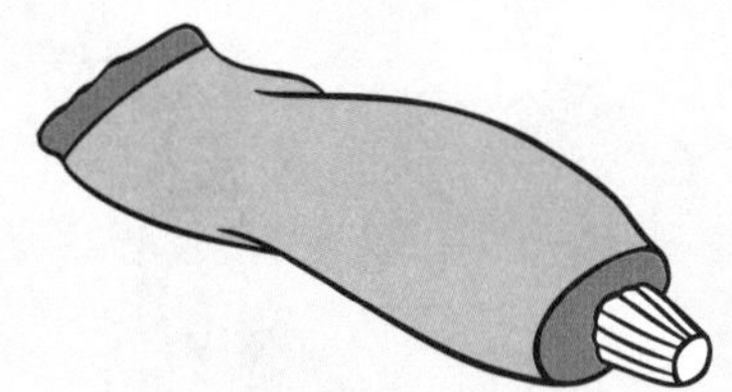

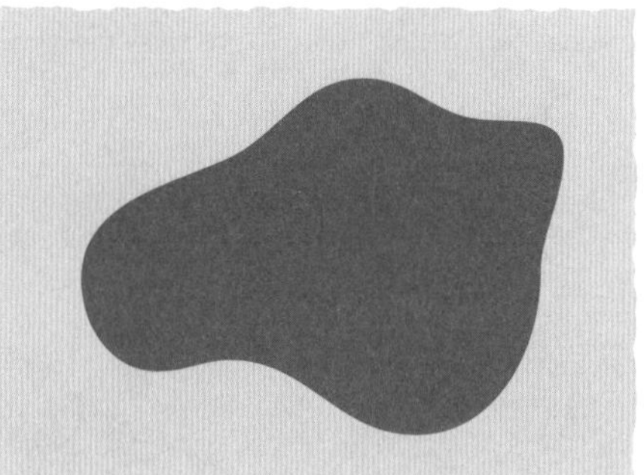

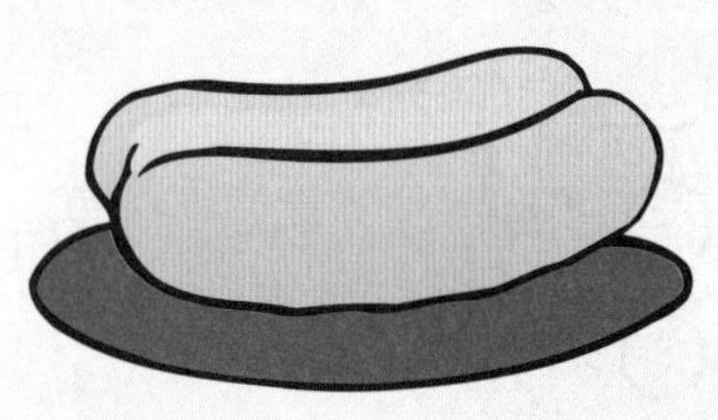

June

		1	2	3	4	5
6	7	8	9	10	11	12
13	14	15	16	17	18	19
20	21	22	23	24	25	26
27	28	28	30			

Name ______________________

Meet Long o

Listen for the sound of long **o** in **rose**. Look for **o__e**.

rose

Directions: Say the name of each picture. Decide whether the vowel sound you hear is long **o** or short **o**. Fill in the circle beside long **o** or short **o**.

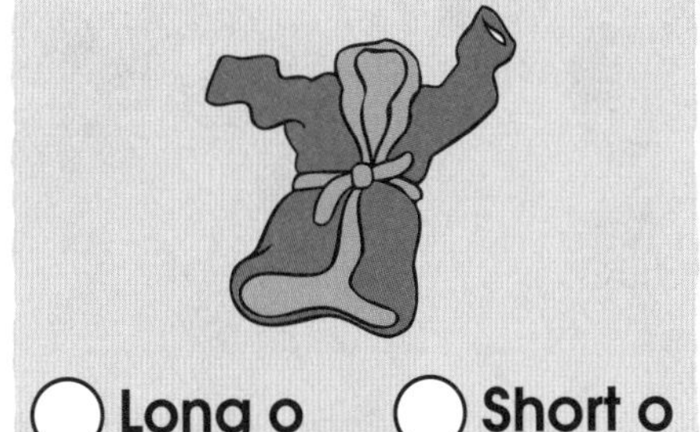

○ Long o ○ Short o

○ Long o ○ Short o

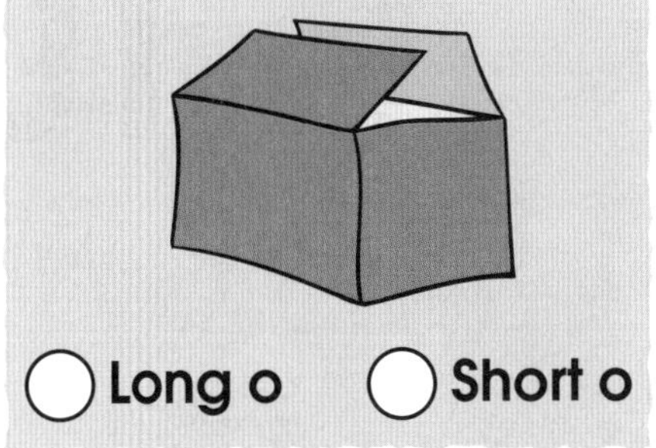

○ Long o ○ Short o

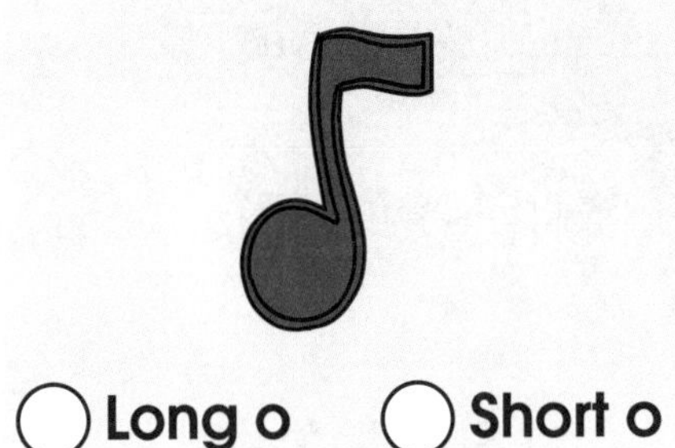

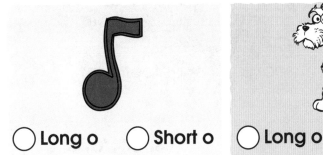

○ Long o ○ Short o

○ Long o ○ Short o

○ Long o ○ Short o

○ Long o ○ Short o

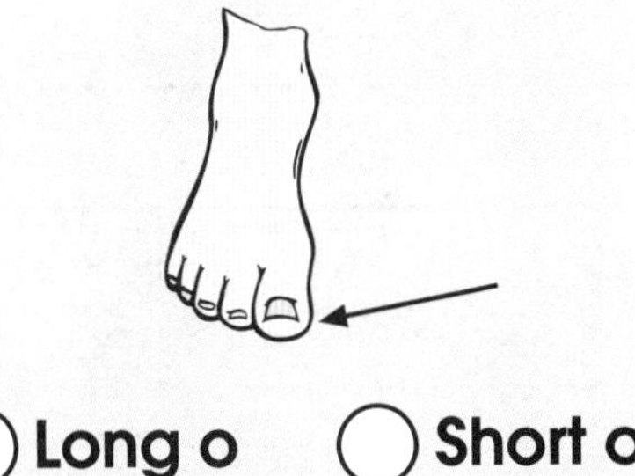

○ Long o ○ Short o

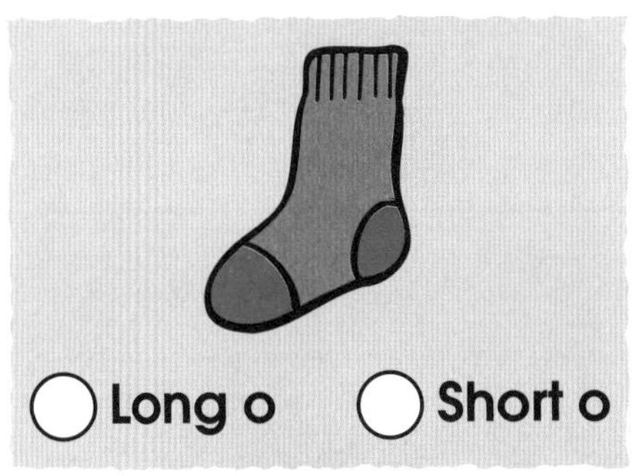

○ Long o ○ Short o

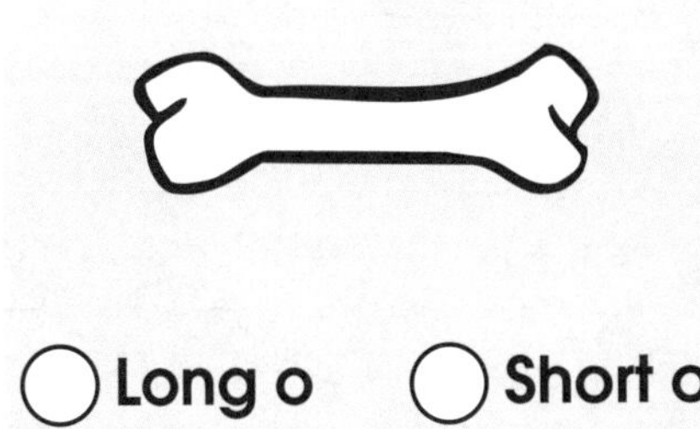

○ Long o ○ Short o

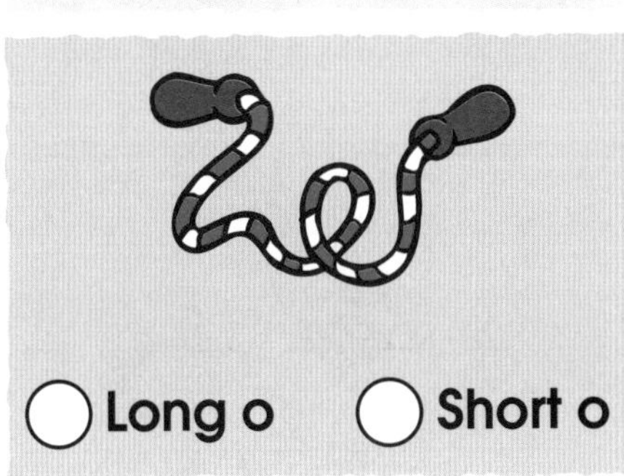

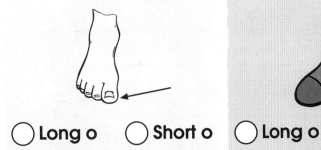

○ Long o ○ Short o

○ Long o ○ Short o

Name ______________________

Meet Long e

Listen for the sound of long **e** in **bee**. The letters **ee** and **ea** usually stand for the long **e** sound.

Directions: Write the name of the picture on the correct line.

ee	**ea**	**Short Vowel e**

Long Vowels

Vowels are the letters **a**, **e**, **i**, **o**, and **u**. Long vowel sounds say their own names. Long **a** is the sound you hear in **hay**. Long **e** is the sound you hear in **me**. Long **i** is the sound you hear in **pie**. Long **o** is the sound you hear in **no**. Long **u** is the sound you hear in **cute**.

Directions: Say the long vowel sound at the beginning of each row. Say the name of each picture. Color the pictures in each row that have the same long vowel sound as that letter.

ā

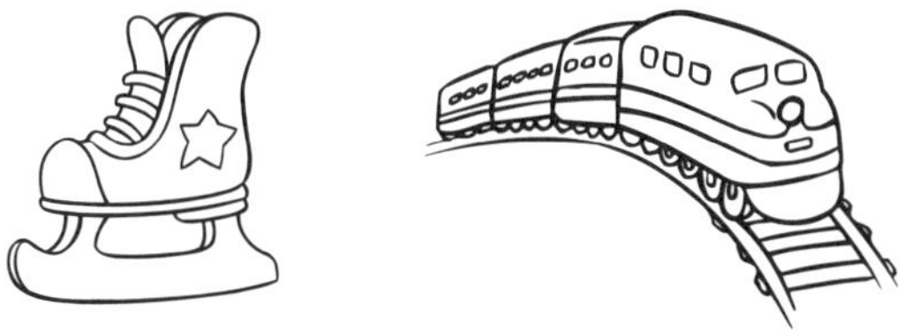

ē

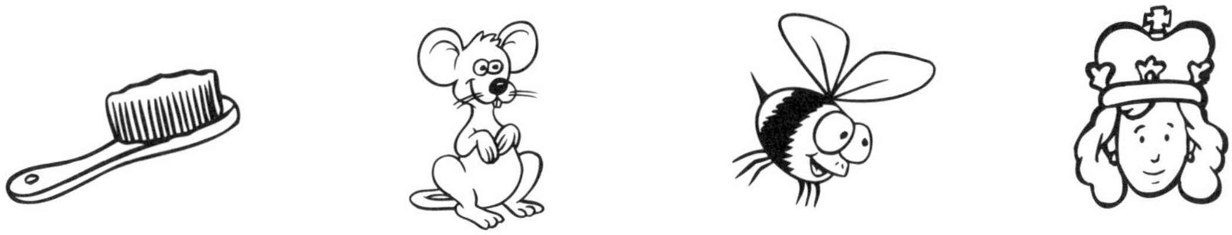

ī

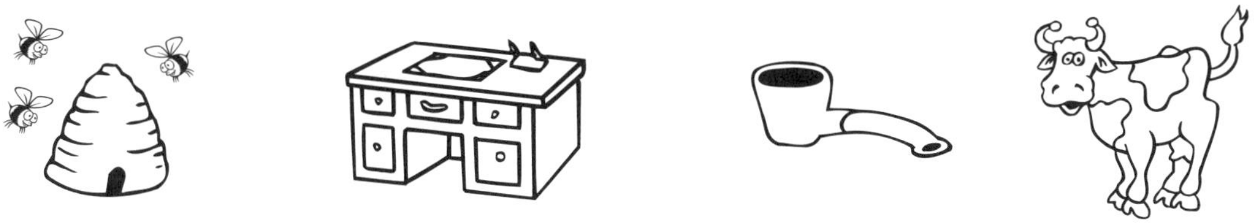

ō

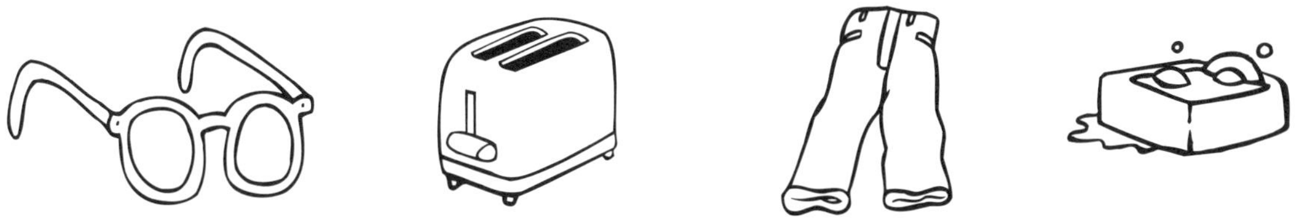

ū

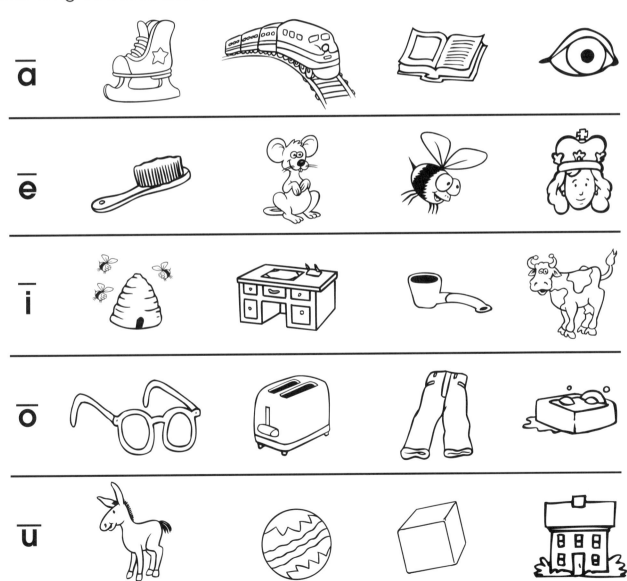

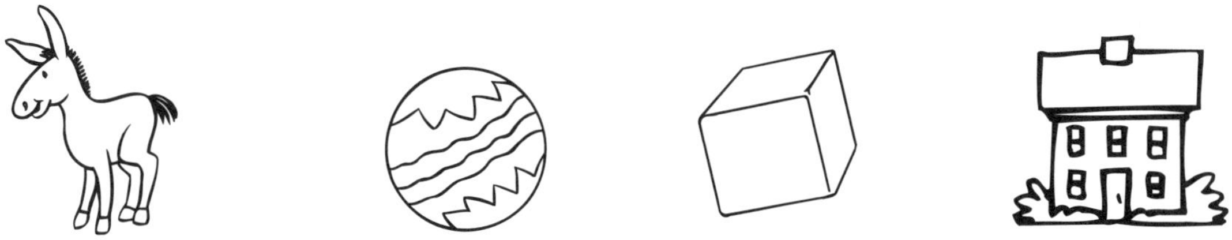

Name ____________________

Super Silent e

When you add an **e** to the end of some words, the vowel changes from a short vowel sound to a long vowel sound. The **e** is silent.

Example: rip + **e** = ripe

Directions: Say the word under the first picture in each pair. Then, add an **e** to the word under the next picture. Say the new word.

can

____

tub

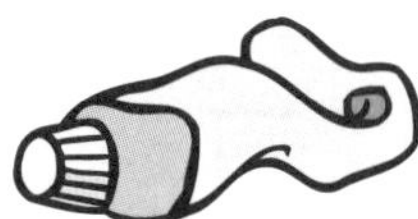

____

man

____

kit

____

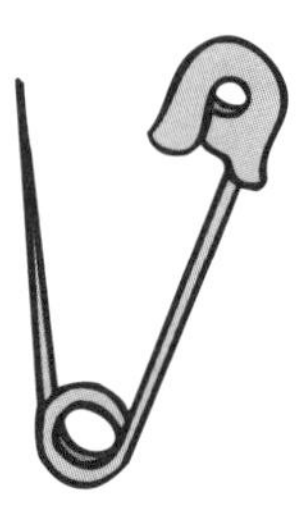

pin

____

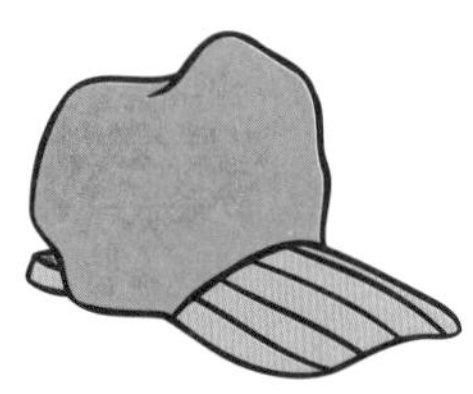

cap

____

Name ______________________

Words with Silent e

When a silent **e** appears at the end of a word, you can't hear it, but it makes the other vowel have a **long** sound. For example, **tub** has a short vowel sound, and **tube** has a long vowel sound.

Directions: Look at the pictures below. Decide if the word has a short or long vowel sound. Circle the correct word. Watch for the silent **e**!

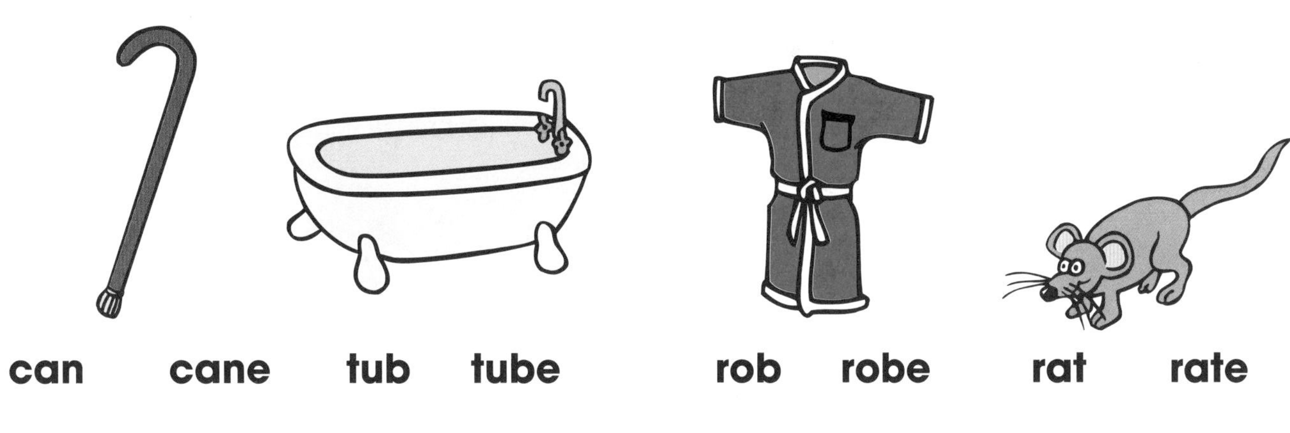

can **cane** **tub** **tube** **rob** **robe** **rat** **rate**

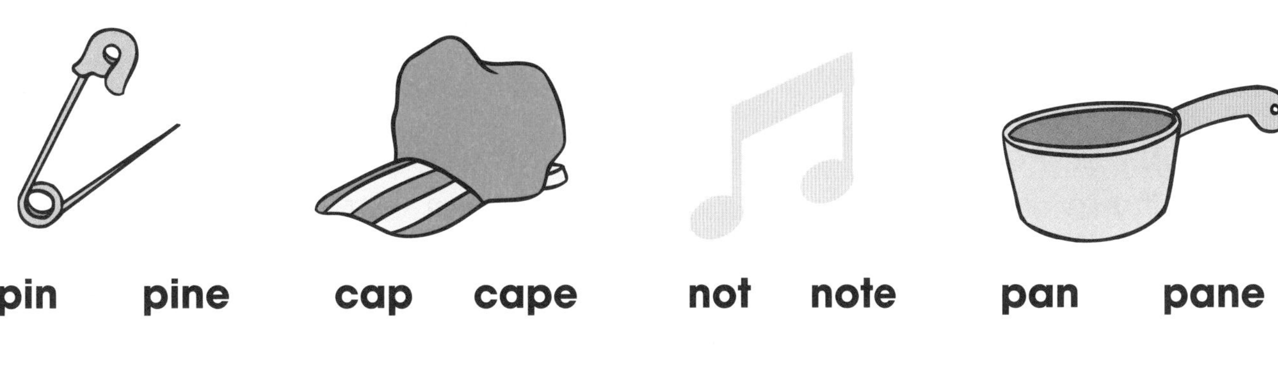

pin **pine** **cap** **cape** **not** **note** **pan** **pane**

slid **slide** **dim** **dime** **tap** **tape** **cub** **cube**

Name ____________________

Final y as a Vowel

Our puppy stays dry in the yard.

You know that **y** is a consonant. When **y** is at the beginning of a word, it makes the sound at the beginning of **yard**.

Y can also be a vowel.

Sometimes, **y** can have the long **e** sound you hear at the end of **puppy**. **Y** has this sound when it is at the end of a word with more than one syllable or part.

Sometimes, **y** can have the long **i** sound you hear at the end of **dry**. **Y** has this sound when it is at the end of a one-syllable word.

Directions: Say each picture name. Circle the word that names the picture. If **y** makes the long **e** sound, color the picture brown. If **y** makes the long **i** sound, color the picture orange.

bail
bay
baby

crazy
cry
crate

bunt
bunny
buy

fry
frosty
frog

pay
pry
pony

fly
feed
fussy

The Sounds of y

A **y** at the end of a word can have the long **i** sound or the long **e** sound. Listen for the long **i** sound in **fly**. Listen for the long **e** sound in **pony**.

fl**y** 

pon**y** 

Directions: Say the name of each picture. Listen for the sound of **y** at the end of the word. Circle either long **i** or long **e**.

sky

Long i **Long e**

baby

Long i **Long e**

bunny

Long i **Long e**

cry

Long i **Long e**

penny

Long i **Long e**

muddy

Long i **Long e**

dry

Long i **Long e**

20

twenty

Long i **Long e**

city

Long i **Long e**

Name ______________________________

Finish-the-Word Puzzles

Directions: Write a vowel in the middle of each puzzle that will make a word across and down.

	w	
p		t
	b	

	m	
d		g
	p	

	f	
m		p
	n	

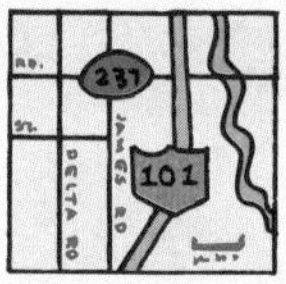

	w	
p		g
	n	

	h	
b		x
	t	

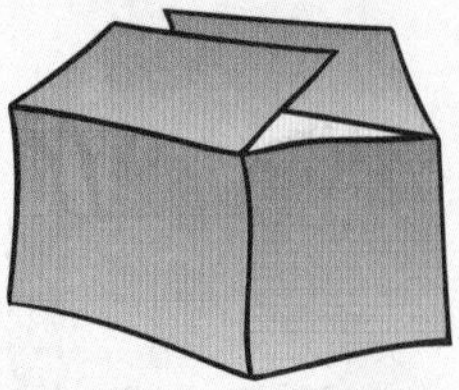

	b	
s		n
	s	

Name ______________________________

Review

Directions: Color all of the vowels black to discover something hidden in the puzzle.

j	e	j	g	w	d	q	n	j	c	g	c	u	b
k	g	u	m	b	j	h	c	h	w	l	o	d	s
r	c	z	i	l	p	q	s	b	k	i	n	z	f
g	k	w	x	e	d	a	e	f	e	l	x	q	k
v	r	f	j	p	i	o	u	a	g	n	f	s	b
d	n	v	m	a	e	e	i	u	u	h	b	s	f
u	a	e	i	e	u	a	i	u	e	a	e	i	u
l	z	k	i	u	u	a	a	e	e	i	m	w	z
q	h	r	a	e	u	e	i	a	e	e	c	c	b
i	u	u	e	o	a	o	u	o	i	i	o	o	u
t	x	b	h	a	i	e	o	u	a	d	v	r	l
c	h	f	s	j	e	i	e	i	f	f	k	j	v
n	m	d	t	e	g	a	o	t	i	j	m	x	h
t	p	g	i	c	v	h	n	g	d	o	p	r	l
l	h	o	k	q	f	r	p	s	j	t	u	g	v

What was hidden?

____

Name ____________________

Review

Directions: Write a vowel on each line to complete each word.

a e i o u

c___t

b__k__ 

 sm__k__

tr____ 

 c___b

 p___n 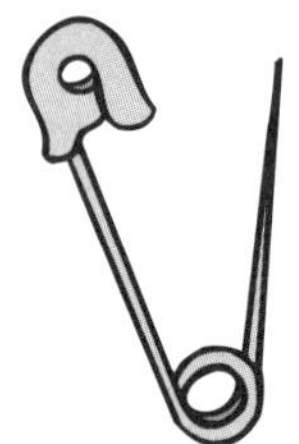

 m___m

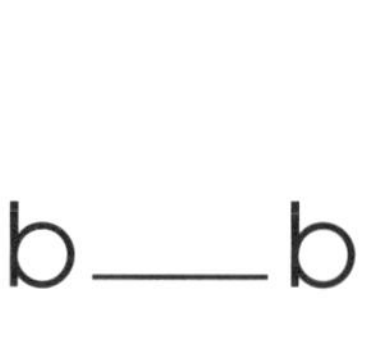 b___b 

 d___d

d___ck 

Name ______________________

Short and Long Vowels

Directions: Say the name of each picture. Write the vowel on each line that completes the word. Color the short vowel pictures. Circle the long vowel pictures.

a e i o u

j ______ g

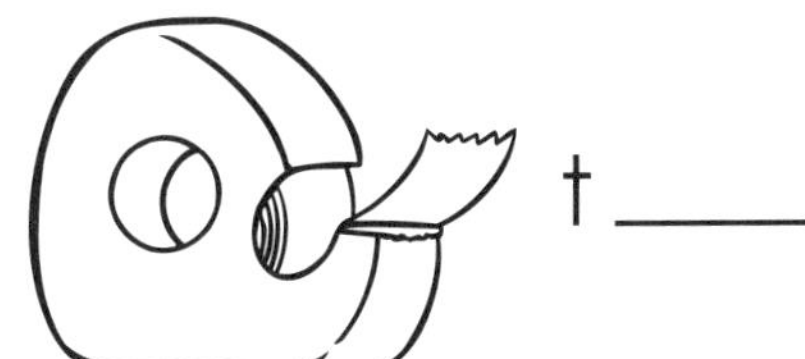

t ______ pe

l ______ af

p______ n

l ______ ck

c______ t

c______ be

b______ ll

k ______ te

r ______ pe

Name ____________________

Consonant Blends with r

Sometimes, two consonants at the beginning of a word blend together. Listen for the **dr** blend in **dragon**. **Gr**, **fr**, **cr**, **tr**, **br**, and **pr** are also **r** blends.

dragon

Directions: Draw a line from each consonant blend to the picture whose name begins with the same sound.

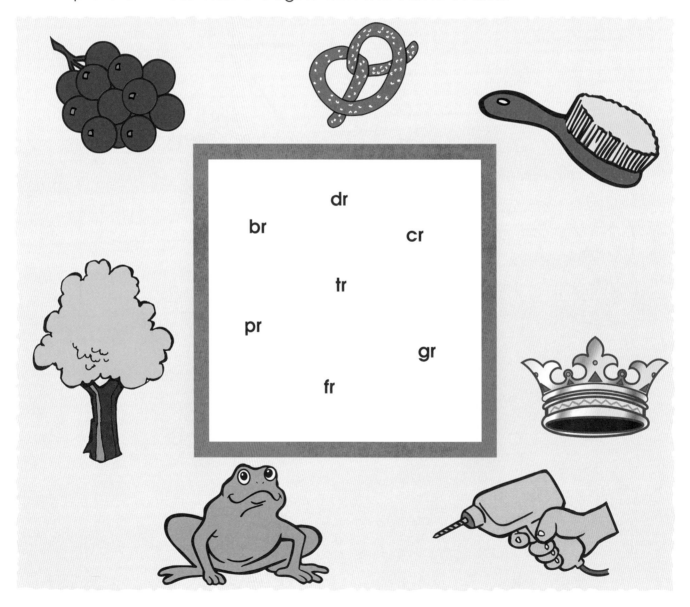

dr

br

cr

tr

pr

gr

fr

Name ______________________________

Fill the Tray

Directions: Read the menu. Circle the words that have **r** blends. On the tray, draw pictures of the foods whose names you circled.

bread	**pretzel**	**meat**
butter	**milk**	**grapes**
salad	**french fries**	**ice cream**

Name ____________________

Consonant Blends with l

Listen for the **cl** blend in **clown**. **Gl**, **pl**, **fl**, and **bl** are also **l** blends.

clown 

Directions: Look at the **l** blend at the beginning of each row. Color the picture whose name begins with that sound.

bl

cl

fl

gl

pl

Name ____________________

Tic-Tac-Toe with l Blends

Directions: Color the pictures whose names begin with **l** blends. Draw a line through three colored pictures in a row to score a Tic-Tac-Toe.

Name ____________________

Consonant Blends with s

Listen for the **sk** blend in **skunk**. **Sm**, **st**, **sp**, **sw**, **sc**, **squ**, **sl**, and **sn** are also **s** blends.

skunk

Directions: Say the name of each picture. Circle the **s** blend you hear at the beginning of the name.

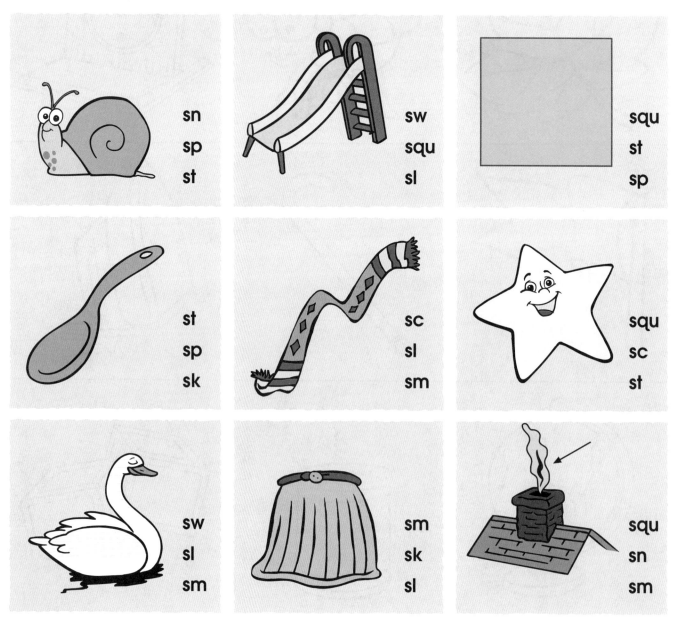

sn sp st	sw squ sl	squ st sp
st sp sk	sc sl sm	squ sc st
sw sl sm	sm sk sl	squ sn sm

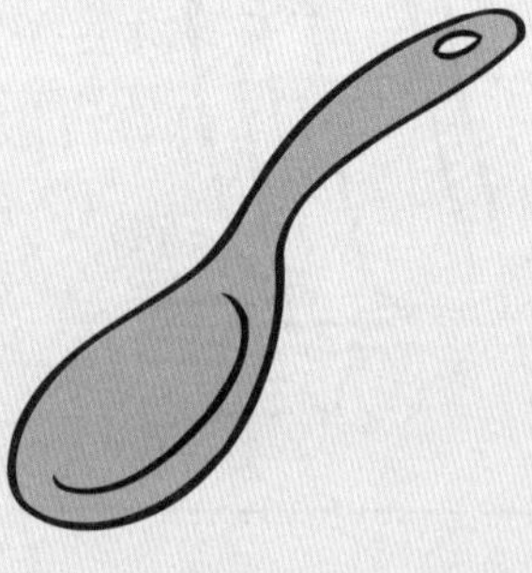

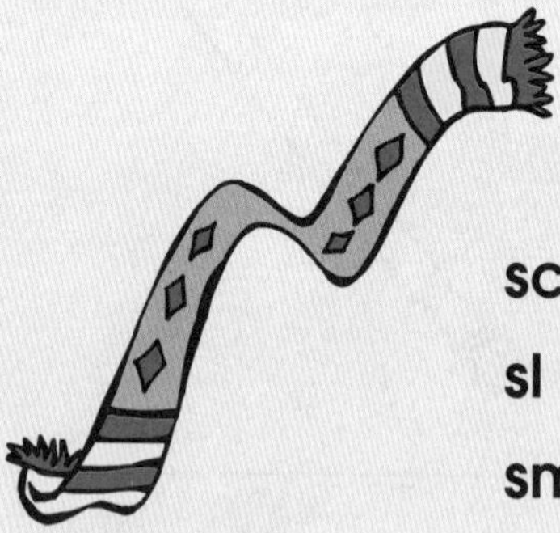

Name ______________________

Match Pictures and Blends

Directions: Draw a line from each **s** blend to the picture whose name begins with that sound.

squ

sp

sw

sl

sk

sn

st

sm

Name ______________________

Blends at the Ends

Some consonant blends come at the ends of words. Listen for the **nd** blend at the end of the word **round**. **Mp**, **ng**, **nt**, **sk**, **nk**, and **st** can also be ending blends.

rou**nd**

Directions: Say the name of each picture. Circle the blend you hear at the end of the name.

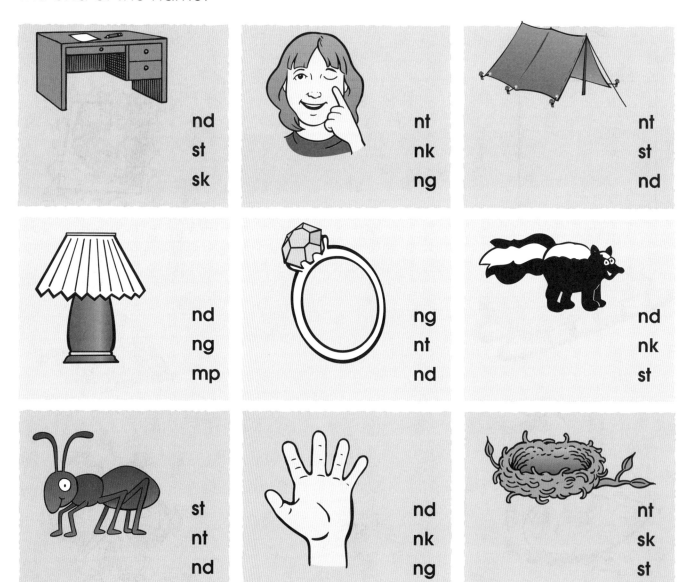

nd **st** **sk**	**nt** **nk** **ng**	**nt** **st** **nd**
nd **ng** **mp**	**ng** **nt** **nd**	**nd** **nk** **st**
st **nt** **nd**	**nd** **nk** **ng**	**nt** **sk** **st**

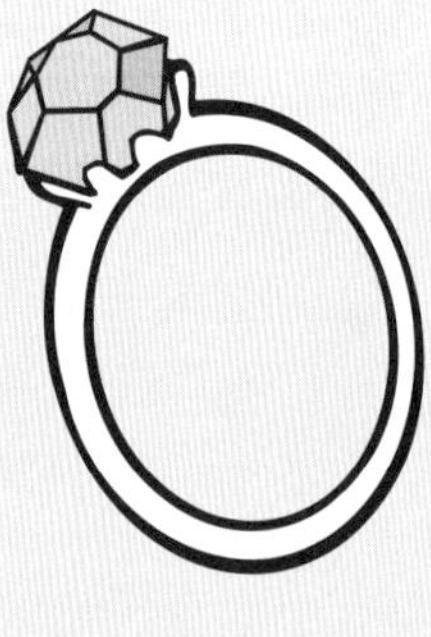

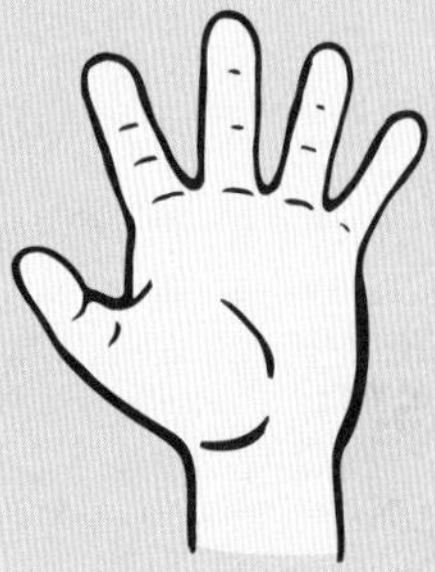

Ending Consonant Blends

Directions: Draw a line from the picture to the blend that ends the word.

lf

lk

sk

st

Name ______________________________

Missing Blends

Directions: Fill in the circle beside the missing blend in each word.

__ain	__an	te__
○ **sk** ○ **tr** ○ **pr**	○ **sl** ○ **sm** ○ **sw**	○ **sk** ○ **nt** ○ **ng**
__ate	__ate	__ide
○ **sk** ○ **sm** ○ **cr**	○ **pl** ○ **pr** ○ **sp**	○ **sk** ○ **cl** ○ **sl**
__ail	__ess	de__
○ **ng** ○ **sn** ○ **st**	○ **pr** ○ **dr** ○ **nd**	○ **st** ○ **nd** ○ **sk**

Name ____________________

More Missing Blends

Directions: Fill in the circle beside the missing blend in each word.

ri__ ○ nt ○ st ○ ng	__y ○ sl ○ fl ○ pl	__apes ○ gr ○ cl ○ sk
__obe ○ sl ○ gl ○ gr	ha__ ○ nd ○ ng ○ sk	__og ○ gr ○ tr ○ fr
__y ○ sk ○ sm ○ nt	__ider ○ pr ○ sl ○ sp	la__ ○ st ○ mp ○ ng

Name ______________________________

Picture Clues

Directions: Read the sentence. Circle the word that makes sense. Use the picture clues to help you. Then, write the word.

I ride on a ____________.

bike hike

I ride on a ____________.

train tree

I ride in a ____________.

car can

I ride on a ____________.

bus bug

I ride in a ____________.

jar jet

I ride in a ____________.

took truck

Picture Clues

Directions: Read the sentence. Circle the word that makes sense. Use the picture clues to help you. Then, write the word.

I see the ____________________.
bird book

I see the ____________________.
fish fork

I see the ____________________.
dogs dig

I see the ____________________.
cats coat

I see the ____________________.
snake snow

I see the ____________________.
rat rake

Name ______________________________

Fun with Directions

Directions: Follow the number code to color the balloons. Color the clown, too.

1 — blue	2 — orange	3 — yellow	4 — green	5 — purple
6 — brown	7 — red	8 — black	9 — blue	10 — pink

one five six three

nine four seven ten

eight two

Name ______________________________

Draw with Directions

Directions: Follow the directions to complete the picture.

1. Draw a smiling yellow face on the sun.
2. Color the fish blue. Draw 2 more blue fish in the water.
3. Draw a brown bird under the cloud. Draw blue raindrops under the cloud.
4. Color the boat purple. Color one sail orange. Color the other sail green.
5. Color the starfish yellow. Draw 2 more yellow starfish.

Name ______________________________

Follow the Course

Directions: Place a penny in the top left corner on page 83. Then, follow the directions below to win the trophy. Check off the directions as you follow them.

1.
- [ ] Go right 7 spaces.
- [ ] Go down 5 spaces.
- [ ] Go left 6 spaces.
- [ ] Go down 4 spaces.
- [ ] Leap through the hoop.

2.
- [ ] Go right 3 spaces.
- [ ] Go up 5 spaces.
- [ ] Go left 4 spaces.
- [ ] Go up 1 space.
- [ ] Do a handstand on your skateboard.

3.
- [ ] Go right 2 spaces.
- [ ] Go up 2 spaces.
- [ ] Go right 3 spaces.
- [ ] Go down 3 spaces.
- [ ] Glide down the ramp.

4.
- [ ] Go right 1 space.
- [ ] Go down 3 spaces.
- [ ] Go left 3 spaces.
- [ ] Go down 2 spaces.
- [ ] Turn the corner.

5.
- [ ] Go right 4 spaces.
- [ ] Go up 8 spaces.
- [ ] Go left 4 spaces.
- [ ] Go down 1 space.
- [ ] Duck! Here's a tunnel.

6.
- [ ] Go left 2 spaces.
- [ ] Go down 6 spaces.
- [ ] Go left 1 space.
- [ ] Go up 2 spaces.
- [ ] You made it! Collect your trophy.

Name ________________________________

Skateboard Course

Name ______________________

Directions for Decorating

Directions: Follow the directions to decorate the bedroom.

Draw a red 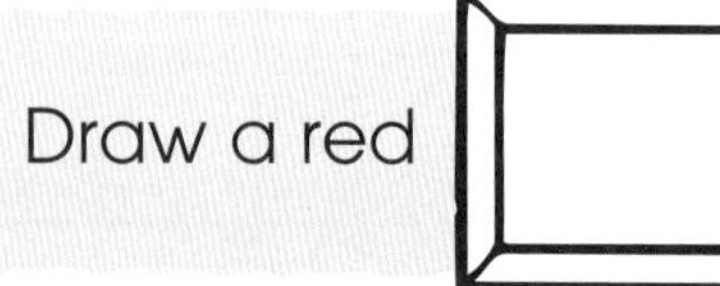 between the two 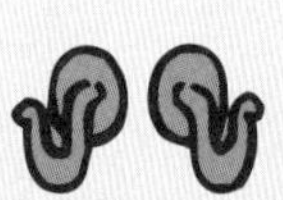.

Draw a under the window. Color it green.

Draw three big  on the wall. Color them orange.

Draw a picture of something you would like to have in your bedroom.

Name ________________

Following Directions

Read the sentences. Then, follow the directions.

Directions: Bob is making a snowman. He needs your help. Draw a black hat on the snowman. Draw red buttons. Now, draw a green scarf. Draw a happy face on the snowman.

Name ______________________

Menu Mix-Up

Directions: Circle names of **drinks** in **red**. Circle names of **vegetables** in **green**. Circle names of **desserts** in **pink**.

Directions: Write each food word on the correct line.

Drinks	Vegetables	Desserts
______	______	______
______	______	______
______	______	______

Name ______________________

Word Sort

Directions: Circle words that name **colors** in **red**.
Circle words that name **shapes** in **yellow**.
Circle words that name **numbers** in **green**.

five blue

ten

square circle

nine

purple

triangle

brown

Directions: Write each word on the correct line.

Colors	Shapes	Numbers
______	______	______
______	______	______
______	______	______

Name ______________________

Classification

Directions: Draw an **X** on the picture that does **not** belong in each group.

Fruit

apple

peach

corn

watermelon

Wild Animals

bear

kitten

gorilla

lion

Pets

cat

goldfish

elephant

dog

Flowers

grass

rose

daisy

tulip

Name ______________________

Classification

Directions: Dapper Dog is going on a camping trip. Draw an **X** on the word in each row that does not belong.

1.	flashlight	candle	radio	fire
2.	shirt	pants	coat	bat
3.	cow	car	bus	train
4.	beans	hot dog	ball	bread
5.	gloves	hat	book	boots
6.	fork	butter	cup	plate
7.	book	ball	bat	milk
8.	dogs	bees	flies	ants

Name ______________________

Things That Go Together

Directions: Draw a line to connect the things that go together.

toothpaste

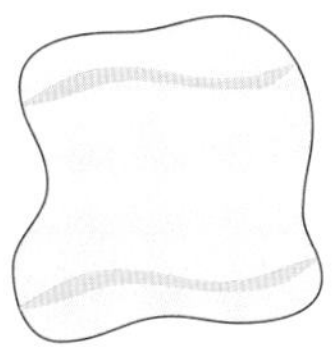
washcloth

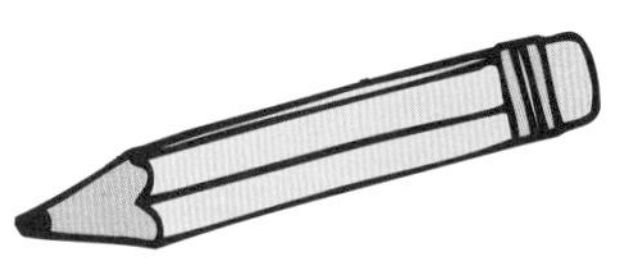
pencil

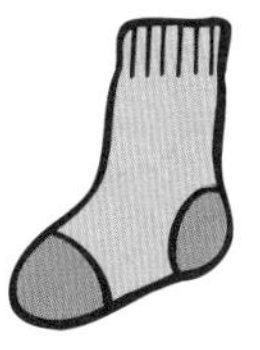
sock

salt

toothbrush

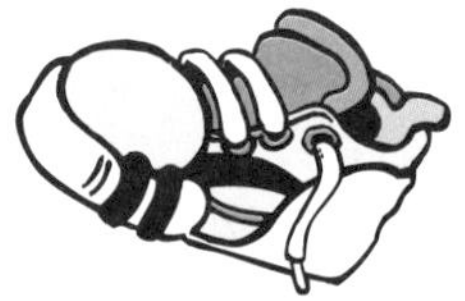
shoe

pepper

soap

paper

pillow

bed

More Things That Go Together

Directions: Draw a line to connect the things that go together.

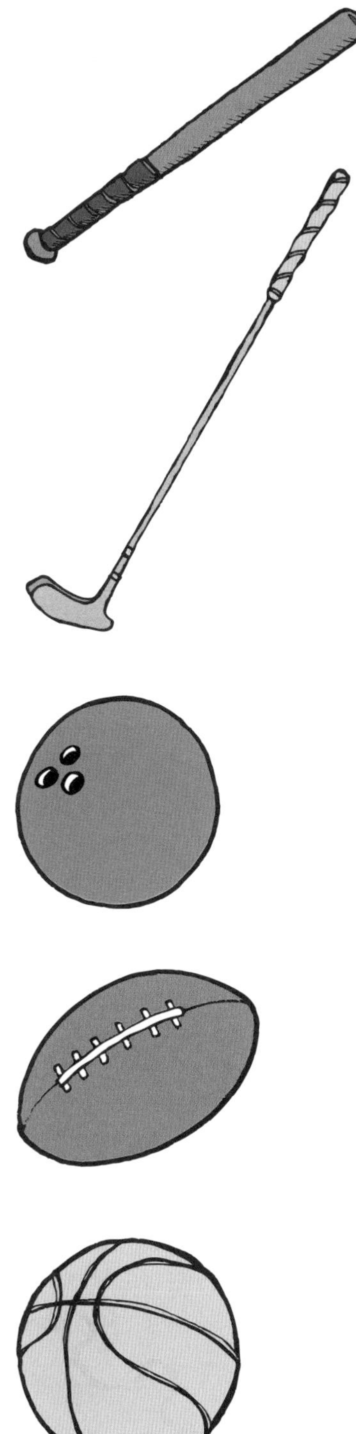

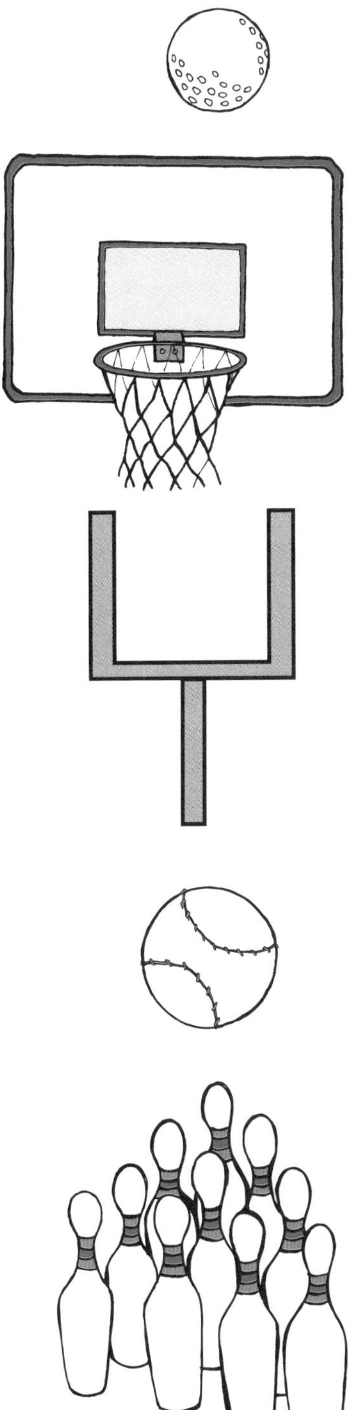

Name ____________________

Same and Different

Reading to find out how things are alike or different can help you picture and remember what you read. Things that are alike are called **similarities**. Things that are not alike are called **differences**.

Similarity: Beth and Michelle are both girls.
Difference: Beth has short hair, but Michelle has long hair.

Directions: Read the story.

Michelle and Beth are wearing new dresses. Both dresses are striped and have four shiny buttons. Each dress has a belt and a pocket. Beth's dress is blue and white, while Michelle's is yellow and white. The stripes on Beth's dress go up and down. Stripes on Michelle's dress go from side to side. Beth's pocket is bigger with room for a kitten.

Directions: Add the details. Color the dresses. Show how the dresses are alike and how they are different.

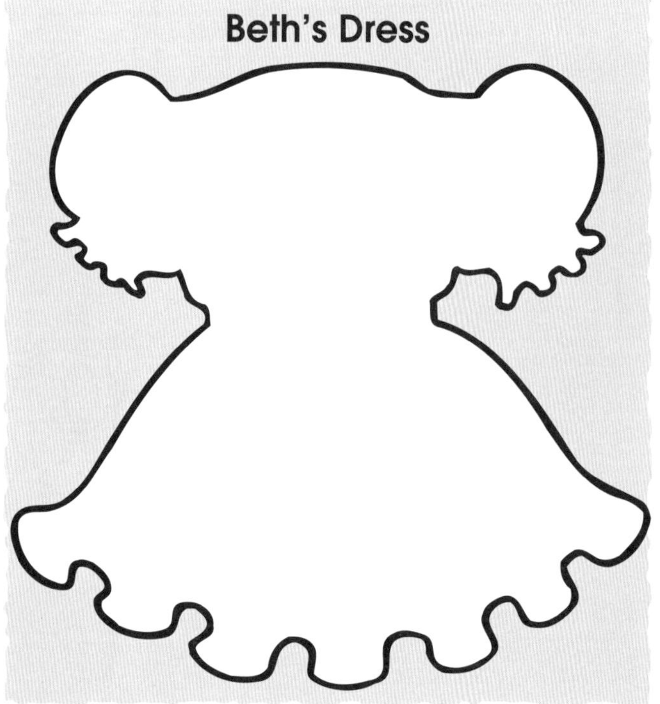

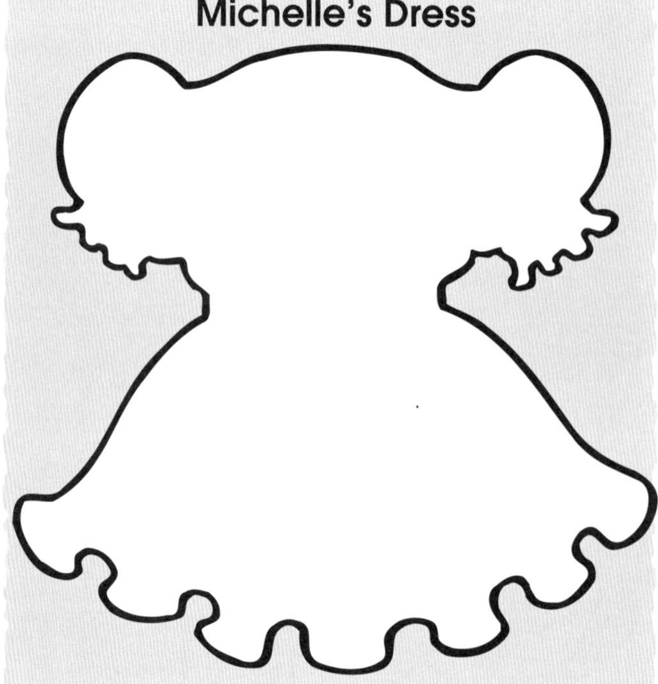

Comparing Cars

Directions: Read the story.

Sarah built a car for a race. Sarah's car has wheels, a steering wheel, and a place to sit just like the family car. It doesn't have a motor, a key, or a gas pedal. Sarah came in second in last year's race. This year, she hopes to win the race.

Directions: Write **S** beside the things Sarah's car has that are like things the family car has. Write **D** beside the things that are different.

_____ steering wheel

_____ motor

_____ gas pedal

_____ seat

_____ wheels

Name ______________________

Sequencing Pictures

Directions: Put the pictures in each column in order. Write **1**, **2**, or **3** next to each picture.

 ___

___

___

 ___

 ___

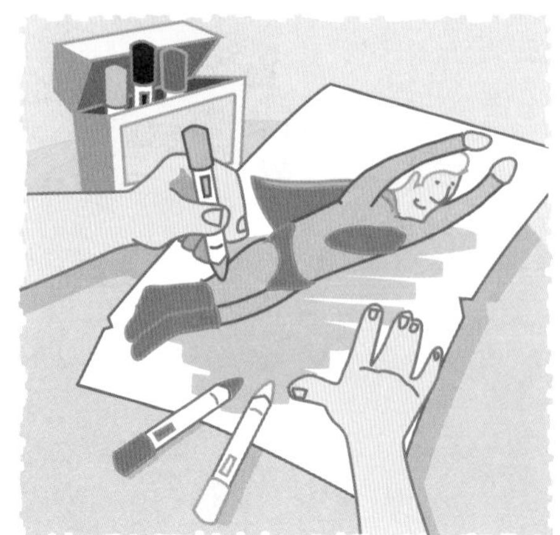 ___

Sequencing Riddles

Directions: To solve the riddles below, look at the letter underneath each line. Next, write the letter that comes **before** each letter.

How do you catch a squirrel?

D M J N C   V Q   B   U S F F

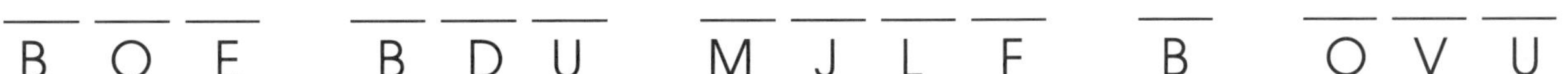

B O E   B D U   M J L F   B   O V U.

What has four wheels and flies?

B   H B S C B H F

U S V D L

Why did the boy run around his bed?

U P   D B U D I   V Q   P O

I J T   T M F F Q

Name ____________________

Story Time

Directions: Write each group of sentences in the correct order.

My cat was full and went to sleep. My cat was hungry.
I filled a bowl with cat food.

1. ____________________
2. ____________________
3. ____________________

I got a gold star. I studied for my spelling test.
My teacher gave us a list of spelling words.

1. ____________________
2. ____________________
3. ____________________

Sequencing

Tom and Tess are making a snack. They are fixing nacho chips and cheese.

Directions: Look at the picture. Then, look at the steps that Tom and Tess use. Put numbers beside each sentence to tell the correct order.

_________ Tom and Tess cook the chips in the microwave oven for 2 minutes.

_________ They get out a plate to cook on.

_________ Tom and Tess get out the nacho chips and cheese.

_________ Tom and Tess eat the food.

_________ They put the chips on a plate.

_________ They put cheese on the chips.

Name ______________________

Boats

Directions: Read about boats. Then, answer the questions.

See the boats! They float on water. Some boats have sails. The wind moves the sails. It makes the boats go. Many people name their sailboats. They paint the name on the side of the boat.

1. What makes sailboats move? ______________________

2. Where do sailboats float? ______________________

3. What would you name a sailboat? ______________________

Name ______________________

Where Flowers Grow

Directions: Read about flowers. Then, answer the questions.

Some flowers grow in pots. Many flowers grow in flower beds. Others grow beside the road. Some flowers begin from seeds. They grow into small buds. Then, they open wide and bloom. Flowers are pretty!

1. Name two places flowers grow.

   ______________________ ______________________

   ____

2. Some flowers begin from ______________________.

3. Then, flowers grow into small ______________________.

4. Flowers then open wide and ______________________.

Name ________________________

Important Signs to Know

Directions: Draw a line from the sign to the sentence that tells about it.

1. If you see this sign, watch out for trains.

2. When cars or bikes come to this sign, they must stop.

3. When this sign is on, do not cross the street.

4. This sign tells you to stay out of the yard.

5. If you see this sign, do not eat or drink what is inside!

6. This sign warns you that it is not safe. Stay away!

7. This sign says you are not allowed to come in.

Comprehension

Directions: Read the story. Write the words from the story that complete each sentence.

Ben and Sue have a bug. It is red with black spots. They call it Spot. Spot likes to eat green leaves and grass. The children keep Spot in a box.

Ben and Sue have a ______________________.

It is ______________________ with black spots.

The bug's name is ______________________.

The bug eats ______________________.

Name ______________________

What's Next?

Directions: Draw a picture of what you think will happen next in the boxes below.

Name ________________________________

What Happens Next?

Directions: Read the story. Predict what will happen and circle your answer choice.

David and Fran go the park. The friendly ice-cream man is there selling ice-cream cones. "Hi kids, would you two like an ice-cream cone?" he asks.

Fran and David reach into their pockets, which are empty. "We don't have any money," says Fran. The ice-cream man smiles at them and reaches into his freezer. Then, he says…

1. Ice cream is bad for children.

2. Today it is my treat. Free ice cream for both of you!

3. I am sorry, maybe next time.

Directions: Draw a picture of what you think will happen.

Name ____________________

Inside Out!

Directions: Can you match the outsides with the insides? Draw a line from each picture on the left to its inside picture on the right.

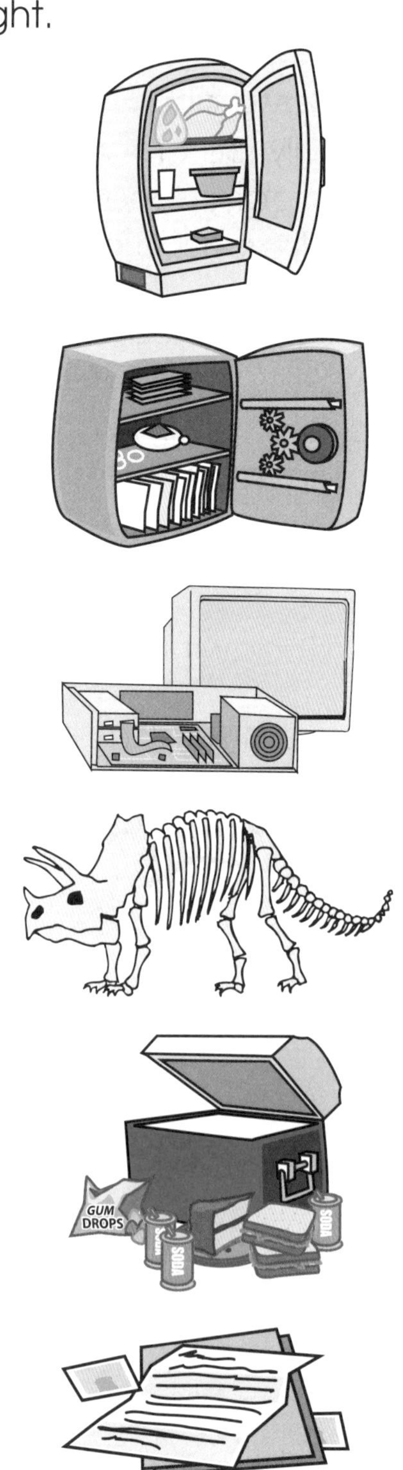

Name ______________________

Books for Gabby!

Gabby loves to read books about many different topics. She loves to read about exotic animals. She loves stories about famous people. Gabby is also interested in becoming a doctor or an actress one day.

Directions: Look at the books below. Circle only the books that Gabby would like to read.

Famous Actresses of the Stage

How to Build a Tree House

Amazing Animals of the Amazon

Baking Muffins With Mom

Abraham Lincoln's Life

Spend a Day With a Doctor!

CARTOON CRAZY

Dogs, Cats, and Other Household Pets

Name ______________________________

Use Your Head!

Directions: Read each sentence below. Then, read each statement that follows it. Using the information in the first sentence, decide which word best completes each statement. Then, write that word on the line.

"Please put on your heavy winter coat before you go sledding," said my mom.

My mom wanted me to keep

____________________. cool warm

I put on my coat ____________________

I went sledding. before after

"Don't forget to bring your glasses, Tom! It will be hard to see the chalkboard if you don't wear them," reminded his dad.

Tom has ____________________ eyesight.

good poor

Tom is ____________________.

forgetful aware

Tom is going to ____________________.

school basketball practice

Name ______________________

Help Hattie!

Help Hattie pick out birthday presents!

Directions: Read the sentences about her friends. Then, write words from the word list on the lines. Draw a picture of each present inside the boxes.

	Word List	
music	airplane	goggles
crayons	journal	

Nancy loves to color pictures.

____

Ray wants to be a pilot.

____

Kristin loves to write.

____

Jared swims every week.

____

Chelsea is a great piano player.

____

Name ____________________

Critical Thinking

Directions: Use your reading skills to answer each riddle. Unscramble the word to check your answer. Write the correct word on the line.

I am a ruler, but I have two feet, not one.

I am a ____________________.
(ngik)

I am very bright, but that doesn't make me smart.

I am the ____________________.
(uns)

You can turn me around, but I won't get dizzy.

I am a ____________________.
(eky)

I can rattle, but I am not a baby's toy.

I am a ____________________.
(nekas)

I will give you milk, but not in a bottle.

I am a ____________________.
(ocw)

I smell, but I have no nose.

I am a ____________________.
(oerflw)

Name ______________________________

Clues About Cats

Directions: Read the clues carefully. Then, number the cats. When you are sure you are correct, color the cats.

1. A gray cat sits on the gate.
2. A cat with orange-and-black spots sits near the tree.
3. A brown cat sits near the bush.
4. A white cat sits between the orange-and-black spotted cat and the gray cat.
5. A black cat sits next to the brown cat.
6. An orange cat sits between the gray cat and the black cat.

Name ______________________

Hey! What's the Big Idea?

Directions: Circle the words that are shown in the picture above.

bowl	spatula	jar	pot	paper towels
oven	pan	scooter	girl	sneakers
mixer	napkins	car	socks	cupcake tin
mitt	phone	cat	milk	
spoon	bed	dog	ink	

Directions: Circle and write the best title for the picture.

Baking With Dad   Chocolate Attack!   Eating Food

____

Tell why the other two titles are not as good.

____

____

Name ______________________________

What's the Main Idea?

The **main idea** tells about the **whole picture**.

Directions: Does the sentence tell the main idea of the picture? Circle **yes** or **no**. Then, write the sentence that best states the main idea for each picture.

The cat wants to play. yes no

The cat takes a nap. yes no

____

____

The brothers play together. yes no

The brothers are smart. yes no

____

____

The dog is hungry. yes no

The dog is playful. yes no

____

____

Name ______________________

Picture This!

Directions: Look at the picture. Circle and write the best title on the lines below.

B-r-r-r, It's Cold! Bears and Birds

Asleep for the Winter Bears Go Shopping

____

____

Fishing Our New Fish

The Pet Store Fish and Chips

____

____

Spring Cleaning My New Toy

Saturday Fun New Shoes

____

____

Name ______________________

Story Time

The **main idea** tells about the **whole story**.

Read the story below.

"Mom, can we build a fort in the dining room?" John asked.

"Sure, honey," said John's mom. Then, John's mom covered the dining room table with a giant sheet. "Do you want to eat lunch in our fort?" asked John's mom.

"Yes!" said John. Then, John's mom brought two peanut butter sandwiches on paper plates and sat under the table, too!

"Mom, making a fort with you is so much fun!" said John, smiling.

Directions: Does the sentence tell the main idea? Write **yes** or **no**.

1. Then, John's mom covered the dining room table with a giant sheet. __________

2. "Do you want to eat lunch in our fort?" asked John's mom.

   ____

3. "Mom, making a fort with you is so much fun!" __________

4. Write a sentence that tells the main idea: ____________________________

   ____

Name ______________________

Caitlin Uses Context Clues

When you read, it is important to know about context clues. **Context clues** can help you figure out the meaning of a word or a missing word just by looking at the **other words** in the sentence.

Directions: Read each sentence below. Circle the context clues, or other words in the sentence that give you hints about the meaning. Choose the answer that fits in each blank. Write it on the line. The first one is done for you.

It was so hot outside that I decided I would go to the beach and **swim**.

play laugh shovel swim

"Swim" is the correct answer because of the context clues "hot" and "beach." Now you try.

1. Last night I went to bed very late and now I feel ______________.

   happy hungry tired yawn

2. When I broke my mom's favorite vase she was ______________.

   worried nice magic angry

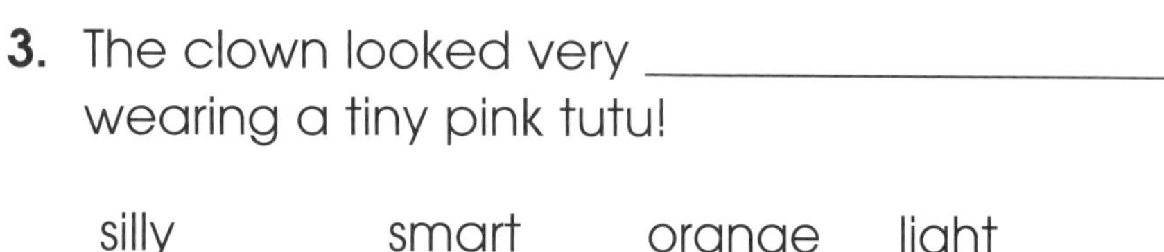

3. The clown looked very ______________ wearing a tiny pink tutu!

   silly smart orange light

Name ______________________

Caitlin Uses More Context Clues

When you read, it is important to know about context clues. **Context clues** can help you figure out the missing word in a sentence, just by looking at the **other words** in the sentence.

Directions: Read each sentence below. Circle the context clues. Choose the answer that fits in each blank. Write it on the line.

1. The cold wind and lack of heat made me wish I had an extra ____________________.

    umbrella   toy   shovel   jacket

2. A whale is a very ____________________ mammal. Sailors often thought whales were actually small islands!

    small   graceful   large   blue

3. Eating fruit is important for ____________________ health. Fruit is full of many important vitamins.

    bad   good   okay   cat

4. The bus was very large and had a lot of seats. It could carry ____________________ people.

    few   hungry   many   tired

Name ____________________

Carlo's Context Clues

Context clues can help you figure out the meaning of a word just by looking at the **other words** in the sentence.

Directions: Read each sentence below. Circle the context clues. Choose a word from the word list to replace each word in **bold**. Write it on the line.

Word List

stop	shined	tease
smart	lively	yummy

1. This prize-winning chocolate cream pie is **delicious**. ____________________

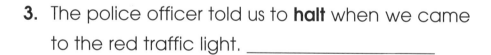

2. Please do not **taunt** your younger brother. Mean words hurt his feelings. ____________________

3. The police officer told us to **halt** when we came to the red traffic light. ____________________

4. The bouncy, happy puppy was very **energetic**. ____________________

5. The silver bowl really **gleamed** after you polished it. ____________________

6. The **intelligent** girl always got 100's on her spelling tests. ____________________

Name ______________________

Carlo's Context Clues Continued

Context clues can help you figure out the meaning of a word just by looking at the **other words** in the sentence.

Directions: Read each sentence below. Circle the context clues. Choose a word from the word list to replace each word in **bold**. Write it on the line.

Word List

petted	understand	tell
little	yelled	

1. "Don't **reveal** the secret! We want the party to be a surprise!" said Mary. ______________

2. I can't **grasp** that hard math problem! It is too difficult. ______________

3. The baby bird was so **tiny** that we could hardly see it. ______________

4. We **stroked** the soft kitten and heard it purr. ______________

5. The crowd **hollered** when the player was called out. ______________

Name ______________________

What Is Cause and Effect?

Cause: An action or act that makes something happen

Effect: Something that happens because of an action or cause

Look at the following example of cause and effect.

Kyle has a spelling test and studies hard.

Kyle's hard work helps him do a super job!

Directions: Now, draw a line connecting each cause on the left side of the page to its effect on the right side of the page.

Name ______________________

We Go Together!

Directions: Draw a line connecting the pictures that go together. Then, figure out which picture is the cause and which is the effect. Write **C** for **cause** or **E** for **effect** under each picture.

____

____

____

____

____

____

Name ____________________

Realistic Story or Fantasy?

Many stories are made-up stories. A made-up story about things that could really happen is a **realistic story**. Some made-up stories, such as fairy tales, tell about things that could never really happen. Those stories are **fantasies**.

Realistic story: A girl hits a home run and wins the game for her team.

Fantasy: A girl hits the ball. It sprouts wings and flies away on an adventure.

Directions: Read the book reviews. Fill in the circle to show whether each story is a realistic story or a fantasy.

The Flying Hippo is about a hippo that flies through the sky. He lands at a busy airport and wanders through New York City.

○ Realistic story ○ Fantasy

A Goose Learns to Fly is about a family who saves an injured baby goose. Later, they teach it to fly on its own.

○ Realistic story ○ Fantasy

The First Airplane is about the Wright Brothers and the airplane they invented.

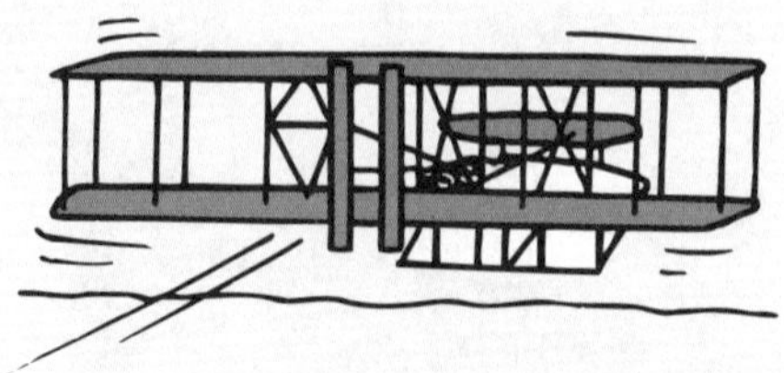

○ Realistic story ○ Fantasy

The Magic Airplane is about a toy airplane that flies to the planet Mars.

○ Realistic story ○ Fantasy

Name ______________________________

Fantasy Tales

If even one thing in a story could not really happen, the whole story is a fantasy.

Directions: Read the stories. Underline the sentence that makes each story a fantasy.

Michelle got a kitten for her birthday. It was soft and cuddly. It liked to chase fuzzy toys. After playing, it napped in Michelle's lap. One day, the kitten said to Michelle, "Would you like me to tell you a story?"

The team lined up. The kicker kicked the football. Up, up it soared. It went up so high that it went into orbit around the Earth. The game was over. The Aardvarks had won.

"This is a great car," the salesperson said. "It can go very fast. It can cook your breakfast. It always starts, even on the coldest day. You really should buy this car."

Chris studied about healthy food in school. He learned that milk could make him grow. Chris drank a glass of milk just before he went to bed. When he got up in the morning, he was so tall, his head went right through the ceiling.

Name ______________________

Starfish

A starfish is not really a fish. It is an animal. It belongs to a group of animals that have skin that is tough and covered with sharp bumps called *spines.*

Starfish live in the ocean.

Most starfish have five "arms" going out from the main body. This makes them look like stars. The mouth of a starfish is on the underside of its body. A starfish can eat in two different ways. It can take food in through its mouth and eat it. It can also eat by pushing its stomach out of its mouth and wrapping it around the food.

If an arm breaks off the starfish, it can grow a new one.

Directions: Read the statements. Decide if each is a fact or an opinion. Write **F** for fact and **O** for opinion.

______ **1.** It would be fun to feel a starfish.

______ **2.** A starfish would be a good pet.

______ **3.** If a starfish "arm" breaks off, it can grow a new one.

______ **4.** Starfish look pretty.

______ **5.** Starfish live in the ocean.

______ **6.** Starfish have tough skin with spines.

Name ______________________

Figs

Fig is the name of a fruit and of the plant the fruit grows on. The plant can look like a bush or like a tree. Fig plants grow where it is warm all year long.

The fig fruit grows in bunches on the stems of fig plants. Some figs can be picked two times each year. They can be picked from old branches in June or July. They can be picked from new branches in August or September.

Many people like to eat figs. They can be eaten in fig cookies or in fig bars. They can be canned or eaten fresh. Sometimes figs are dried.

Directions: Color the fig **red** if the sentence is a **fact**. Color the fig **blue** if the sentence is an **opinion**.

 **1.** A fig is a plant and a fruit.

 **2.** The fig tree is very pretty.

 **3.** Fig plants do not grow where it is very cold.

 **4.** Figs grow in a bunch.

 **5.** You can pick figs two times each year.

 **6.** Figs taste very good.

 **7.** You can eat figs in many ways.

 **8.** The best way to eat a fig is in a fig cookie.

Name ____________________

What's My Name?

Different words have different jobs. A **naming word** names a person, place, or thing. Naming words are also called **nouns**.

Example: person — nurse
place — store
thing — drum

Directions: In the word box below, circle only the words that name a person, place, or thing. Then, use the nouns you circled to name each picture.

teacher	up	dog	the	library
runs	is	cowhand	cap	zoo

Name ______________________

Person, Place, or Thing?

Directions: Write each noun in the correct box below.

girl	park	truck	vase
artist	tree	doctor	zoo
school	store	ball	baby

Person

Place

Thing

Name ______________________

Finding Nouns

A **noun** names a person, place, or thing.

Directions: Circle two nouns in each sentence below. The first one is done for you.

The (pig) has a curly (tail.)

The hen is sitting on her nest.

A horse is in the barn.

The goat has horns.

The cow has a calf.

The farmer is painting the fence.

Name ______________________

Nouns at Play

Directions: Complete each sentence with the correct noun from the word box. Write the noun on the line.

ducks	**sun**	**tree**
dog	**boys**	**bird**

1. A big ______________________ grows in the park.
2. The ______________________ is in the sky.
3. A ______________________ digs a hole.
4. Three ______________________ swim in the water.
5. A ______________________ sits on its nest.
6. Two ______________________ fly a kite.

Name ______________________

Verbs

Directions: Look at the picture and read the words. Write an action word in each sentence below.

1. The two boys like to ______________________ together.

2. The children ______________________ the soccer ball.

3. Some children like to ______________________ on the swing.

4. The girl can ______________________ very fast.

5. The teacher ______________________ the bell.

Name ______________________

Ready, Set, Go!

An **action word** tells what a person or thing can do.

Example: Fred **kicks** the ball.

Directions: Read the words below. Circle words that tell what the children are doing.

jump

boy

sleep

bed

hello

talk

skate

mittens

hop

sidewalk

sing

song

swim

deep

story

read

Name ______________________

Action Words

Directions: Underline the action word in each sentence. Then, draw a line to match each sentence with the correct picture. The first one is done for you.

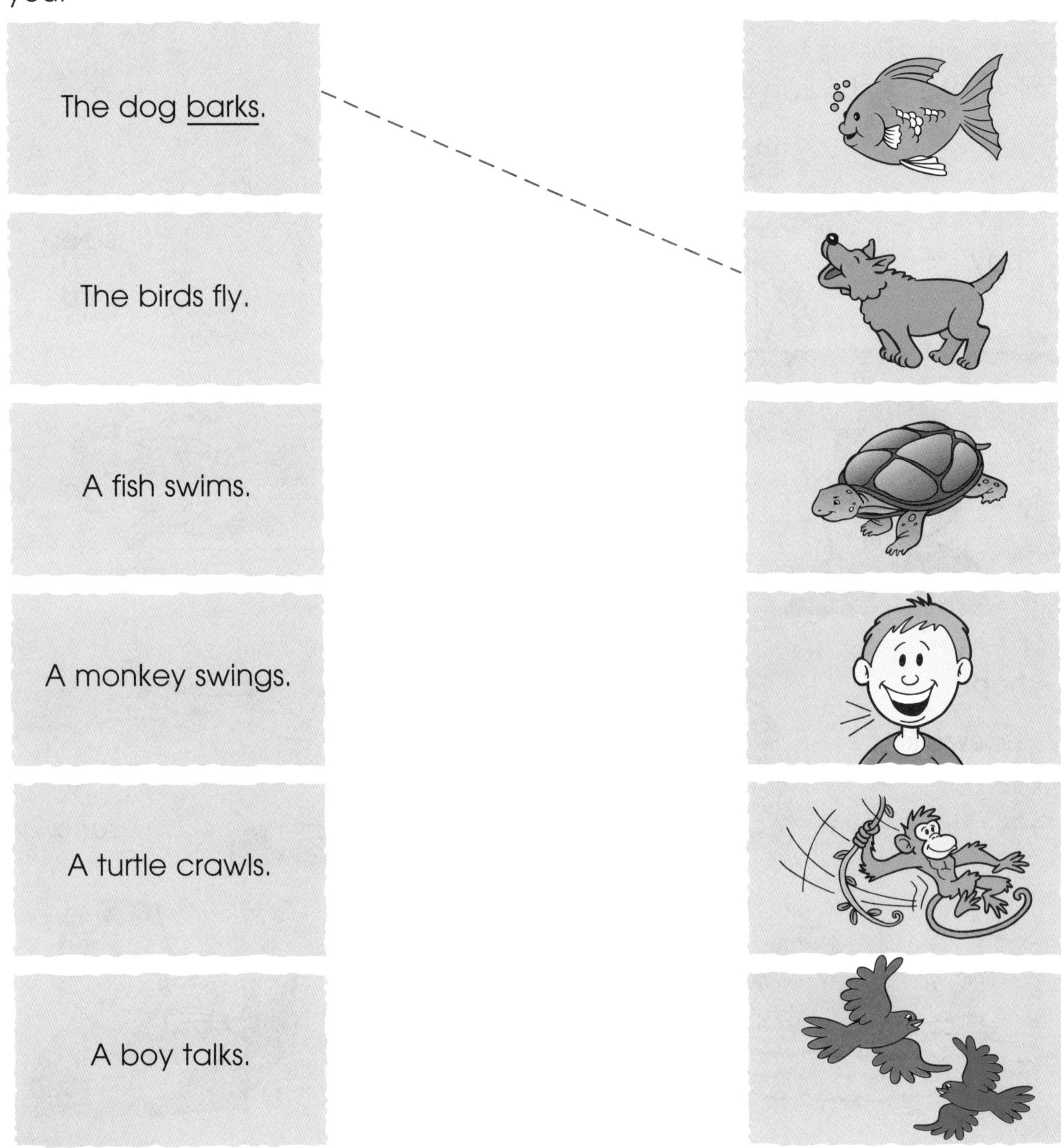
The dog barks.
The birds fly.
A fish swims.
A monkey swings.
A turtle crawls.
A boy talks.

Name ______________________

What Is a Verb?

A **verb** is an action word. A verb tells what a person or thing does.

Example: Jane **reads** a book.

Directions: Circle the verb in each sentence below.

Two tiny dogs dance.

The bear climbs a ladder.

The clown falls down.

A tiger jumps through a ring.

A boy eats popcorn.

A woman swings on a trapeze.

Name ____________________

Review

Directions: Read the sentences below. Draw a **red** circle around the **nouns**. Draw a **blue** line under the **verbs**.

1. The boy runs fast.

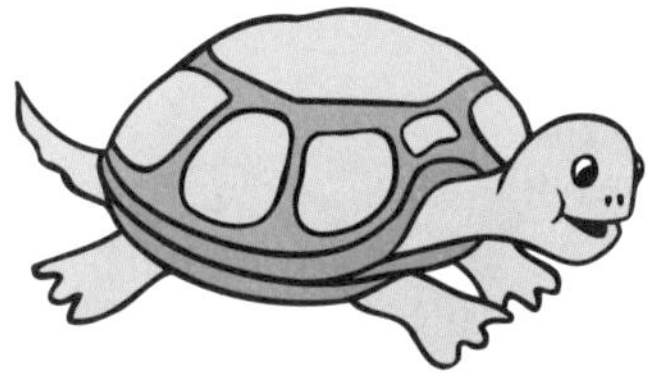

2. The turtle eats leaves.

3. The fish swim in the tank.

4. The girl hits the ball.

Name ______________________

Review

Directions: Cut out the words below. Glue naming words in the **Nouns** box. Glue action words in the **Verbs** box.

Nouns	Verbs

cut ✂ -

boy	jump	cat	sit
throw	house	swim	fork

Name ______________________

Words That Describe

Directions: Read the words in the box. Choose the word that describes, or tells about, the picture. Write it next to the picture.

wet	round	funny	soft	sad	tall

______________	______________
______________	______________
______________	______________

Name ______________________

Words That Describe

Describing words tell us more about a person, place, or thing.

Directions: Read the words in the box. Choose a word that describes the picture. Write it next to the picture.

happy **round** **sick** **cold** **long**

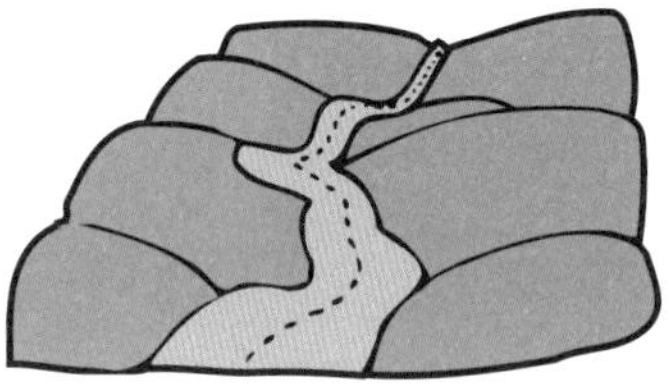

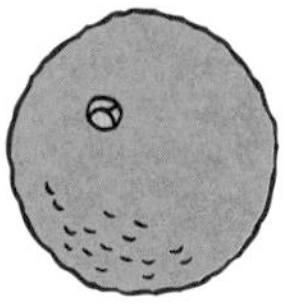

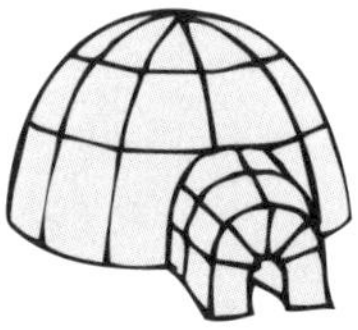

Adjectives

Describing words are also called **adjectives**.

Directions: Circle the describing words in the sentences.

1. The juicy apple is on the plate.

2. The furry dog is eating a bone.

3. It was a sunny day.

4. The kitten drinks warm milk.

5. The baby has a loud cry.

Name ____________________

We're the Same!

Words that mean the **same** thing, or close to the same thing, are called **synonyms**.

Directions: Write a word from the word list that has the same meaning as each word below.

Word List			
bright	hop	dad	fast
pretty	plate	silly	center

sunny ____________________

beautiful ____________________

middle ____________________

dish ____________________

quick ____________________

jump ____________________

goofy ____________________

father ____________________

Name ______________________

Take My Place

Directions: Choose the word from the word list below that could take the place of the underlined word in each sentence. Write it on the line.

Word List

pick	tired	cut
porch	pull	bag

1. I was so <u>sleepy</u>! I couldn't wait to go to bed! ______________________

2. Please put all your books in this <u>sack</u>.

   ____

3. Please <u>choose</u> a present you would like to open. ______________________

4. Are you strong enough to <u>drag</u> this heavy crate? ______________________

5. "It is important to <u>trim</u> the extra fabric on your art project," said my art teacher.

   ____

6. We sipped lemonade on the <u>deck</u>.

   ____

Name ____________________

Antonym Artists!

Antonyms are words that have **opposite** meanings. Abby and Abe are Antonym Artists! They like to draw opposite pictures.

Directions: Help Abe draw the opposite of Abby's pictures.

Name ______________________

Antonyms Are Opposites!

Words with **opposite** meanings are called **antonyms**.

Directions: Circle an antonym for the underlined word in each sentence.

1. The sky was very <u>dark</u>.	purple	old	light
2. Turn <u>left</u> at the light.	right	sideways	yellow
3. The shelf was very <u>high</u>.	pretty	low	loud
4. The turtle walked <u>slowly</u>.	silly	quickly	nicely
5. I <u>whispered</u> at the circus.	laughed	coughed	shouted
6. Bobby is an <u>adult</u>.	child	fan	principal
7. The clown was very <u>strong</u>.	weak	silly	hungry
8. The library is a <u>quiet</u> place.	fun	messy	noisy

Name ______________________

Batty Bats!

Some words have more than one meaning.

The word **bat** has more than one meaning.

Directions: Look at the words and their meanings below. Next to each picture, write the number that has the correct meaning.

can: **1.** a metal container
2. to know how

____  ____ 

band: **1.** a group of musicians
2. a strip of material

____  ____ 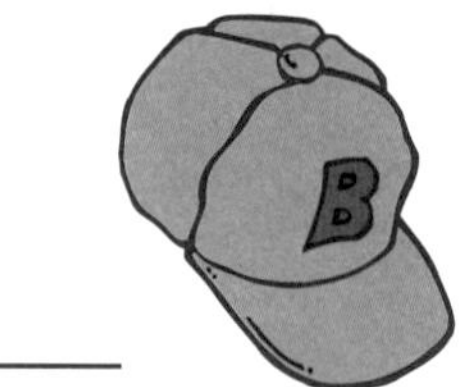

cap: **1.** a soft hat with a visor
2. lid or cover

____ 

____ 

crow: **1.** a large black bird
2. the loud cry of a rooster

____ ____

Name ____________________

Match That Meaning!

Some words have more than one meaning. Look at the list of words.

Directions: Match the word's correct meaning to the pictures below.

cross: **1.** to draw a line through
2. angry

fall: **3.** the season between summer and winter
4. to trip or stumble

land: **5.** to bring to a stop or rest
6. the ground

____

____

____

____

____

____

Name ______________________

Homonyms

Homonyms are words that sound the same, but are spelled differently and have different meanings. For example, **sun** and **son** are homonyms.

Directions: Look at the word. Circle the picture that goes with the word.

1. sun

2. hi

3. ate

4. four

5. buy

6. hear

Homonyms

Directions: Look at each picture. Circle the homonym that is spelled the correct way.

deer dear

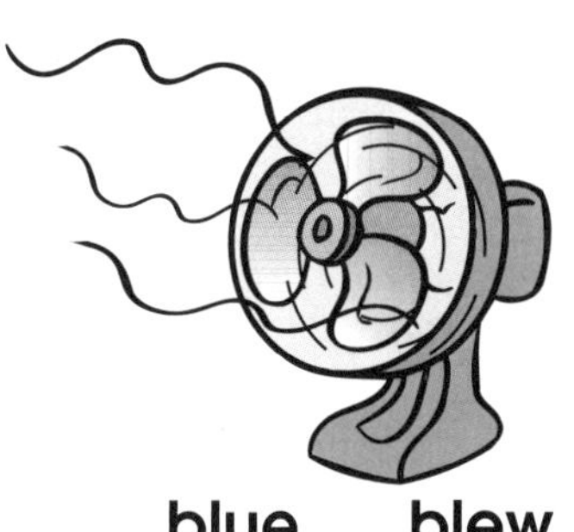

blue blew

to two

hi high

by bye

new knew

ate eight

red read

Name ______________________

Homonyms

Directions: Write the word from the box that has the same sound but a different meaning next to each picture.

ball	see	blew	pear

bawl ______________________

pair ______________________

sea ______________________

blue ______________________

Name ______________________

Homonyms

Directions: Jane is having a birthday party. Complete each sentence with a homonym from the box. Then, write the word in the puzzle.

blew	son
blue	two
too	to
sun	write
right	bee
be	knew
new	

1. 2. 3. 4. 5.

Across:

1. Jane ______________ out the candles.

4. Two days ago, she was stung by a ______________ .

5. But after ______________ days, she felt better.

Down:

1. She has on a ______________ dress for her party.

2. She will ______________ a letter to her grandma.

3. Jane is a girl, so she is not a ______________.

Name ______________________

Make Compound Words

Some short words can be put together to make one new word. The new word is called a **compound word**.

cow + hand = cowhand

Directions: Look at each pair of pictures and words below. Join the two words to make a compound word. Write it on the line.

rain + coat = ______________________

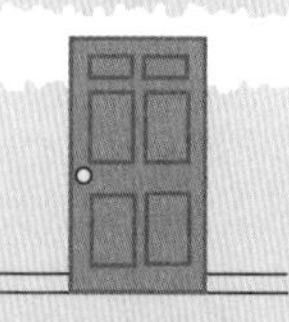 

door + bell = ______________________

dog + house = ______________________

pan + cake = ______________________

horse + shoe = ______________________

Name ______________________________

Two Words in One

Directions: Write the two words that make up each compound word.

snowball ______ ______

raincoat ______ ______

airplane ______ ______

watermelon ______ ______

haircut ______ ______

football ______ ______

sunshine ______ ______

Name ____________________

Compound Word Riddles

Directions: Underline the two words in each sentence that can make a compound word. Write the compound word on the line to complete the sentence.

A kind of bird that is black is a ____________________.

A horse that can race is a ____________________.

A cloth that covers a table is a ____________________.

A room with a bed is a ____________________.

A book with a story is a ____________________.

A bowl that holds fish is a ____________________.

Name ____________________

Compound Words

Directions: Cut out the pictures and words at the bottom of the page. Put two words together to make a compound word. Write the new word.

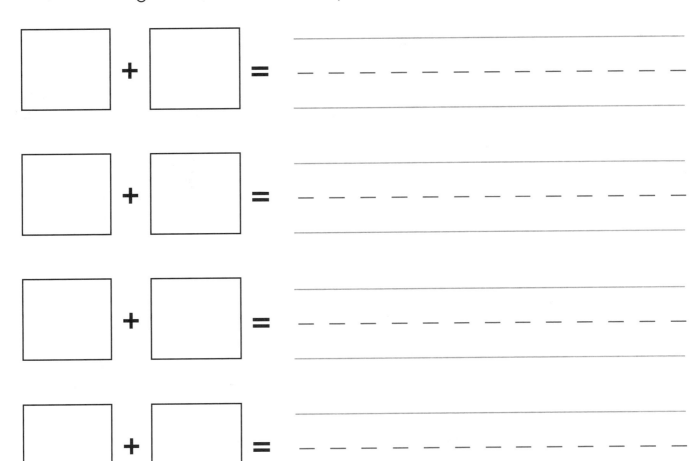

☐ + ☐ = ____________________

☐ + ☐ = ____________________

☐ + ☐ = ____________________

☐ + ☐ = ____________________

cut ✂ -

Name ______________________

Compound Words

Directions: Circle the compound word that completes each sentence. Write each word on the line.

1. The ______________________ brings us letters.

   mailman   snowman

2. A ______________________ grows tall.

   sunlight   sunflower

3. The snow falls ______________________.

   outside   inside

4. A ______________________ fell on my head.

   raindrop   rainbow

5. I put the letter in a ______________________.

   mailbox   shoebox

Name ______________________

One or More Than One?

Directions: Circle the correct word under each picture. The first one is done for you.

Name ______________________

How Many Toys?

Directions: Read the nouns under the pictures. Write each noun under **One** or **More Than One**.

yo-yos

jet

doll

blocks

boat

cars

drum

balls

One	More Than One

Name ____________________

Making Nouns Plural

A **plural noun** means more than one. Add **s** to most nouns to make plural nouns.

Example: Penny has one **dog**.
Jerry has two **dogs**.

Directions: Write the plural form of the nouns below.

flower

girl

squirrel

toy

wagon

turtle

Name ____________________

More Than One

Some nouns name more than one person, place, or thing.

Directions: Add **s** to make the words tell about the picture.

frog ______

pan ______

boy ______

egg ______

horn ______

girl ______

Name ______________________

One Is Not Enough!

A plural noun means more than one. To make nouns that end in **x**, **s**, **ss**, **sh**, or **ch** plural, add **es**.

Example: Barry filled one **box** with sand.
Barry filled four **boxes** with sand.

Directions: Write the plural form of each noun below.

peach

____

brush

____

fox

____

dress

____

bus

____

watch

____

Name ______________________________

Use the Clues

Directions: Write each word from the word box in the correct place. Remember that plural forms usually end in **s**.

kites **star** **chick** **foxes** **matches** **lunch**

One

More Than One (Plural)

Name ____________________

Sentences That Tell

Some sentences tell something. Every **telling sentence** ends with a **period**.

Example: The bird sings.

Directions: Circle only the sentences that tell something.

1. Two turtles sat on a log.
2. One turtle fell off.
3. Did you see her?
4. She swam away.
5. The water is cold.
6. Can you swim?

Name ____________________

Statements

A **statement** is a sentence that tells something. It begins with a capital letter and ends with a period.
Example: The Moon orbits the Earth.

Directions: If the sentence is a statement, color the space black. If it is not, color the space yellow.

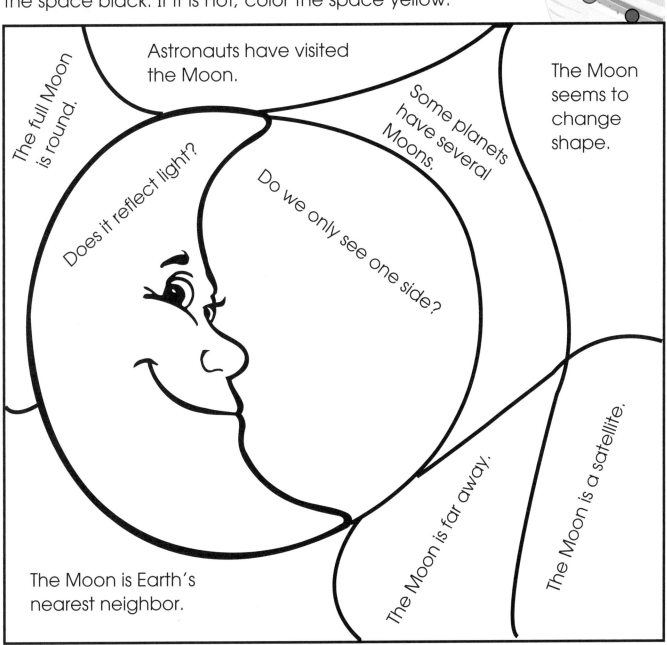

The full Moon is round.

Astronauts have visited the Moon.

Some planets have several Moons.

The Moon seems to change shape.

Does it reflect light?

Do we only see one side?

The Moon is Earth's nearest neighbor.

The Moon is far away.

The Moon is a satellite.

Name ____________________

Sentences

Sentences begin with capital letters.

Directions: Read the sentences and write them below. Begin each sentence with a capital letter.

Example: the cat is fat.

The cat is fat.

my dog is big.

the boy is sad.

bikes are fun!

dad can bake.

Name ____________________

Writing Sentences

A **sentence** begins with a capital letter and ends with a period.

Directions: Read the two sentences on each line. Draw a line between the two sentences. Then, write each sentence correctly.

i have a new bike it is red

we are twins we look just alike

the baby is crying she wants a bottle

Name ____________________

Completing Sentences

A **sentence** must make sense.

Directions: Match each sentence with an ending which makes sense. Circle the correct ending.

1. Today is
   - the first day of school.
   - on the window.

2. I like to
   - around the corner.
   - walk to school with my friend.

3. We eat lunch
   - at noon every day.
   - on the roof.

4. My class
   - under the old tree.
   - is learning to read.

5. I put my
   - pencil on my desk.
   - in the small box.

6. Our classroom
   - three more times.
   - has a map on the wall.

Name ______________________

Making Sentences

A **sentence** tells a whole idea.

Directions: Cut out and glue each picture and group of words together to make a sentence.

has four carrots.
makes a web.
are on the cake.
is on a dish.

Name ______________________________

Sentence Building

Sentences can tell a story.

Directions: Read each sentence. Cut out and glue the sentence that tells what happened next. Write a sentence that tells what could happen after that.

Mary went to bed and quickly fell asleep.

Glue

Brad saw something shiny in the grass.

Glue

PET STORE

OPEN

Sally wanted a pet for her birthday.

Glue

He bent down to see what it was.

Her mom took her to the pet store.

She began to have an amazing dream.

Subjects of Sentences

The **subject** of a sentence tells who or what does something.

Examples: Polar bears love cold weather.
The bear's coat is thick.

Directions: Circle the subject of each sentence.

1. Polar bears live in the Arctic.
2. The Arctic is very cold.
3. The polar bear's coat is white.
4. The fur coat keeps the bear warm.
5. The bear has a layer of fat under its skin.
6. The fat is called blubber.
7. Blubber keeps the bear warm, too.
8. Polar bears eat seals.
9. A polar bear can sneak up on a seal.
10. The bear's white coat makes it hard to see.

Name ________________________

Predicates of Sentences

The **predicate** of a sentence tells what the subject is or does.

Examples: Parrots **are not all alike**.
Some parrots **can learn tricks**.

Directions: Circle the predicate of each sentence.

1. Parrots live in hot places.
2. Some macaws are three-feet long.
3. Macaws live in rainforests.
4. Other parrots build nests in desert cactuses.
5. Most parrots have long beaks.
6. They use their beaks for cracking nuts.
7. Some parrots cannot crack nuts.
8. They eat seeds and fruits instead.
9. Parrots are colorful birds.
10. These birds have loud voices.

Questions

A **question** is a sentence that asks something. It begins with a capital letter and ends with a question mark.

Example: Have you ever visited a farm? What animals lived on the farm?

Directions: If the sentence is a question, put a **question mark** at the end and color the barn red. If it is not, draw an **X** on the barn.

 1. I'm going to visit my grandma

 2. Would you like to go with me

 3. Will you ask your mother

 4. Did she say you could go

 5. What would you like to do first

 6. Do you want to see the ducks

 7. There are four of them on the pond

 8. We'll see the baby chicks next

 9. Are you glad you came with me

 10. Maybe you can come again

Name ______________________

More Questions

Directions: A **question** begins with a capital letter and ends with a question mark. Look at each picture of Panda. Ask Panda a question to go with each picture.

Name ______________________

Changing Sentences

The order of words can change a sentence.

Directions: Read each telling sentence. Change the order of the words to make an asking sentence. **Example:**

The clown is happy.

Is the clown happy?

The boy can swim.

____

The bell will ring.

____

The popcorn is hot.

____

The flowers are lovely.

____

Name ____________________

Sentences That Ask

Some sentences ask something. An **asking sentence** is called a **question**. A question ends with a **question mark**.

Example: What is your name?

Directions: Circle only the questions.

1. Is that your house?
2. There are two pictures on the wall.
3. Where do you sleep?
4. Do you watch TV in that room?
5. Which coat is yours?
6. The kitten is asleep.

Name ______________________

Questions, Questions

A **question** begins with a capital letter and ends with a question mark.

Directions: Write each question correctly on the line.

is our class going to the Science Museum

will we see dinosaur bones

does the museum have a mummy

Name ___________________________

I'm So Excited!

The end mark **!** shows that you are excited.
Use it to end a sentence that shows strong feelings.

Example: What a beautiful day this is**!**

Directions: Read these sentences. Write **?** or **!** after each sentence.

? or !

1. What a great day this is for a race ☐
2. Who is running in this race ☐
3. How fast they run ☐
4. Who will finish first ☐
5. The runners are off ☐
6. Run faster ☐
7. Can you see the finish line ☐
8. I won the race ☐

Name ____________________

Sentence Sequence

The words in a sentence must be in the correct order.

Directions: Cut out and glue the words in the correct order to tell about each picture.

1.

2.

3.

1.	2.	3.
is going	We are taking	to swim
to the beach.	of food.	It's fun
My family	a basket	in the ocean.

Word Order

Word order is the order of words in a sentence which makes sense.

Directions: Cut out the words and put them in the correct order. Glue each sentence on another sheet of paper.

I	like	bike.	to ride my

hot.	It is	and	sunny

drink	I can	water.

My	me.	with	plays	mom

tricks.	do	can	The	dog

you	go	store?	to	the	Can

Name ______________________

Surprising Sequence

Some sentences show a strong feeling and end with an **exclamation mark (!)**. A surprising sentence may be only one or two words showing fear, surprise, or pain, such as "Oh, no!"

Directions: Put a **period** at the end of the sentences that tell something. Put an **exclamation mark** at the end of the sentences that show a strong feeling. Put a **question mark** at the end of the sentences that ask a question.

1. The cheetah can run very fast

2. Wow

3. Look at that cheetah go

4. Can you run fast

5. Oh, my

6. You're faster than I am

7. Let's run together

8. We can run as fast as a cheetah

9. What fun

10. Do you think cheetahs get tired

Name ______________________

ABC Order

Sometimes, words are put in **ABC order**. That means that if a word starts with **a**, it comes first. If it starts with **b**, it comes next, and so on in the order of the alphabet.

Directions: Circle the first letter of each word below. Then, put the words in ABC order. The first one is done for you.

car bird

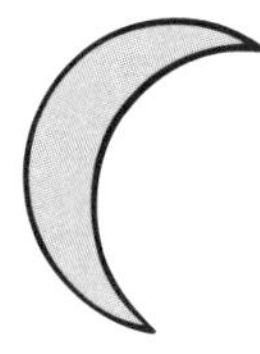

moon two

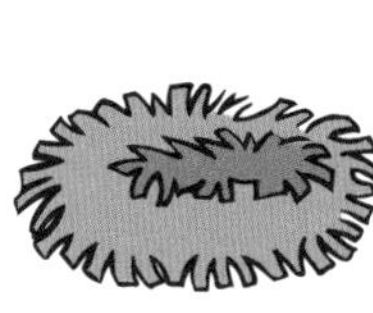

nest fan

bird ______________ ______________

car ______________ ______________

card dog

pig bike

sun pie

______________ ______________ ______________

______________ ______________ ______________

Name ____________________

ABC Order

Directions: Put each row of words in ABC order. If the first letters of two words are the same, look at the second or third letters.

Example:

1. __1__ candy __2__ carrot __4__ duck __3__ dance

2. ____ cold ____ hot ____ carry ____ hit

3. ____ flash ____ fan ____ fun ____ garden

4. ____ seat ____ sun ____ saw ____ sit

5. ____ row ____ ring ____ rock ____ run

6. ____ truck ____ turn ____ twin ____ talk

7. ____ seven ____ shoe ____ soap ____ smell

8. ____ pay ____ penny ____ pocket ____ plant

How to Help Your Child Prepare for Standardized Testing

Preparing All Year Round
Perhaps the most valuable way you can help your child prepare for standardized achievement tests is by providing enriching experiences. Keep in mind also that test results for younger children are not as reliable as for older students. If a child is hungry, tired, or upset, this may result in a poor test score. Here are some tips on how you can help your child do his or her best on standardized tests.

Read aloud with your child. Reading aloud helps develop vocabulary and fosters a positive attitude toward reading. Reading together is one of the most effective ways you can help your child succeed in school.

Share experiences. Baking cookies together, planting a garden, or making a map of your neighborhood are examples of activities that help build skills that are measured on the tests, such as sequencing and following directions.

Become informed about your state's testing procedures. Ask about or watch for announcements of meetings that explain about standardized tests and statewide assessments in your school district. Talk to your child's teacher about your child's individual performance on these state tests during a parent-teacher conference.

Help your child know what to expect. Read and discuss with your child the test-taking tips in this book. Your child can prepare by working through a couple of strategies a day so that no practice session takes too long.

Help your child with his or her regular school assignments. Set up a quiet study area for homework. Supply this area with pencils, paper, markers, a calculator, a ruler, a dictionary, scissors, glue, and so on. Check your child's homework and offer to help if he or she gets stuck. But remember, it's your child's homework, not yours. If you help too much, your child will not benefit from the activity.

Keep in regular contact with your child's teacher. Attend parent-teacher conferences, school functions, PTA or PTO meetings, and school board meetings. This will help you get to know the educators in your district and the families of your child's classmates.
Learn to use computers as an educational resource. If you do not have a computer and Internet access at home, try your local library.
Remember—simply getting your child comfortable with testing procedures and helping him or her know what to expect can improve test scores!

Getting Ready for the Big Day

There are lots of things you can do on or immediately before test day to improve your child's chances of testing success. What's more, these strategies will help your child prepare him- or herself for school tests, too, and promote general study skills that can last a lifetime.

Provide a good breakfast on test day. Instead of sugar cereal, which provides immediate but not long-term energy, have your child eat a breakfast with protein or complex carbohydrates, such as an egg, whole grain cereal or toast, or a banana-yogurt shake.

Promote a good night's sleep. A good night's sleep before the test is essential. Try not to overstress the importance of the test. This may cause your child to lose sleep because of anxiety. Doing some exercise after school and having a quiet evening routine will help your child sleep well the night before the test.

Assure your child that he or she is not expected to know all of the answers on the test. Explain that other children in higher grades may take the same test, and that the test may measure things your child has not yet learned in school. Help your child understand that you expect him or her to put forth a good effort—and that this is enough. Your child should not try to cram for these tests. Also avoid threats or bribes; these put undue pressure on children and may interfere with their best performance.

Keep the mood light and offer encouragement. To provide a break on test days, do something fun and special after school—take a walk around the neighborhood, play a game, read a favorite book, or prepare a special snack together. These activities keep your child's mood light—even if the testing sessions have been difficult—and show how much you appreciate your child's effort.

TEST PRACTICE Name ____________________

READING: WORD ANALYSIS

Lesson 1: Letter Recognition

Directions: Look at the word your teacher reads. Mark the letter the word begins with. Example A is done for you. Practice with example B.

Examples

A. Which letter does the word sand begin with?

- (A) b
- (B) l
- (C) s
- (D) c

B. Which letter does the word large begin with?

- (F) p
- (G) q
- (H) m
- (J) l

If you are not sure which answer is correct, take your best guess. Eliminate answer choices you know are wrong.

Practice

1. Which letter does the word park begin with?

- (A) v
- (B) w
- (C) b
- (D) p

2. Which letter does the word dog begin with?

- (F) d
- (G) b
- (H) y
- (J) o

3. Which letter does the word nice begin with?

- (A) s
- (B) n
- (C) u
- (D) k

4. Which letter does the word talk begin with?

- (F) j
- (G) f
- (H) t
- (J) l

Name ______________________

READING: WORD ANALYSIS

Lesson 2: Beginning Sounds

Directions: Look at the picture. Listen to your teacher read the word. Listen to your teacher read the words to the right of the picture. Mark the word with the same beginning sound as the picture. Practice with example A.

Example

A. desk

Ⓐ chair
Ⓑ den
Ⓒ bat
Ⓓ man

Say the name of the picture to yourself. Listen closely to the word choices.

Practice

1. rabbit

Ⓐ man
Ⓑ bike
Ⓒ paper
Ⓓ ring

2. mop

Ⓕ miss
Ⓖ hill
Ⓗ clock
Ⓙ win

3. bag

Ⓐ vase
Ⓑ top
Ⓒ bell
Ⓓ fish

4. tie

Ⓕ tag
Ⓖ girl
Ⓗ shell
Ⓙ pin

Name ____________________

READING: WORD ANALYSIS

Lesson 3: Ending Sounds

Directions: Listen to your teacher read all the words. Mark the word with the same ending sound as the first word. Practice with examples A and B.

Examples

A. make

- Ⓐ cat
- Ⓑ rock
- Ⓒ worm
- Ⓓ pen

B. hive

- Ⓕ web
- Ⓖ fun
- Ⓗ glove
- Ⓙ tip

Listen carefully to the ending sound of each word.

Practice

1. star

- Ⓐ mop
- Ⓑ leaf
- Ⓒ jar
- Ⓓ five

2. leg

- Ⓕ rug
- Ⓖ gone
- Ⓗ rich
- Ⓙ grab

3. stew

- Ⓐ net
- Ⓑ wheel
- Ⓒ barn
- Ⓓ now

4. hit

- Ⓕ dish
- Ⓖ win
- Ⓗ not
- Ⓙ hear

5. bell

- Ⓐ rest
- Ⓑ hill
- Ⓒ boat
- Ⓓ cab

Name ______________________

READING: WORD ANALYSIS

Lesson 4: Rhyming Words

Directions: Listen to your teacher read the word. Choose the picture that rhymes with the word. Practice with example A.

Example

A. mop

Ⓐ 

Ⓑ 

Ⓒ 

Clue

Look at the pictures. Say the words to yourself. Listen for the ending sound.

Practice

1. dog

Ⓐ 

Ⓑ 

Ⓒ 

2. hat

Ⓕ 

Ⓖ 

Ⓗ 

3. rock

Ⓐ 

Ⓑ 

Ⓒ 

STOP

TEST PRACTICE

Name ____________________

READING: WORD ANALYSIS

Lesson 5: Word Recognition

Directions: Listen to your teacher read the word. Notice the underlined part. Then, listen as your teacher reads the word choices. Listen for the word with the same sound as the underlined part and mark it. Practice with examples A and B.

Examples

A. mud

- (A) but
- (B) sock
- (C) shell
- (D) cat

B. pound

- (F) snow
- (G) spent
- (H) loud
- (J) rider

Do numbers 1–4 the same way. You may ask your teacher to repeat an item after all of the word choices have been read one time.

Practice

1. rose

- (A) rule
- (B) bake
- (C) pony
- (D) nine

2. spoon

- (F) here
- (G) smooth
- (H) after
- (J) chip

3. peach

- (A) quiet
- (B) push
- (C) last
- (D) need

4. ride

- (F) miss
- (G) line
- (H) street
- (J) horse

Name ______________________________

READING: WORD ANALYSIS

Lesson 6: Vowel Sounds and Sight Words

Directions: Listen as your teacher reads the question and says the name of the picture. Then, listen as your teacher reads the word choices. Choose the best answer. Example A is done for you. Practice with example B.

Examples

A. What word has the same vowel sound as the picture?

- (A) pen (filled in)
- (B) spoon
- (C) kite
- (D) chip

B. What word rhymes with shell?

- (F) smell
- (G) dog
- (H) rode
- (J) mile

Listen to all choices before you mark your answer.

Practice

1. What word has the same vowel sound as the picture?

- (A) mouse
- (B) long
- (C) tick
- (D) spoon

2. What word has the same vowel sound as the picture?

- (F) bead
- (G) hive
- (H) quilt
- (J) apple

3. What word has the same vowel sound as might?

- (A) pin
- (B) time
- (C) from
- (D) soul

4. What word rhymes with tough?

- (F) crow
- (G) pool
- (H) puff
- (J) ton

TEST PRACTICE

Name ____________________

READING: WORD ANALYSIS

Lesson 7: Word Study

Directions: Listen as your teacher reads the word choices. Mark the word that is a compound word. Practice with example A.

Directions: Listen as your teacher reads the sentence and the word choices. One will fill in the blank. Mark your choice. Practice with example B.

Examples

A.

Ⓐ airplane
Ⓑ ringer
Ⓒ tune

B. The dog _______ its food.

Ⓕ eat
Ⓖ ate
Ⓗ eating

Listen carefully each time your teacher reads directions. The directions may change.

Practice

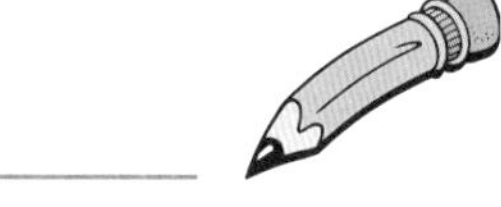

1.

Ⓐ toolbox
Ⓑ kitchen
Ⓒ gate

2.

Ⓕ warning
Ⓖ flowerpot
Ⓗ glasses

3.

Ⓐ teacup
Ⓑ pencil
Ⓒ jumping

4. I am _______ than you.

Ⓕ big
Ⓖ bigger
Ⓗ biggest

5. I _______ books.

Ⓐ readed
Ⓑ reads
Ⓒ read

6. He _______ hot.

Ⓕ weren't
Ⓖ wasn't
Ⓗ won't

Name ______________________________ TEST PRACTICE

READING: VOCABULARY

Lesson 8: Picture Vocabulary

Directions: Listen to your teacher read the sentence. Choose the picture that finishes the sentence. Practice with example A.

Example

A. Bill drinks ________ .

Ⓐ Ⓑ Ⓒ

Practice

Listen carefully. Think about what you hear while you look at each picture.

1. I like to read a ________ .

Ⓐ     

2. The ________ ran fast.

Ⓕ  Ⓖ  Ⓗ 

3. The baby ________ in her bed.

Ⓐ  Ⓑ  Ⓒ 

4. The ________ rings.

 Ⓖ   

STOP

Name ____________________

READING: VOCABULARY

Lesson 9: Word Reading

Directions: Look at the picture. Listen as your teacher reads the word choices. Mark the word that matches the picture. Practice with examples A and B.

Examples

A.

Ⓐ cat
Ⓑ flower
Ⓒ bird

B.

Ⓕ sing
Ⓖ bark
Ⓗ read

Listen to all answer choices before you choose.

Practice

1. Ⓐ mom
Ⓑ dog
Ⓒ book

2. Ⓕ hug
Ⓖ cry
Ⓗ run

3. Ⓐ sit
Ⓑ love
Ⓒ eat

4. Ⓕ land
Ⓖ shelf
Ⓗ water

5. Ⓐ run
Ⓑ skip
Ⓒ swim

6. Ⓕ skin
Ⓖ scales
Ⓗ cloth

Name ______________________

READING: VOCABULARY

Lesson 10: Word Meaning

Directions: Listen to your teacher read each phrase and the word choices. Mark the word that matches the phrase. Practice with examples A and B.

Examples

A. to move fast...

- (A) crawl
- (B) run
- (C) walk
- (D) sit

B. a cold thing...

- (F) ice
- (G) fire
- (H) sun
- (J) stove

Be sure about your answer.

Practice

1. a thing that flies...

- (A) pen
- (B) book
- (C) bird
- (D) cup

2. a thing that sings...

- (F) chair
- (G) girl
- (H) nest
- (J) paper

3. to drink a little...

- (A) spill
- (B) tip
- (C) sip
- (D) toss

4. to stay on top of water...

- (F) float
- (G) sink
- (H) pin
- (J) zip

5. noise a dog makes...

- (A) bark
- (B) purr
- (C) cut
- (D) land

6. a food...

- (F) wood
- (G) cart
- (H) apple
- (J) bed

Name ____________________

READING: VOCABULARY

Lesson 11: Synonyms

Directions: Listen to your teacher read the sentence and word choices. Look at the underlined part. Mark the word that means about the same. Practice with examples A and B.

Examples

A. I was sleepy.

- (A) tired
- (B) running
- (C) tall
- (D) purple

B. Jill was in the center.

- (F) bowl
- (G) middle
- (H) end
- (J) side

Clue Think about what the sentence means.

Practice

1. The car was speedy.

- (A) better
- (B) heavy
- (C) fast
- (D) able

2. She is lovely.

- (F) pretty
- (G) sharp
- (H) sad
- (J) near

3. The soup is steaming.

- (A) soft
- (B) spilling
- (C) hot
- (D) cold

4. Kida washes dishes.

- (F) hides
- (G) cuts
- (H) sleeps
- (J) cleans

5. It is a small city.

- (A) house
- (B) bus
- (C) town
- (D) road

6. We took a boat ride.

- (F) car
- (G) balloon
- (H) ship
- (J) bike

STOP

Name ____________________

READING: VOCABULARY

Lesson 12: Antonyms

Directions: Listen to your teacher read the sentence and word choices. Look at the underlined part. Mark the word that means the opposite. Practice with examples A and B.

Examples

A. This is wet.

- (A) big
- (B) brown
- (C) dry
- (D) soaked

B. The rock is heavy.

- (F) cold
- (G) hard
- (H) dirty
- (J) light

Remember, the correct answer is the opposite of the underlined part.

Practice

1. The bear is tame.

- (A) black
- (B) wild
- (C) hungry
- (D) big

2. Susie whispered the secret.

- (F) yelled
- (G) tapped
- (H) cried
- (J) wrote

3. Why is it so little?

- (A) loud
- (B) bad
- (C) big
- (D) short

4. I run very fast.

- (F) slow
- (G) quick
- (H) around
- (J) loud

5. This is easy.

- (A) less
- (B) home
- (C) simple
- (D) hard

6. Jordan was sick.

- (F) ill
- (G) happy
- (H) well
- (J) tiny

Name ____________________

READING: VOCABULARY

Lesson 13: Words in Context

Directions: Listen to your teacher read the sentence and word choices. Choose the word that completes the sentence. Practice with examples A and B.

Examples

A. The ________ was green. It hopped far.

- (A) dog
- (B) rabbit
- (C) frog
- (D) boy

B. The ________ was long. It had 13 cars.

- (F) string
- (G) train
- (H) paper
- (J) hair

Clue **When you think you hear the correct answer, put your finger next to it. Listen to all of the choices.**

Practice

1. Sam sat on the ________ . He soon fell asleep.

- (A) ice
- (B) chair
- (C) hammer
- (D) nail

2. The bee flew to its ________ . It went inside.

- (F) corner
- (G) cup
- (H) hive
- (J) honey

3. There are four ________ on the shelf. Tuti read them all.

- (A) cats
- (B) animals
- (C) suns
- (D) books

4. The joke was ________ . We all smiled.

- (F) funny
- (G) sad
- (H) blue
- (J) bread

STOP

Name ______________________

READING: COMPREHENSION

Lesson 14: Listening Comprehension

Directions: Listen to your teacher read each story. Choose the best answer for each question. Practice with example A.

Example

A. Henry Turtle was in a jam. He had been taking his walk when suddenly an owl landed on his head. What a surprise! What was on Henry's head?

(A) 

 (B) 

 (C) 

Practice

Listen to each story. Think about what you hear, then mark your choice.

1. Carol was going to ride her bike. She would go to the park. She asked Ray to go. His bike had a flat tire. What was wrong with Ray's bike?

(A) 

 (B) 

 (C) 

2. Carol and Ray walked to the park. They walked by the pond. They slid on the slide. They sat on the bench. On what did the children sit to rest?

(F) 

 (G) 

 (H) 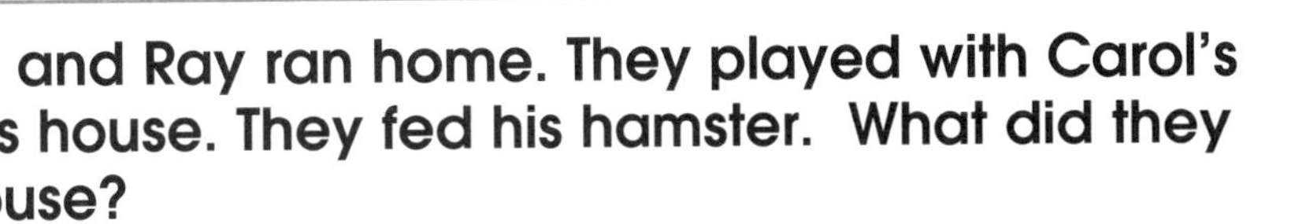

3. It started to rain. Carol and Ray ran home. They played with Carol's cat. They went to Ray's house. They fed his hamster. What did they play with at Carol's house?

 (A) 

 (B) 

 (C) 

Name ________________________

READING: COMPREHENSION

Lesson 15: Picture Comprehension

Directions: Look at the picture. Listen to your teacher read the words next to the picture. Mark the choice that best describes the picture. Practice with example A.

Example

A.

Ⓐ Butterflies have wings.
Ⓑ I saw five butterflies.
Ⓒ The plane was huge.

The correct answer says the most about the picture.

Practice

1.

Ⓐ He reads books here.
Ⓑ Three toys are by the chair.
Ⓒ It was dark.

2.

Ⓕ Tiger got a bath.
Ⓖ It was muddy.
Ⓗ I hate to take baths.

3.

Ⓐ Tina has a cat.
Ⓑ Buster chased the kitten.
Ⓒ The cat is hungry.

4.

Ⓕ I gave Mom a hug.
Ⓖ He was sitting.
Ⓗ Gifts are fun to get.

Name ____________________

READING: COMPREHENSION

Lesson 16: Sentence Comprehension

Directions: Listen to your teacher read the sentence. Mark the picture that completes or matches the sentence. Practice with examples A and B.

Examples

A. This is made of wood. You can write with it.

Ⓐ 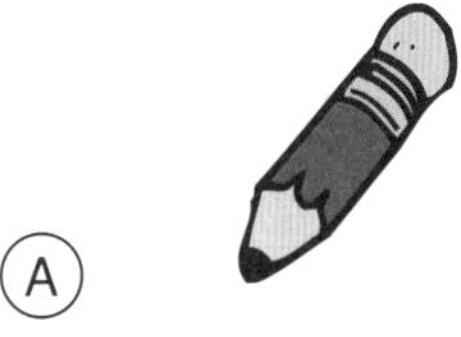 Ⓑ  Ⓒ 

B. I ate a ________.

Ⓕ book
Ⓖ cookie
Ⓗ mop

Listen to the sentence. Think before you make your choice.

Practice

1. This is hot. It helps things grow.

Ⓐ     

2. You smell with this. It is on your face.

 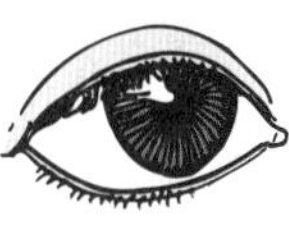 Ⓖ 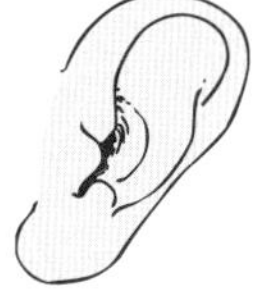 Ⓗ 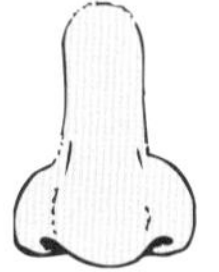

3. This is my ________ .

Ⓐ dog
Ⓑ school
Ⓒ lake

4. There is a ________ in front of school.

Ⓕ bike
 frog
Ⓗ flag

Name ____________________

READING: COMPREHENSION

Lesson 17: Fiction

Directions: Listen to your teacher read the story. Choose the best answers for the questions about the story. Practice with example A.

Example

The boy ran fast. He did not want to be late. Mom was making chicken. It was his favorite food.

A. What was Mom making?

(A) shoes
(B) chicken
(C) puddles

Listen carefully to the whole story.

Practice

Steve and his sister were playing. They were in the yard. A bird landed on the fence.

They watched the bird fly to the ground. It picked up some grass. Then, it flew to a tree. Steve said the bird was making a nest.

1. Who was with Steve?

(A) Steve's mother
(B) Steve's sister
(C) Steve's dog

2. Where did the bird land?

(F) on the fence
(G) on the roof
(H) under the tree

READING: COMPREHENSION

Lesson 18: Fiction

Directions: Listen to your teacher read the story. Mark the best answers to the questions.

Get Warm

Brenda Butterfly was cold. She did not like it. She liked the sunny, warm weather. But it was autumn. "What can I do to get warm?"

Her friend Buddy knew what to do. "I think you should follow the birds. They fly to warm places in winter."

Brenda liked the idea. "That sounds great! Will you come with me, Buddy?"

They followed a flock of birds. It was a long trip. But it was so warm and sunny! Brenda and Buddy smiled. What a good idea!

There were many butterflies in this place. The flowers were colorful. Maybe Brenda and Buddy would stay.

1. Brenda did not like ________ .

- (A) sunny weather
- (B) being cold
- (C) her friend Buddy

2. What did Buddy think Brenda should do?

- (F) follow the birds
- (G) light a fire
- (H) get new coats

3. Why should she follow the birds?

- (A) to find water
- (B) to see snow
- (C) to get to a warm place

4. Two things Brenda and Buddy liked now were ________ .

- (F) their bird friends and fish
- (G) colorful flowers and being warm
- (H) flying far and the moon

Name ______________________________

READING: COMPREHENSION

Lesson 19: Nonfiction

Directions: Listen to your teacher read the story. Choose the best answers to the questions about the story.

Spiders

Spiders are animals. The special name for their animal family is "arachnid." One spider is the tarantula. Another is the wolf spider. All spiders have eight legs. Most spiders spin webs of silk. The webs help the spider catch food. They eat mostly insects. Some spiders are big. There is one as big as a man's hand. Some spiders are very small. One spider is as small as the tip of a pin. This animal is helpful to people. Spiders eat harmful or pesky insects. They eat flies and mosquitoes.

1. Spiders are __________ .

- Ⓐ insects
- Ⓑ animals
- Ⓒ plants

2. Spider webs are made of __________ .

- Ⓕ silk
- Ⓖ rope
- Ⓗ wire

3. Why are spiders helpful?

- Ⓐ Spiders are big and small.
- Ⓑ A tarantula is a kind of spider.
- Ⓒ Spiders eat harmful insects.

4. Why was this story written?

- Ⓕ to tell about spiders
- Ⓖ to tell about mosquitoes
- Ⓗ to scare you

READING: COMPREHENSION

Lesson 20: Nonfiction

Directions: Listen to your teacher read the story. Choose the best answers to the questions.

Statue of Liberty

The Statue of Liberty is in New York. It is a famous statue. People in France gave the United States the statue. This happened in 1884. They wanted to show their friendship.

It is one of the biggest statues ever made. The statue is made from copper. It shows a lady. She is dressed in a robe. She is wearing a crown. The lady is holding a torch and a tablet. A poet wrote a famous poem about the statue. It is on a bronze plaque. People read it when they visit.

Long ago, millions of immigrants, people coming to live in the United States, saw the statue. They felt like she welcomed them. It seemed like her torch was lighting the way to their new home. Millions of other people, called tourists, have also visited. They can climb up to the crown. They can see New York City. Many people around the world know about this great statue.

1. **Who gave the Statue of Liberty to the United States?**
   - Ⓐ the people of France
   - Ⓑ many immigrants
   - Ⓒ the queen

2. **Why did they give the statue to the United States?**
   - Ⓕ to make money
   - Ⓖ so the United States would give them one
   - Ⓗ to show friendship

3. **The statue is made from copper because ________ .**
   - Ⓐ copper is ugly
   - Ⓑ it is strong
   - Ⓒ it smells nice

4. **Immigrants felt like the statue ________ .**
   - Ⓕ worked like a flashlight
   - Ⓖ welcomed them
   - Ⓗ was too tall

Name ______________________________

READING PRACTICE TEST ANSWER SHEET

STUDENT'S NAME																		SCHOOL
LAST											FIRST						MI	TEACHER
																		FEMALE ◯ MALE ◯
A	A	A	A	A	A	A	A	A	A	A	A	A	A	A	A	A	A	
B	B	B	B	B	B	B	B	B	B	B	B	B	B	B	B	B	B	
C	C	C	C	C	C	C	C	C	C	C	C	C	C	C	C	C	C	
D	D	D	D	D	D	D	D	D	D	D	D	D	D	D	D	D	D	
E	E	E	E	E	E	E	E	E	E	E	E	E	E	E	E	E	E	
F	F	F	F	F	F	F	F	F	F	F	F	F	F	F	F	F	F	
G	G	G	G	G	G	G	G	G	G	G	G	G	G	G	G	G	G	
H	H	H	H	H	H	H	H	H	H	H	H	H	H	H	H	H	H	
I	I	I	I	I	I	I	I	I	I	I	I	I	I	I	I	I	I	
J	J	J	J	J	J	J	J	J	J	J	J	J	J	J	J	J	J	
K	K	K	K	K	K	K	K	K	K	K	K	K	K	K	K	K	K	
L	L	L	L	L	L	L	L	L	L	L	L	L	L	L	L	L	L	
M	M	M	M	M	M	M	M	M	M	M	M	M	M	M	M	M	M	
N	N	N	N	N	N	N	N	N	N	N	N	N	N	N	N	N	N	
O	O	O	O	O	O	O	O	O	O	O	O	O	O	O	O	O	O	
P	P	P	P	P	P	P	P	P	P	P	P	P	P	P	P	P	P	
Q	Q	Q	Q	Q	Q	Q	Q	Q	Q	Q	Q	Q	Q	Q	Q	Q	Q	
R	R	R	R	R	R	R	R	R	R	R	R	R	R	R	R	R	R	
S	S	S	S	S	S	S	S	S	S	S	S	S	S	S	S	S	S	
T	T	T	T	T	T	T	T	T	T	T	T	T	T	T	T	T	T	
U	U	U	U	U	U	U	U	U	U	U	U	U	U	U	U	U	U	
V	V	V	V	V	V	V	V	V	V	V	V	V	V	V	V	V	V	
W	W	W	W	W	W	W	W	W	W	W	W	W	W	W	W	W	W	
X	X	X	X	X	X	X	X	X	X	X	X	X	X	X	X	X	X	
Y	Y	Y	Y	Y	Y	Y	Y	Y	Y	Y	Y	Y	Y	Y	Y	Y	Y	
Z	Z	Z	Z	Z	Z	Z	Z	Z	Z	Z	Z	Z	Z	Z	Z	Z	Z	

BIRTH DATE				
MONTH	DAY		YEAR	
JAN ◯	0	0	0	0
FEB ◯	1	1	1	1
MAR ◯	2	2	2	2
APR ◯	3	3		3
MAY ◯		4		4
JUN ◯		5		5
JUL ◯		6		6
AUG ◯		7		7
SEP ◯		8		8
OCT ◯		9		9
NOV ◯				
DEC ◯				

GRADE
1 2 3 4 5

Part 1: WORD ANALYSIS

A (A) (B) (C) (D)
1 (A) (B) (C) (D)
2 (F) (G) (H) (J)
3 (A) (B) (C) (D)
4 (F) (G) (H) (J)
5 (A) (B) (C) (D)
B (F) (G) (H)
C (A) (B) (C)
6 (F) (G) (H)
7 (A) (B) (C)
8 (F) (G) (H)
9 (A) (B) (C)
D (F) (G) (H)
10 (F) (G) (H)
11 (A) (B) (C)
12 (F) (G) (H)
13 (A) (B) (C)
14 (F) (G) (H)
15 (A) (B) (C)
E (A) (B) (C)
F (F) (G) (H)
16 (F) (G) (H)
17 (A) (B) (C)
18 (F) (G) (H)
19 (A) (B) (C)

Part 2: VOCABULARY

A (A) (B) (C)
1 (A) (B) (C)
2 (F) (G) (H)
3 (A) (B) (C)
4 (F) (G) (H)
B (F) (G) (H)
C (A) (B) (C)
5 (A) (B) (C)
6 (F) (G) (H)
7 (A) (B) (C)
8 (F) (G) (H)
9 (A) (B) (C)
10 (F) (G) (H)
11 (A) (B) (C)
12 (F) (G) (H)
D (A) (B) (C) (D)
13 (A) (B) (C) (D)
14 (F) (G) (H) (J)
15 (A) (B) (C) (D)
16 (F) (G) (H) (J)
17 (A) (B) (C) (D)
18 (F) (G) (H) (J)
19 (A) (B) (C) (D)
20 (F) (G) (H) (J)
21 (A) (B) (C) (D)
22 (F) (G) (H) (J)

Part 3: READING COMPREHENSION

A (A) (B) (C)
1 (A) (B) (C)
2 (F) (G) (H)
B (F) (G) (H)
3 (A) (B) (C)
4 (F) (G) (H)
5 (A) (B) (C)
6 (F) (G) (H)
C (A) (B) (C)
7 (A) (B) (C)
8 (F) (G) (H)
9 (A) (B) (C)
10 (F) (G) (H)
D (F) (G) (H)
11 (A) (B) (C)
12 (F) (G) (H)
13 (A) (B) (C)
14 (F) (G) (H)
15 (A) (B) (C)
16 (F) (G) (H)
17 (A) (B) (C)
18 (F) (G) (H)
19 (A) (B) (C)
20 (F) (G) (H)
21 (A) (B) (C)
22 (F) (G) (H)
23 (A) (B) (C)
24 (F) (G) (H)
25 (A) (B) (C)
26 (F) (G) (H)

Name ______________________

READING PRACTICE TEST

Part 1: Word Analysis

Directions: Listen to your teacher read each question and the answer choices. Choose the best answer. Practice with example A. Do numbers 1–5 the same way.

Example

A. Which letter does the word water begin with?

(A) t
(B) v
(C) m
(D) w

1. Which letter does the word heart begin with?

(A) p
(B) b
(C) d
(D) h

2. Which letter does the word take begin with?

(F) t
(G) b
(H) a
(J) e

3. Which letter does the word sunny begin with?

(A) c
(B) s
(C) y
(D) l

4. Which letter does the word bottle begin with?

(F) d
(G) h
(H) b
(J) p

5. Which letter does the word money begin with?

(A) m
(B) n
(C) w
(D) j

Name ____________________

READING PRACTICE TEST

Part I: Word Analysis (cont.)

Directions: Listen closely as your teacher reads each question and the answer choices. Choose the word with the same beginning or ending sound. Practice with examples B and C. Do the same for numbers 6–9.

Examples

B. Which picture has the same beginning sound as beet?

(F) 

(G) 

(H) 

C. Which word has the same ending sound as slip?

(A) truck
(B) sash
(C) map

6. Which picture has the same beginning sound as cup?

(F) 

(G) 

(H) 

7. Which picture has the same ending sound as Mike?

(A) 

(B) 

(C) 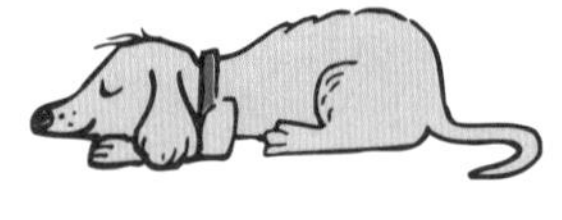

8. Which word has the same beginning sound as table?

(F) cash
(G) shoot
(H) try

9. Which word has the same ending sound as frog?

(A) gray
(B) tag
(C) begin

READING PRACTICE TEST

Part 1: Word Analysis (cont.)

Directions: Listen to your teacher say the words. Notice the underlined part. Listen as your teacher reads the word choices. Listen for the word with the same sound as the underlined part and mark it. Practice with example D. Do the same for numbers 10–15.

Example

D. wig

- (F) time
- (G) swam
- (H) tip

10. pat

- (F) from
- (G) mad
- (H) goes

11. mine

- (A) dime
- (B) into
- (C) hurt

12. pump

- (F) child
- (G) cutting
- (H) shark

13. shout

- (A) loud
- (B) crow
- (C) pill

14. made

- (F) bake
- (G) puddle
- (H) line

15. beg

- (A) mass
- (B) kelp
- (C) broke

STOP

Name ______________________________

READING PRACTICE TEST

Part 1: Word Analysis (cont.)

Directions: Listen to your teacher read the words. Choose the picture that rhymes with the word. Practice with examples E and F. Do the same for numbers 16–19.

Examples

E. Which picture rhymes with barn?

Ⓐ 

Ⓑ 

Ⓒ 

F. Which word rhymes with tool?

Ⓕ pool
Ⓖ book
Ⓗ lamp

16. Which picture rhymes with dish?

17. Which picture rhymes with car?

Ⓑ 

Ⓒ 

18. Which word rhymes with chance?

Ⓕ dance
Ⓖ make
Ⓗ patch

19. Which word rhymes with how?

Ⓐ show
Ⓑ now
Ⓒ zoom

Name ____________________

READING PRACTICE TEST

Part 2: Vocabulary

Directions: Listen to your teacher read the group of words and answer choices. Choose the picture that matches the words. Practice with example A. Do the same for 1–4.

Example

A. Something to eat

Ⓐ  Ⓑ  Ⓒ 

1. Something that rings

Ⓐ  Ⓑ  Ⓒ 

2. Something to ride in

Ⓕ  Ⓖ 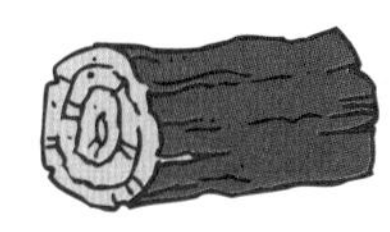 Ⓗ 

3. To get taller

Ⓐ shrink
Ⓑ grow
Ⓒ empty

4. A place for clothes

Ⓕ closet
Ⓖ desk
Ⓗ doghouse

Name ______________________

READING PRACTICE TEST

Part 2: Vocabulary (cont.)

Directions: Look at the picture. Listen as your teacher reads the word choices. Mark the word that goes with the picture. Practice with examples B and C. Do the same for numbers 5–12.

Examples

B.

(F) cap
(G) box
(H) jacket

C.

(A) kick
(B) throw
(C) swing

5.

(A) dance
(B) run
(C) sleep

6.

(F) blanket
(G) coat
(H) hat

7.

(A) one
(B) two
(C) three

8.

(F) dog
(G) girl
(H) boy

9.

(A) sledding
(B) camping
(C) shopping

10.

(F) tent
(G) car
(H) van

11.

(A) hot
(B) snowing
(C) raining

12.

(F) sandcastle
(G) toothpicks
(H) jelly

Name ____________________

READING PRACTICE TEST

Part 2: Vocabulary (cont.)

Directions: Listen closely as your teacher reads the sentences and word choices. Choose the word that completes the sentence. Practice with example D. Do the same for numbers 13–16.

Example

D. Camila ________ the phone.

Ⓐ ringing
Ⓑ answered
Ⓒ went
Ⓓ shouted

13. My mother drinks ________ .

Ⓐ tea
Ⓑ nails
Ⓒ watermelon
Ⓓ sandwiches

14. The ________ on the radio was loud.

Ⓕ sun
Ⓖ water
Ⓗ music
Ⓙ computer

15. Lucy walked all the way to the ________ .

Ⓐ over
Ⓑ cut
Ⓒ jar
Ⓓ park

16. Maisie sat on the ________ .

Ⓕ touch
Ⓖ something
Ⓗ bench
Ⓙ large

STOP

Name ______________________

READING PRACTICE TEST

Part 2: Vocabulary (cont.)

Directions: Listen closely as your teacher reads the sentences and word choices. Choose the answer that means the same or about the same as the underlined word for numbers 17–19.

17. Do you <u>like</u> watermelon?

- (A) make
- (B) enjoy
- (C) hate
- (D) pat

18. His ideas are always <u>great</u>!

- (F) wonderful
- (G) crazy
- (H) boring
- (J) bunny

19. <u>Listen to</u> the story.

- (A) taste
- (B) hear
- (C) look
- (D) sit

Directions: Listen closely as your teacher reads the sentences and word choices. Choose the answer that means the opposite of the underlined word for numbers 20–22.

20. I am <u>wet</u>.

- (F) soaked
- (G) dry
- (H) yellow
- (J) quiet

21. Sammy is a <u>tiny</u> mouse.

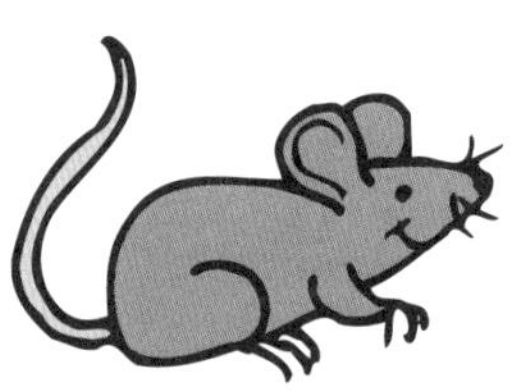

- (A) large
- (B) small
- (C) friendly
- (D) brown

22. The glass is <u>full</u>.

- (F) mine
- (G) Teri's
- (H) empty
- (J) broken

STOP

Name ____________________

READING PRACTICE TEST

Part 3: Reading Comprehension

Directions: Listen to your teacher read each story. Choose the best answer for the question. Practice with example A. Do the same for numbers 1 and 2.

Example

A. Grandfather has a farm. He has many animals. He has pigs, chicks, and horses. He loves pigs the most. Which animal does Grandfather love the most?

Ⓐ 

Ⓑ 

Ⓒ 

1. Katie packed her backpack. She took things to eat. She took things to drink. Which item wouldn't she put in her bag?

Ⓐ 

Ⓑ 

Ⓒ 

2. Lilo was planting a garden. She had many tools. The tools helped her plant. Which picture shows something that Lilo didn't need when planting?

Ⓕ 

Ⓖ 

Ⓗ 

STOP

Name ______________________

READING PRACTICE TEST

Part 3: Reading Comprehension (cont.)

Directions: Listen to your teacher read the sentences. Look at the pictures. Choose the sentence that matches the picture. Practice with example B. Do 3–6 the same way.

Example

B.
- (F) Todd ate cereal.
- (G) I love my horse.
- (H) The weather is nice.

3.
- (A) The boat sunk.
- (B) My pen does not work.
- (C) Tanika swims every day.

4.
- (F) Lee gave him a car.
- (G) My dad has a new watch.
- (H) I see the clock.

5.
- (A) We read together.
- (B) I ran away from my brother.
- (C) He plays the flute.

6.
- (F) It was snowing.
- (G) Parker was singing.
- (H) I go to the library.

STOP

READING PRACTICE TEST

Part 3: Reading Comprehension (cont.)

Directions: Listen to your teacher read the sentences. Match a picture to the sentences. Practice with example C. Do the same for numbers 7–10.

Example

C. This floats high. Some people ride them.

Ⓐ  Ⓑ  Ⓒ 

7. It was very cold. Mother said to wear these.

 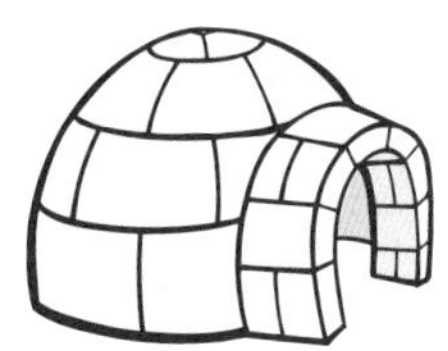    

8. It was time. We had to get there fast!

9. One boy is ________ .

Ⓐ whispering
Ⓑ jumping
Ⓒ eating

10. One boy is ________ .

Ⓕ listening
Ⓖ awake
Ⓗ sleeping

Name ____________________

READING PRACTICE TEST

Part 3: Reading Comprehension (cont.)

Directions: Listen to your teacher read the story and the questions. Choose the best answer to the questions. Practice with example D. Do the same for numbers 11–14.

Example

Kida's party started at 2 o'clock. It was a pool party. People brought towels. They brought sunscreen.

D. What kind of party did Kida have?

Ⓕ birthday party
Ⓖ pool party
Ⓗ sunscreen party

The box was heavy. Simon needed help to move it. He asked Tom. He asked Kate. They went to help. The box was full. It had books in it. Tom and Kate decided to read. Simon sat down to read too. The box stayed.

11. What was in the box?

Ⓐ Simon
Ⓑ books
Ⓒ boxes

12. How many people came to help Simon?

Ⓕ 1
Ⓖ 2
Ⓗ 3

13. What did Tom and Kate do?

Ⓐ read books
Ⓑ moved the box
Ⓒ ran away

14. Why didn't they move the box?

Ⓕ It was purple.
Ⓖ They wanted to read.
Ⓗ Kate went home.

Name ____________________

READING PRACTICE TEST

Part 3: Reading Comprehension (cont.)

Directions: Listen to your teacher read the story and the questions. Choose the best answer to the questions.

Riley's Racer

"I want to make a car," Riley said to his father. "Will you help?"

"Yes! We can make a car. We need a plan. We need the tools. Then, we will buy the things we need to make it."

Riley and his father drew a plan for the car. They decided on the size and color. Riley was so happy! It would be big! He could sit in it. It would roll down the hill in the yard. He would wear a helmet.

It took two weeks to make. They had fun. Mom took pictures. She even helped paint the car red. It was a fun family project.

15. What did Riley want to make?

- Ⓐ tools
- Ⓑ a car
- Ⓒ pictures

16. What did they do first?

- Ⓕ made a plan
- Ⓖ painted
- Ⓗ wore a helmet

17. Why would Riley wear a helmet when riding in the car?

- Ⓐ to be safe
- Ⓑ to hide his hair
- Ⓒ to show his friend

18. How did the family feel?

- Ⓕ sad
- Ⓖ happy
- Ⓗ angry

STOP

Name ______________________

READING PRACTICE TEST

Part 3: Reading Comprehension (cont.)

Directions: Listen to your teacher read the story and the questions. Choose the best answer to the questions.

Ship Shape

A ship is a very large boat. It can travel in the ocean. Some take trips across the whole ocean. Ships carry people and things from one place to another. They have people to work on them. These workers are called the crew.

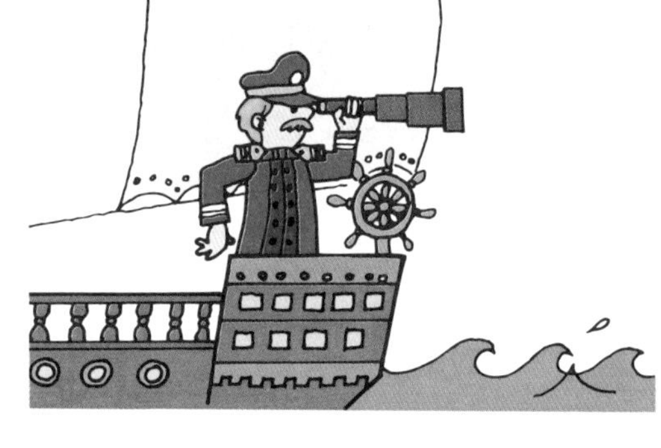

A ship has many parts. The stern is the back of the ship. The bow is the front. On some ships masts hold the sails. The sails are like big sheets. They catch the wind and help ships go fast. Up on the mast might be a crow's nest. A sailor can sit there. He can watch the ocean.

Another important part is the helm. This is the ship's steering wheel. It can turn the ship to the left and right.

19. What is a ship?

- Ⓐ a train
- Ⓑ a very large boat
- Ⓒ a raft

20. Where do many ships travel?

- Ⓕ across the ocean
- Ⓖ in rivers
- Ⓗ to dark places

21. What do sails do?

- Ⓐ carry people
- Ⓑ cover people
- Ⓒ help the ship go

22. Why did the author write this story?

- Ⓕ to tell about sailors
- Ⓖ to tell about ships
- Ⓗ so people would buy boats

STOP

READING PRACTICE TEST

Part 3: Reading Comprehension (cont.)

Directions: Listen to your teacher read the story and the questions. Choose the best answer to the questions.

What About Rabbits?

Rabbits are small animals. They have short, fluffy tails. Some have long ears that can hear very well. These ears can be floppy. Some also stick right up!

Rabbits eat all kinds of plants. They eat in fields. They eat in gardens. Some farmers do not like rabbits. They eat the vegetables farmers grow. Sometimes the rabbits eat young trees.

When a mother rabbit is having babies, she digs a hole. She puts in soft grass. She adds her own fur. This will keep the babies warm. She may have two to ten babies. Baby rabbits are called kits.

Some people have pet rabbits. They keep them in pens or cages. They might enter them in contests. Some pet rabbits can be trained to do tricks. Grains, vegetables, and grass are good foods for them.

23. What is this story mostly about?

Ⓐ rabbits
Ⓑ plants rabbits eat
Ⓒ farming

24. Why do some farmers not like rabbits?

Ⓕ They run on the grass.
Ⓖ They eat their trees and vegetables.
Ⓗ They make too much noise.

25. Where might pet rabbits sleep?

Ⓐ in a field
Ⓑ a pen or cage
Ⓒ under the blanket

26. What are good foods for pet rabbits?

Ⓕ vegetables and grass
Ⓖ hot dogs and candy
Ⓗ vegetables and meat

Answer Key

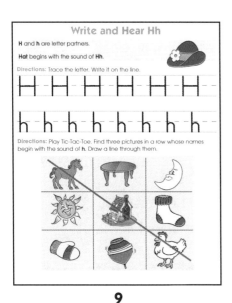

Write and Hear Mm

M and **m** are letter partners.

Map begins with the sound of **Mm**.

Directions: Trace the letter. Write it on the line.

M M M M M

m m m m m m

Directions: Color the pictures whose names begin with the sound of **m**.

6

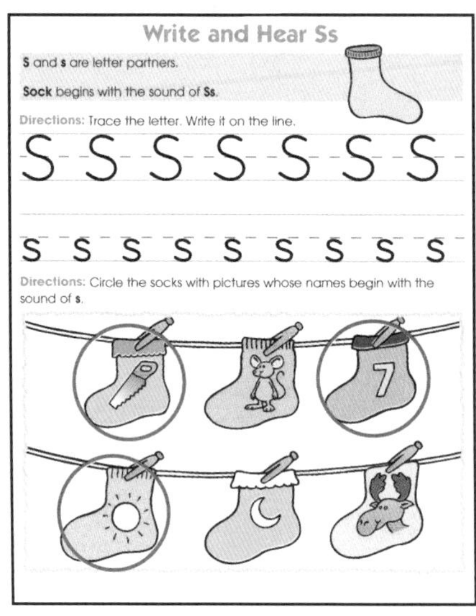

Write and Hear Ss

S and **s** are letter partners.

Sock begins with the sound of **Ss**.

Directions: Trace the letter. Write it on the line.

S S S S S S S

s s s s s s s s s

Directions: Circle the socks with pictures whose names begin with the sound of **s**.

7

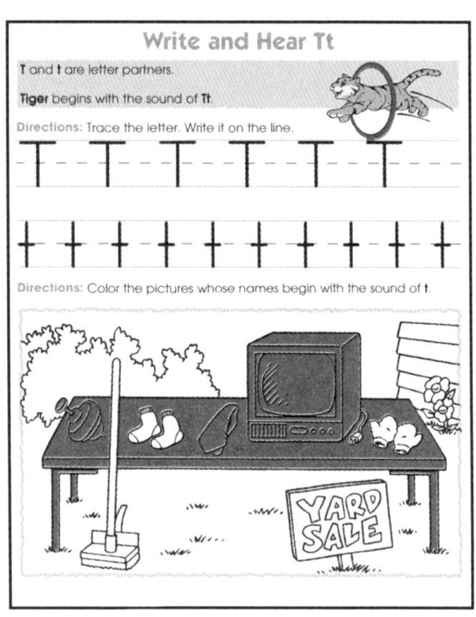

Write and Hear Tt

T and **t** are letter partners.

Tiger begins with the sound of **Tt**.

Directions: Trace the letter. Write it on the line.

T T T T T T

t t t t t t t t t t

Directions: Color the pictures whose names begin with the sound of **t**.

8

Write and Hear Hh

H and **h** are letter partners.

Hat begins with the sound of **Hh**.

Directions: Trace the letter. Write it on the line.

H H H H H H

h h h h h h h h

Directions: Play Tic-Tac-Toe. Find three pictures in a row whose names begin with the sound of **h**. Draw a line through them.

9

Write and Hear Kk

K and **k** are letter partners.

Kitten begins with the sound of **Kk**.

Directions: Trace the letter. Write it on the line.

K K K K K K K

k k k k k k k k

Directions: Color the pictures whose names begin with the sound of **k**.

10

Write and Hear Bb

B and **b** are letter partners.

Ball begins with the sound of **Bb**.

Directions: Trace the letter. Write it on the line.

B B B B B B

b b b b b b b b

Directions: Color the bow if the name of the picture on the box begins with the sound of **b**.

11

Answer Key

Write and Hear Ff

F and **f** are letter partners.

Fox begins with the sound of **Ff**.

Directions: Trace the letter. Write it on the line.

F F F F F F F

f f f f f f f f

Directions: Help the farmer find the fox. Draw a line through the pictures whose names begin with the sound of **f**.

12

Write and Hear Gg

G and **g** are letter partners.

Goat begins with the sound of **Gg**.

Directions: Trace the letter. Write it on the line.

G G G G G G G

g g g g g g g g

Directions: Write **g** if the name of the picture begins with the sound of **g**.

g g g g

13

Write and Hear Ll

L and **l** are letter partners.

Leaf begins with the sound of **Ll**.

Directions: Trace the letter. Write it on the line.

L L L L L L L

l l l l l l l l l l l

Directions: Color the leaves with pictures whose names begin with the sound of **l**.

14

Write and Hear Nn

N and **n** are letter partners.

Nest begins with the sound of **Nn**.

Directions: Trace the letter. Write it on the line.

N N N N N N

n n n n n n n n

Directions: Color the pictures whose names begin with the sound of **n**.

15

Write and Hear Dd

D and **d** are letter partners.

Desk begins with the sound of **Dd**.

Directions: Trace the letter. Write it on the line.

D D D D D D

d d d d d d d d

Directions: Color the pictures whose names begin with the sound of **d**.

16

Write and Hear Ww

W and **w** are letter partners.

Window begins with the sound of **Ww**.

Directions: Trace the letter. Write it on the line.

W W W W

w w w w w w w

Directions: Color the curtains if the name of the picture begins with the sound of **w**.

17

Answer Key

Write and Hear Cc

C and c are letter partners.

Cap begins with the sound of Cc.

Directions: Trace the letter. Write it on the line.

Directions: Play Tic-Tac-Toe. Find three pictures in a row whose names begin with the sound of c. Draw a line through them.

18

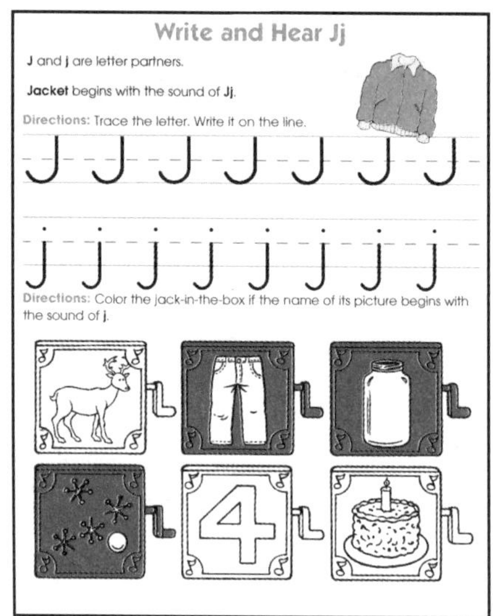

Write and Hear Jj

J and j are letter partners.

Jacket begins with the sound of Jj.

Directions: Trace the letter. Write it on the line.

Directions: Color the jack-in-the-box if the name of its picture begins with the sound of j.

19

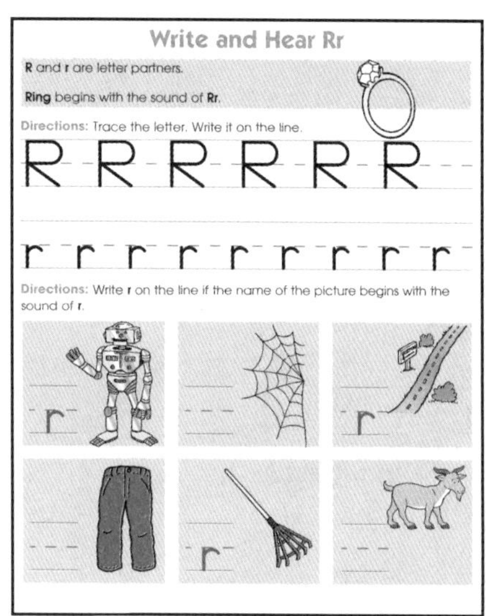

Write and Hear Rr

R and r are letter partners.

Ring begins with the sound of Rr.

Directions: Trace the letter. Write it on the line.

Directions: Write r on the line if the name of the picture begins with the sound of r.

20

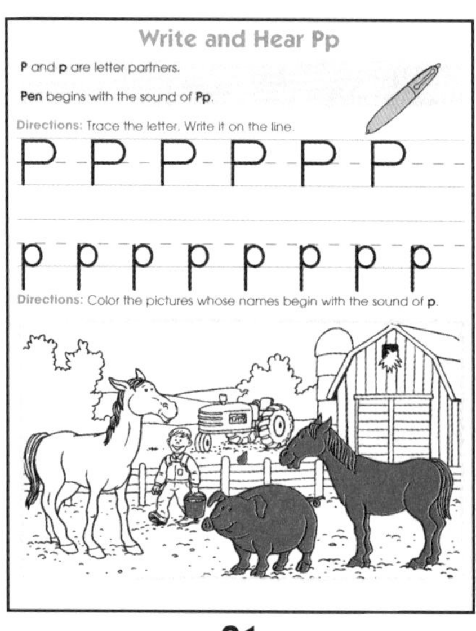

Write and Hear Pp

P and p are letter partners.

Pen begins with the sound of Pp.

Directions: Trace the letter. Write it on the line.

Directions: Color the pictures whose names begin with the sound of p.

21

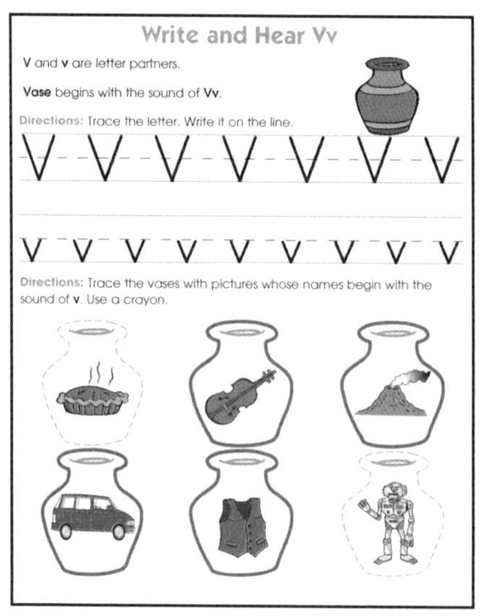

Write and Hear Vv

V and v are letter partners.

Vase begins with the sound of Vv.

Directions: Trace the letter. Write it on the line.

Directions: Trace the vases with pictures whose names begin with the sound of v. Use a crayon.

22

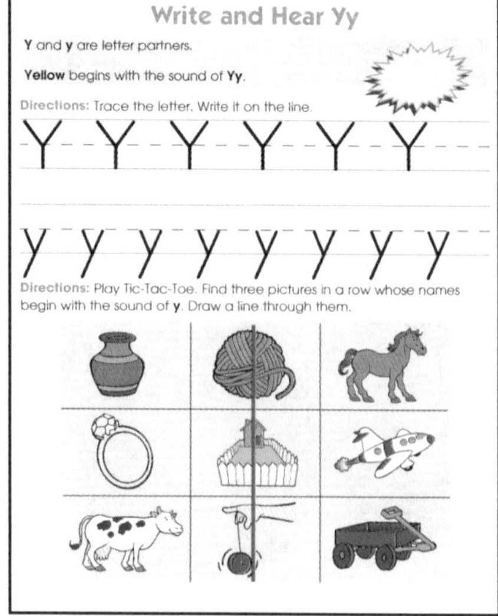

Write and Hear Yy

Y and y are letter partners.

Yellow begins with the sound of Yy.

Directions: Trace the letter. Write it on the line.

Directions: Play Tic-Tac-Toe. Find three pictures in a row whose names begin with the sound of y. Draw a line through them.

23

Answer Key

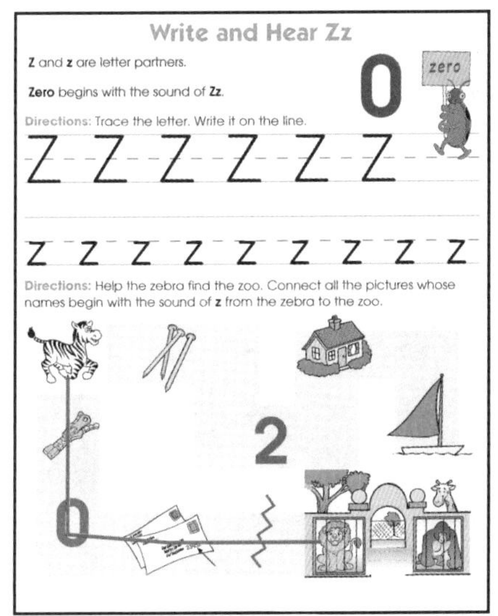

Write and Hear Zz

Z and z are letter partners.

Zero begins with the sound of Zz.

Directions: Trace the letter. Write it on the line.

Z Z Z Z Z Z

z z z z z z z z z

Directions: Help the zebra find the zoo. Connect all the pictures whose names begin with the sound of z from the zebra to the zoo.

24

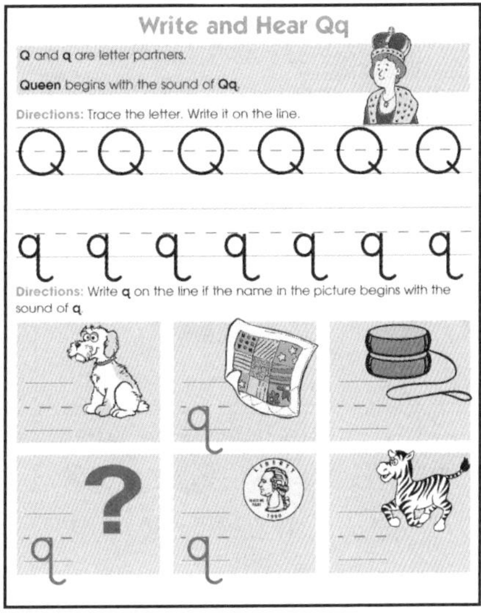

Write and Hear Qq

Q and q are letter partners.

Queen begins with the sound of Qq.

Directions: Trace the letter. Write it on the line.

Q Q Q Q Q Q

q q q q q q q

Directions: Write q on the line if the name in the picture begins with the sound of q.

25

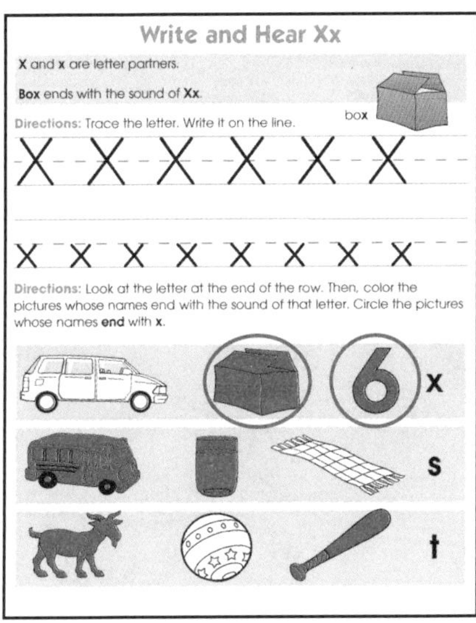

Write and Hear Xx

X and x are letter partners.

Box ends with the sound of Xx.

Directions: Trace the letter. Write it on the line.

X X X X X X

x x x x x x x x

Directions: Look at the letter at the end of the row. Then, color the pictures whose names end with the sound of that letter. Circle the pictures whose names end with x.

26

How Do I Begin?

Directions: Say the name of each picture. Write the beginning sound for each picture.

h at, g oat, k ite, j am, j acks, g ate, k ey, h appy

Directions: Write each word next to its beginning sound.

g	goat	g	gate
h	hat	h	happy
j	jam	j	jacks
k	kite	k	key

27

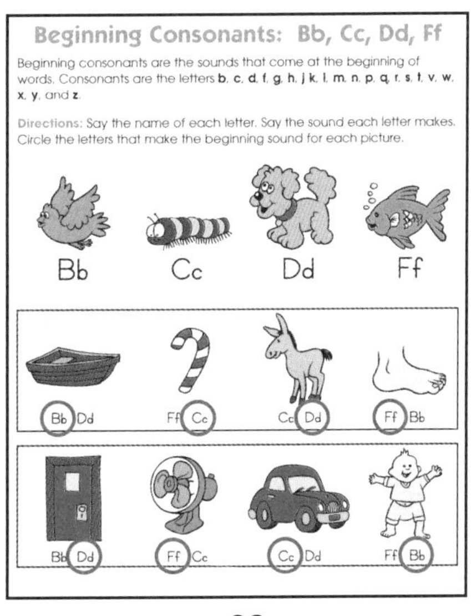

Beginning Consonants: Bb, Cc, Dd, Ff

Beginning consonants are the sounds that come at the beginning of words. Consonants are the letters b, c, d, f, g, h, j, k, l, m, n, p, q, r, s, t, v, w, x, y, and z.

Directions: Say the name of each letter. Say the sound each letter makes. Circle the letters that make the beginning sound for each picture.

Bb Cc Dd Ff

Bb Dd · Ff Cc · Cc Dd · Ff Bb

Bb Dd · Ff Cc · Cc Dd · Ff Bb

28

Beginning Consonants: Gg, Hh, Jj, Kk

Directions: Say the name of each letter. Say the sound each letter makes. Trace the letter pair that makes the beginning sound in each picture.

Gg Hh Jj Kk

Kk Hh · Gg Kk

Gg Hh · Jj Gg

29

Answer Key

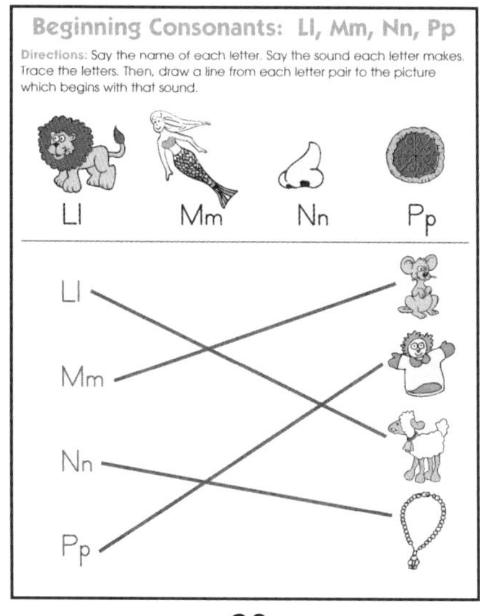

Beginning Consonants: Ll, Mm, Nn, Pp

Directions: Say the name of each letter. Say the sound each letter makes. Trace the letters. Then, draw a line from each letter pair to the picture which begins with that sound.

Ll Mm Nn Pp

Ll

Mm

Nn

Pp

30

Beginning Consonants: Qq, Rr, Ss, Tt

Directions: Say the name of each letter. Say the sound each letter makes. Trace the letter pair in the boxes. Then, color the picture which begins with that sound.

Qq Rr Ss Tt

Tt Qq

Rr Ss

31

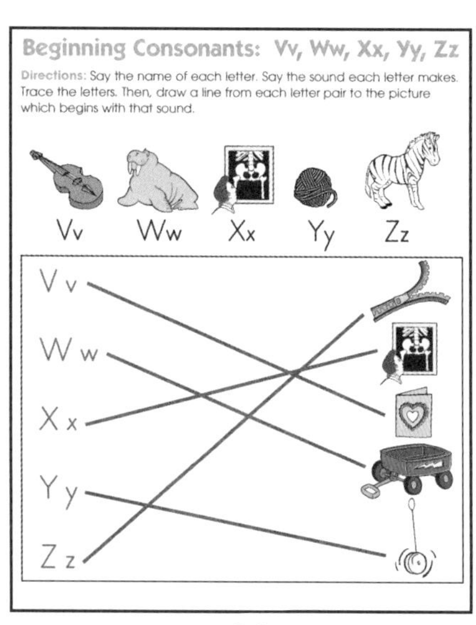

Beginning Consonants: Vv, Ww, Xx, Yy, Zz

Directions: Say the name of each letter. Say the sound each letter makes. Trace the letters. Then, draw a line from each letter pair to the picture which begins with that sound.

Vv Ww Xx Yy Zz

V v

W w

X x

Y y

Z z

32

How Do I Begin Again?

Directions: Say each letter sound. Color the pictures in each row that begin with that sound.

b

c

d

f

Directions: Say the name of each picture. Write the beginning sound for each picture.

b ed d og f eet c up

33

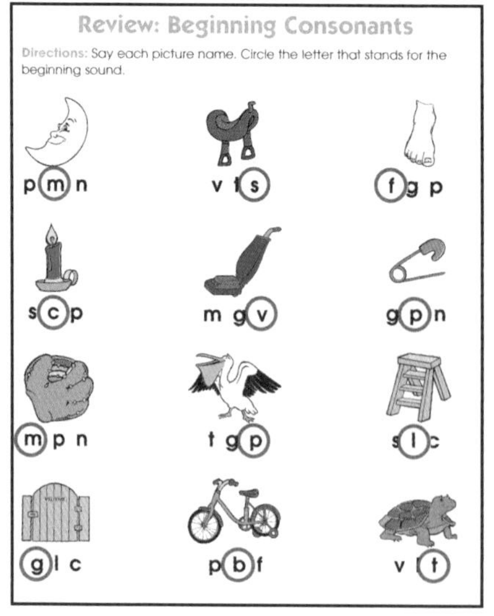

Review: Beginning Consonants

Directions: Say each picture name. Circle the letter that stands for the beginning sound.

p m n — v f s — f g p

s c p — m g v — g p n

m p n — t g p — s l c

g l c — p b f — v t

34

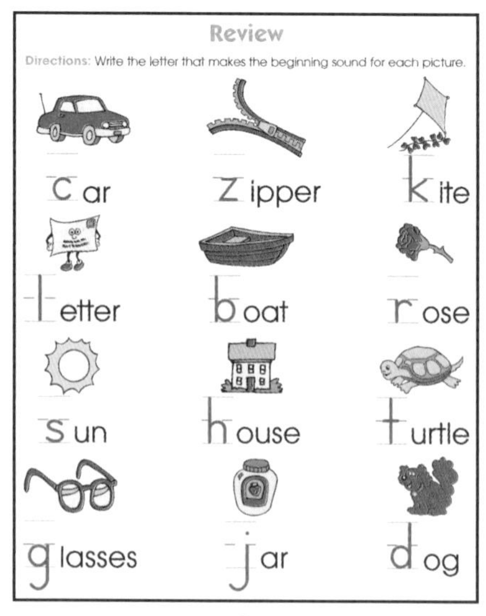

Review

Directions: Write the letter that makes the beginning sound for each picture.

c ar — z ipper — k ite

l etter — b oat — r ose

s un — h ouse — t urtle

g lasses — j ar — d og

35

Answer Key

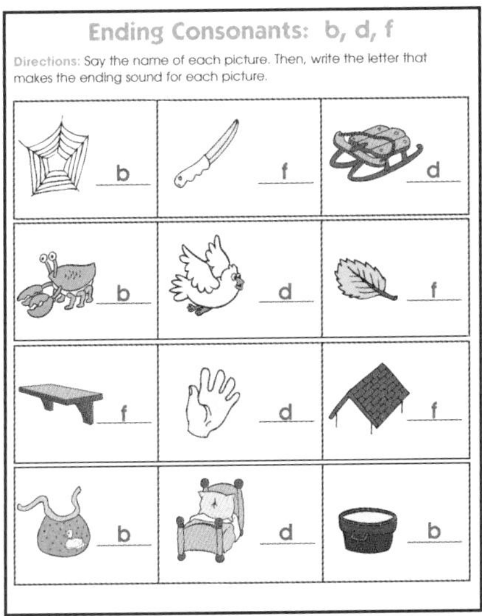

Ending Consonants: b, d, f

Directions: Say the name of each picture. Then, write the letter that makes the ending sound for each picture.

b	f	d
b	d	f
f	d	f
b	d	b

36

Ending Consonants: g, m, n

Directions: Say the name of each picture. Draw a line from each letter to the pictures which end with that sound.

g m n

g

m

n

37

Ending Consonants: k, l, p

Directions: Trace the letters in each row. Say the name of each picture. Then, color the pictures in each row which end with that sound.

k

l

p

38

Ending Consonants: r, s, t, x

Directions: Say the name of each picture. Then, circle the ending sound for each picture.

(r) s t x — r (s) t x

(r) s t x — r s (t) x

r s (t) x — r (s) t x

r s t (x) — r s (t) x

39

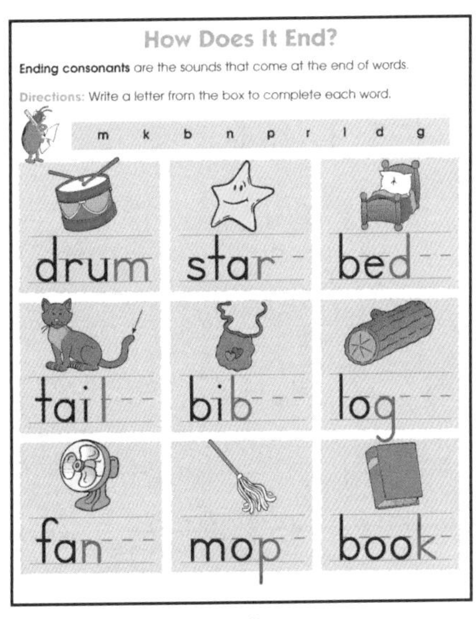

How Does It End?

Ending consonants are the sounds that come at the end of words.

Directions: Write a letter from the box to complete each word.

m k b n p r l d g

drum	star	bed
tail	bib	log
fan	mop	book

40

And Finally...

Directions: Say each picture name. Write the ending sound for each picture.

tu b	pai l	pa d
lo g	hoo k	mu g
boo k	ha m	shel f
lea f	cra b	li d
gir l	bea k	broo m

41

Answer Key

Consonant Review

Directions: One letter is missing in each word. Write the missing letter on the line.

dog box sun
hen tulip top
log leaf wagon

42

Consonant Review

Directions: Write all the missing consonants.

man fox pig
bed jar camel
goat car cap

43

Meet Short a

Listen for the sound of short **a** in **van**.

Directions: Trace the letter. Write it on the line.

A A A A A A

a a a a a a a a

Directions: Color the pictures whose names have the short **a** sound.

44

Short a Maze

Directions: Help the cat get to the bag. Connect all the pictures whose names have the short **a** sound from the cat to the bag.

45

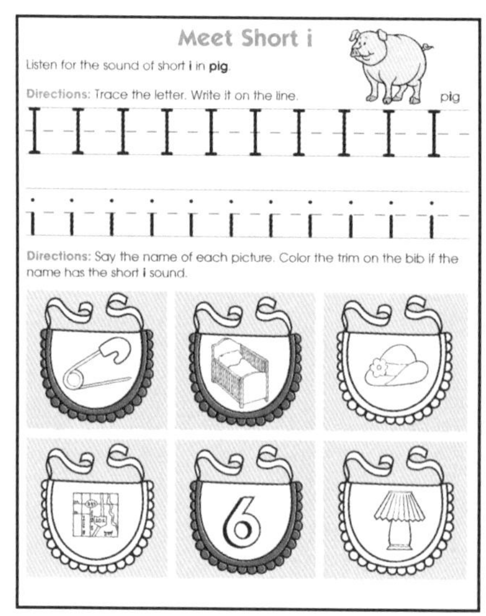

Meet Short i

Listen for the sound of short **i** in **pig**.

Directions: Trace the letter. Write it on the line.

I I I I I I I I I I

i i i i i i i i i i

Directions: Say the name of each picture. Color the trim on the bib if the name has the short **i** sound.

46

Read and Color Short i

Directions: Say the name of each picture. Color the pictures whose names have the short **i** sound. The words in the box will give you hints.

milk	crib	bib
pig	kitten	fish

47

Answer Key

Meet Short u

Listen for the sound of short **u** in **bug**.

Directions: Trace the letter. Write it on the line.

Directions: Say the name of each picture. Color the sun yellow if you hear the short **u** sound in the name.

48

Short u Tic-Tac-Toe

Directions: Color the pictures whose names have the short **u** sound. Then, play Tic-Tac-Toe. Draw a line through three colored pictures in a row.

49

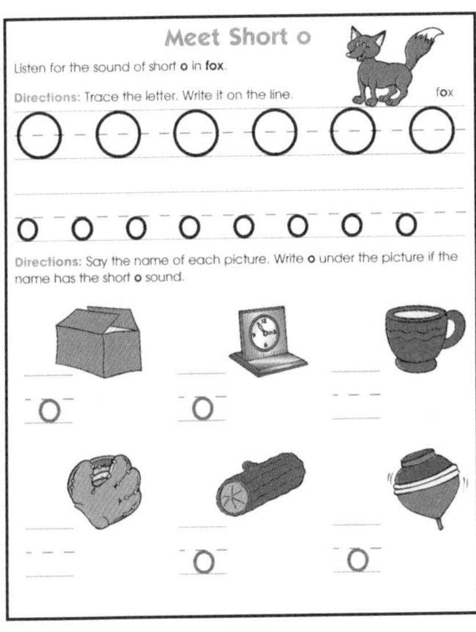

Meet Short o

Listen for the sound of short **o** in **fox**.

Directions: Trace the letter. Write it on the line.

Directions: Say the name of each picture. Write **o** under the picture if the name has the short **o** sound.

50

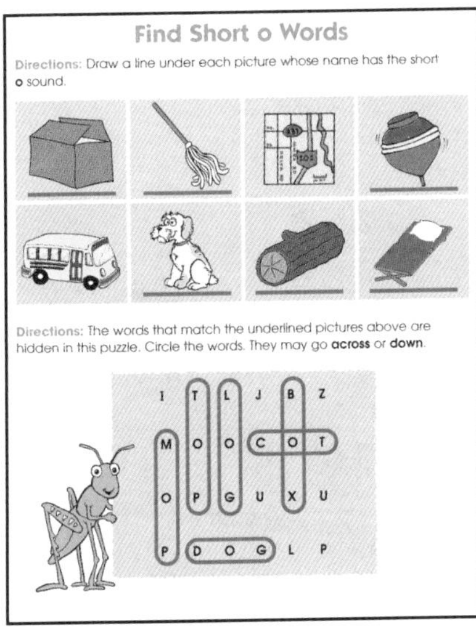

Find Short o Words

Directions: Draw a line under each picture whose name has the short **o** sound.

Directions: The words that match the underlined pictures above are hidden in this puzzle. Circle the words. They may go **across** or **down**.

I	T	L	J	B	Z
M	O	O	C	O	T
O	P	G	U	X	U
P	D	O	G	L	P

51

Meet Short e

Listen for the sound of short **e** in **hen**.

Directions: Trace the letter. Write it on the line.

Directions: Color the pictures whose names have the short **e** sound.

52

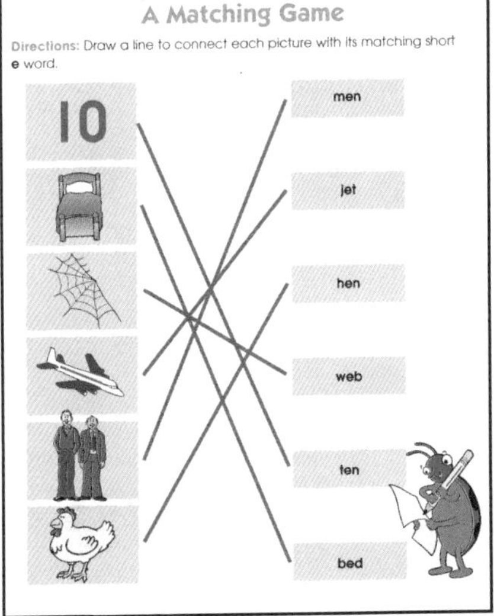

A Matching Game

Directions: Draw a line to connect each picture with its matching short **e** word.

53

Answer Key

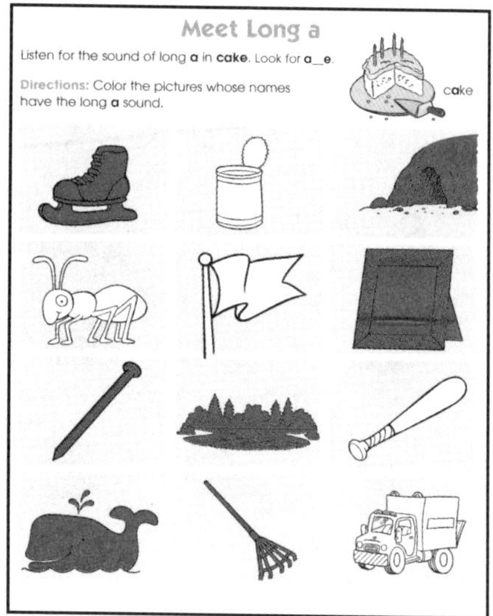

Meet Long a

Listen for the sound of long **a** in **cake**. Look for **a_e**.

Directions: Color the pictures whose names have the long **a** sound.

cake

54

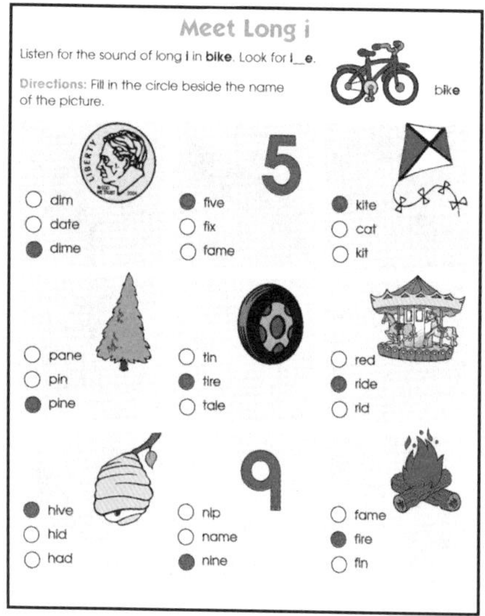

Meet Long i

Listen for the sound of long **i** in **bike**. Look for **i_e**.

Directions: Fill in the circle beside the name of the picture.

bike

○ dim ○ date ● dime	● five ○ fix ○ fame	● kite ○ cat ○ kit
○ pane ○ pin ● pine	○ tin ● tire ○ tale	○ red ● ride ○ rid
● hive ○ hid ○ had	○ nip ○ name ● nine	○ fame ● fire ○ fin

55

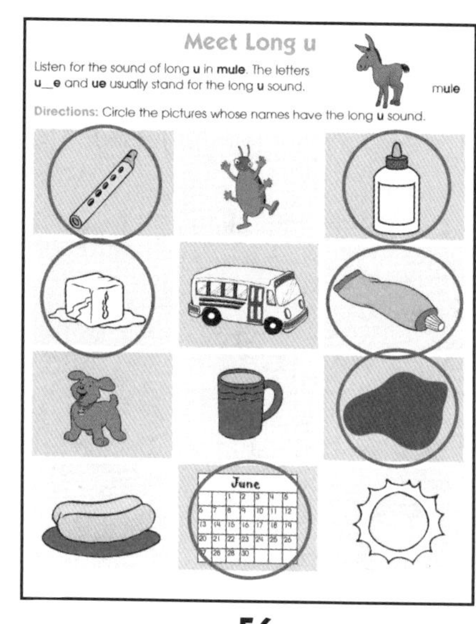

Meet Long u

Listen for the sound of long **u** in **mule**. The letters **u_e** and **ue** usually stand for the long **u** sound.

mule

Directions: Circle the pictures whose names have the long **u** sound.

56

Meet Long o

Listen for the sound of long **o** in **rose**.

Directions: Say the name of each picture. Decide whether the vowel sound you hear is long **o** or short **o**. Fill in the circle beside long **o** or short **o**.

rose

● Long o ○ Short o	○ Long o ● Short o	○ Long o ● Short o
● Long o ○ Short o	○ Long o ● Short o	● Long o ○ Short o
○ Long o ● Short o	● Long o ○ Short o	○ Long o ● Short o
● Long o ○ Short o	● Long o ○ Short o	○ Long o ● Short o

57

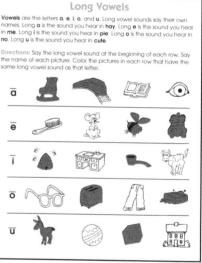

Meet Long e

Listen for the sound of long **e** in **bee**. The letters **ee** and **ea** usually stand for the long **e** sound.

Directions: Write the name of the picture on the correct line.

bee

seal ten beet jeep leaf

bed red seat feet

ee	ea	Short Vowel e
beet	seal	ten
jeep	leaf	bed
feet	seat	red

58

Long Vowels

Vowels are the letters **a**, **e**, **i**, **o**, and **u**. Long vowel sounds say their own names. Long **a** is the sound you hear in **hay**. Long **e** is the sound you hear in **me**. Long **i** is the sound you hear in **pie**. Long **o** is the sound you hear in **no**. Long **u** is the sound you hear in **cute**.

Directions: Say the long vowel sound at the beginning of each row. Say the name of each picture. Color the pictures in each row that have the same long vowel sound as that letter.

ā

ē

ī

ō

ū

59

Answer Key

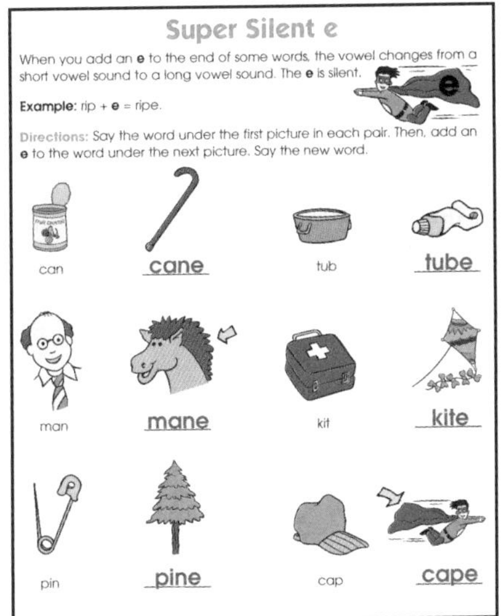

Super Silent e

When you add an **e** to the end of some words, the vowel changes from a short vowel sound to a long vowel sound. The **e** is silent.

Example: rip + **e** = ripe.

Directions: Say the word under the first picture in each pair. Then, add an **e** to the word under the next picture. Say the new word.

can cane tub tube

man mane kit kite

pin pine cap cape

60

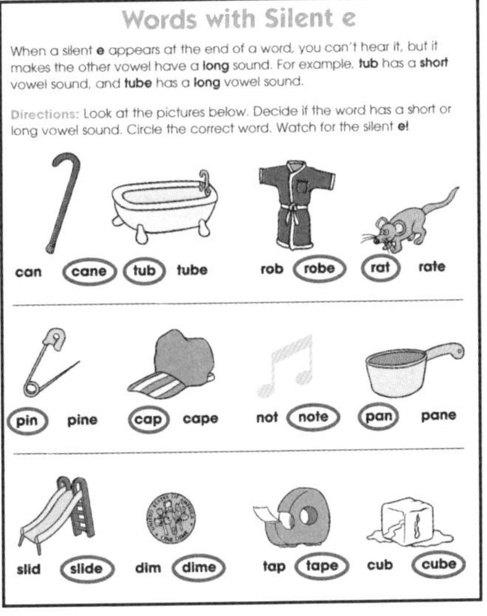

Words with Silent e

When a silent **e** appears at the end of a word, you can't hear it, but it makes the other vowel have a **long** sound. For example, **tub** has a **short** vowel sound, and **tube** has a **long** vowel sound.

Directions: Look at the pictures below. Decide if the word has a short or long vowel sound. Circle the correct word. Watch for the silent **e**!

can cane tub tube rob robe rat rate

pin pine cap cape not note pan pane

slid slide dim dime tap tape cub cube

61

Final y as a Vowel

Our puppy stays dry in the yard.

You know that **y** is a consonant. When **y** is at the beginning of a word, it makes the sound at the beginning of **yard**.

Y can also be a vowel.

Sometimes **y** can have the long **e** sound you hear at the end of **puppy**. **Y** has this sound when it is at the end of a word with more than one syllable or part.

Sometimes **y** can have the long **i** sound you hear at the end of **dry**. **Y** has this sound when it is at the end of a one-syllable word.

Directions: Say each picture name. Circle the word that names the picture. If **y** makes the long **e** sound, color the picture brown. If **y** makes the long **i** sound, color the picture orange.

bail bay baby crazy cry crate bunt bunny buy

fry frosty frog pay pry pony fly feed fussy

62

The Sounds of y

A **y** at the end of a word can have the long **i** sound or the long **e** sound. Listen for the long **i** sound in **fly**. Listen for the long **e** sound in **pony**.

fly pony

Directions: Say the name of each picture. Listen for the sound of **y** at the end of the word. Circle either long **i** or long **e**.

sky Long i Long e | baby Long i Long e | bunny Long i Long e

cry Long i Long e | penny Long i Long e | muddy Long i Long e

dry Long i Long e | 20 twenty Long i Long e | city Long i Long e

63

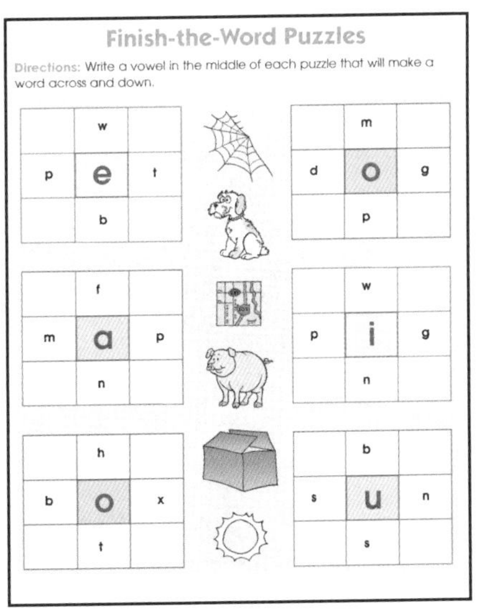

Finish-the-Word Puzzles

Directions: Write a vowel in the middle of each puzzle that will make a word across and down.

	w	
p	e	t
	b	

	m	
d	o	g
	p	

	f	
m	a	p
	n	

	w	
p	i	g
	n	

	h	
b	o	x
	t	

	b	
s	u	n
	s	

64

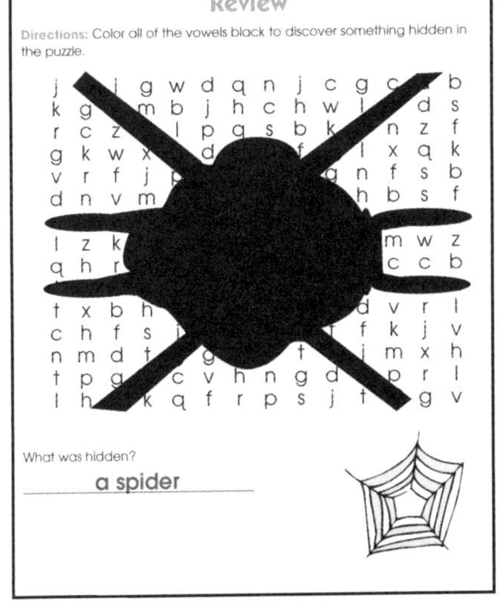

Review

Directions: Color all of the vowels black to discover something hidden in the puzzle.

What was hidden? a spider

65

Answer Key

Review

Directions: Write a vowel on each line to complete each word.

a e i o u

c a t — b i k e
sm o k e — tr ee
c u b — p i n
m o m — b i b
d a d — d u ck

66

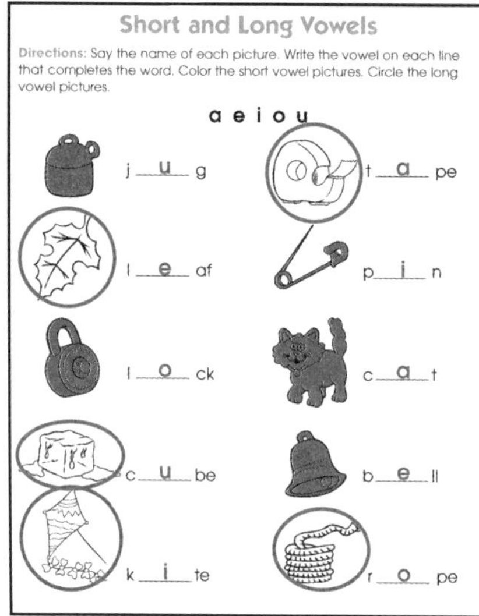

Short and Long Vowels

Directions: Say the name of each picture. Write the vowel on each line that completes the word. Color the short vowel pictures. Circle the long vowel pictures.

a e i o u

j u g — t a pe
l e af — p i n
l o ck — c a t
c u be — b e ll
k i te — r o pe

67

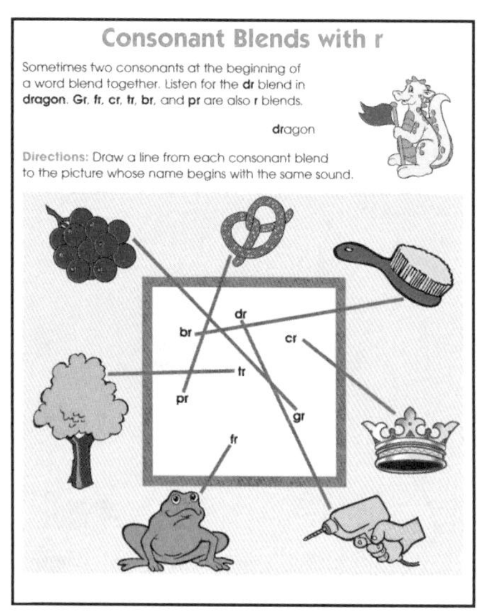

Consonant Blends with r

Sometimes two consonants at the beginning of a word blend together. Listen for the **dr** blend in **dragon**. **Gr**, **fr**, **cr**, **tr**, **br**, and **pr** are also **r** blends.

dragon

Directions: Draw a line from each consonant blend to the picture whose name begins with the same sound.

68

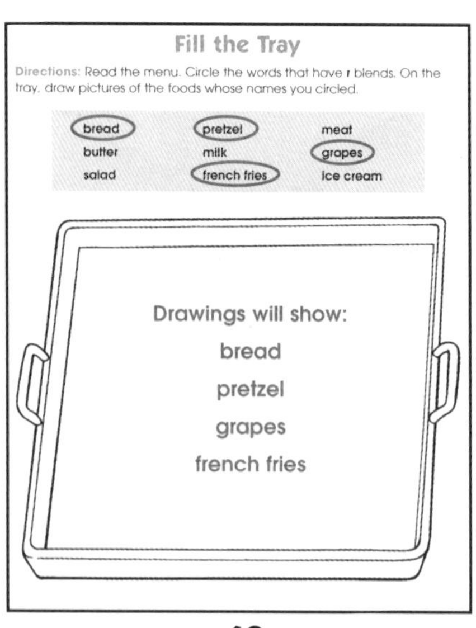

Fill the Tray

Directions: Read the menu. Circle the words that have **r** blends. On the tray, draw pictures of the foods whose names you circled.

(bread)	(pretzel)	meat
butter	milk	(grapes)
salad	(french fries)	ice cream

Drawings will show:
bread
pretzel
grapes
french fries

69

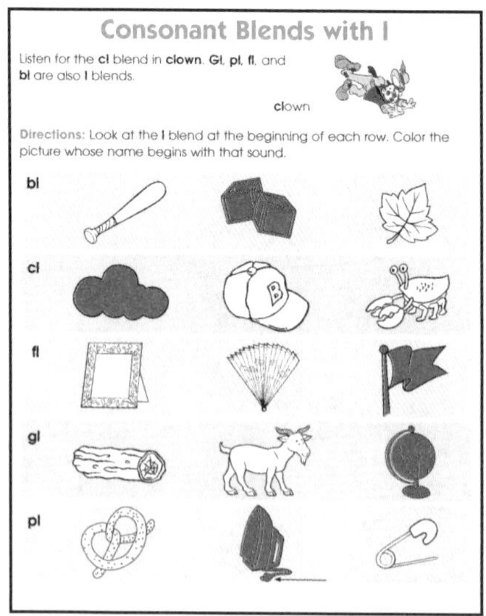

Consonant Blends with l

Listen for the **cl** blend in **clown**. **Gl**, **pl**, **fl**, and **bl** are also **l** blends.

clown

Directions: Look at the **l** blend at the beginning of each row. Color the picture whose name begins with that sound.

bl
cl
fl
gl
pl

70

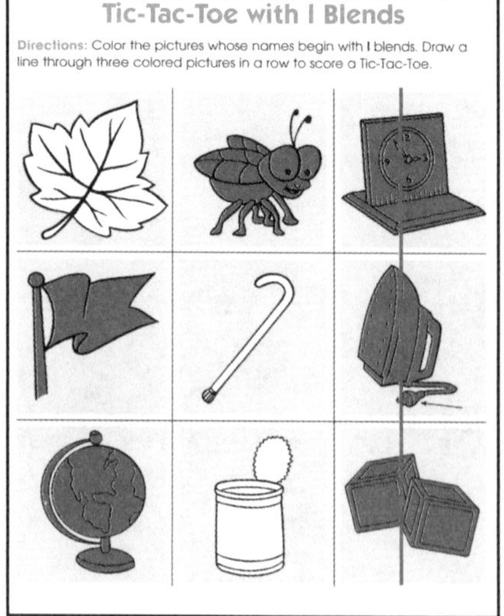

Tic-Tac-Toe with l Blends

Directions: Color the pictures whose names begin with **l** blends. Draw a line through three colored pictures in a row to score a Tic-Tac-Toe.

71

Answer Key

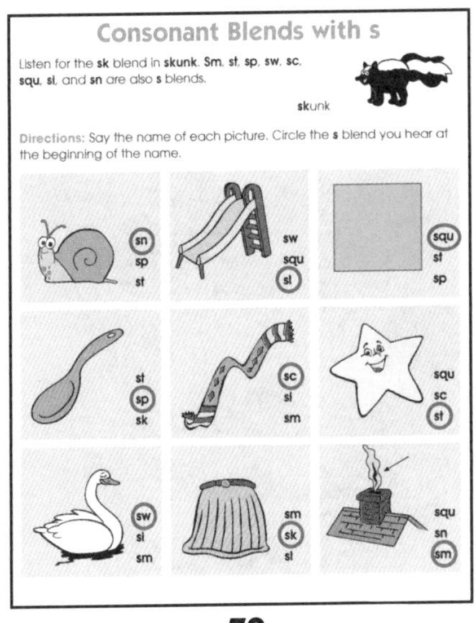

Consonant Blends with s

Listen for the **sk** blend in **skunk**. **Sm**, **st**, **sp**, **sw**, **sc**, **squ**, **sl**, and **sn** are also **s** blends.

skunk

Directions: Say the name of each picture. Circle the **s** blend you hear at the beginning of the name.

sn sp st	sw squ sl	squ st sp
st sp sk	sc sl sm	squ sc st
sw sl sm	sm sk sl	squ sn sm

72

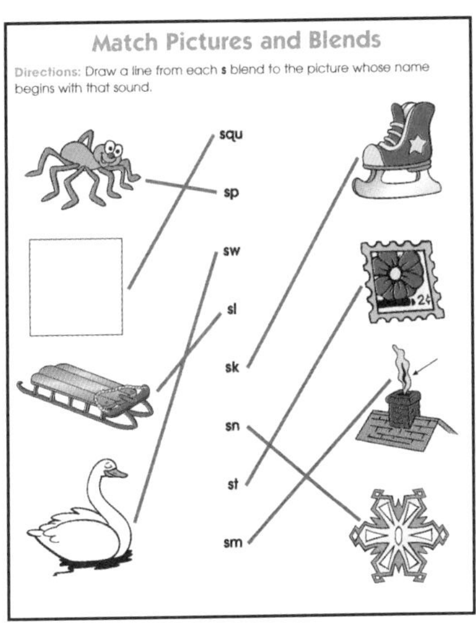

Match Pictures and Blends

Directions: Draw a line from each **s** blend to the picture whose name begins with that sound.

squ
sp
sw
sl
sk
sn
st
sm

73

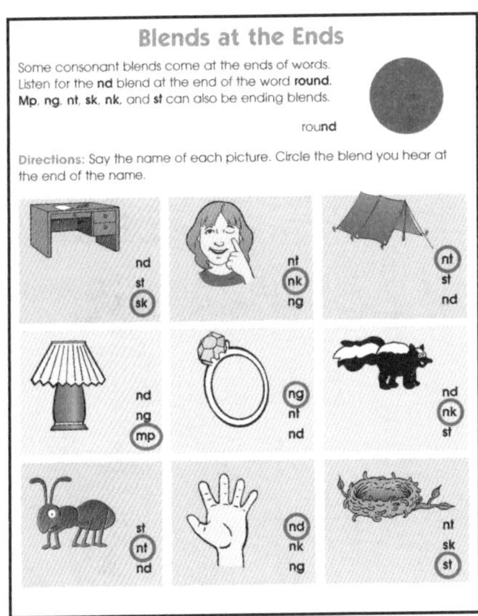

Blends at the Ends

Some consonant blends come at the ends of words. Listen for the **nd** blend at the end of the word **round**. **Mp**, **ng**, **nt**, **sk**, **nk**, and **st** can also be ending blends.

round

Directions: Say the name of each picture. Circle the blend you hear at the end of the name.

nd st sk	nt nk ng	nt st nd
nd ng mp	ng nt nd	nd nk st
st nt nd	nd nk ng	nt sk st

74

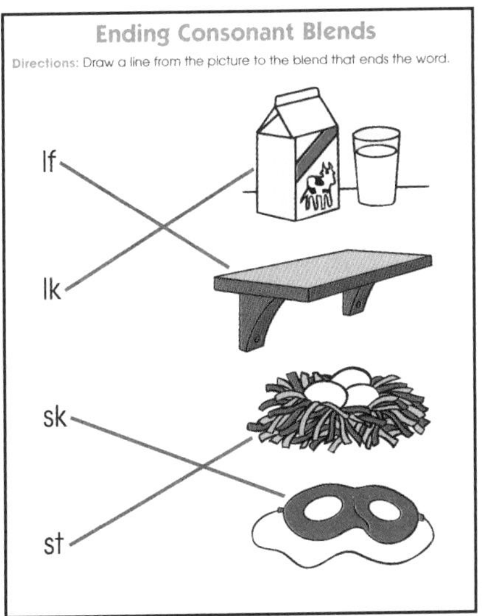

Ending Consonant Blends

Directions: Draw a line from the picture to the blend that ends the word.

lf
lk
sk
st

75

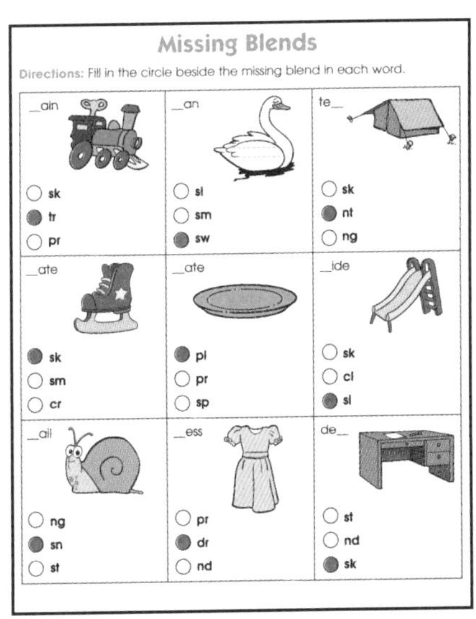

Missing Blends

Directions: Fill in the circle beside the missing blend in each word.

_ain sk tr pr	_an sl sm sw	te_ sk nt ng
_ate sk sm cr	_ate pl pr sp	_ide sk cl sl
_ail ng sn st	_ess pr dr nd	de_ st nd sk

76

More Missing Blends

Directions: Fill in the circle beside the missing blend in each word.

ri_ nt st ng	_y sl fl pl	_apes gr cl sk
_obe sl gl gr	ha_ nd ng sk	_og gr tr fr
_y sk sm nt	_ider pr sl sp	la_ st mp ng

77

Answer Key

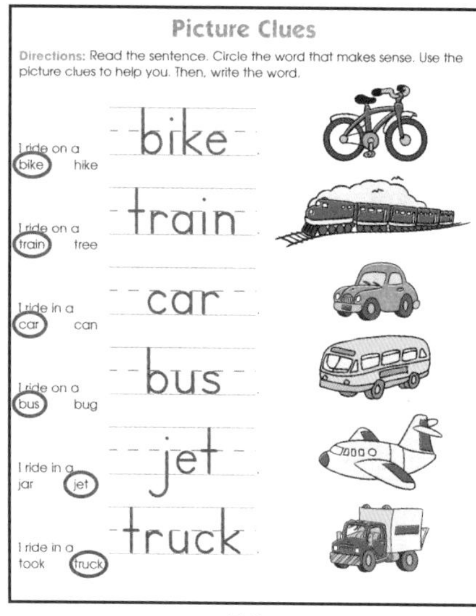

Picture Clues

Directions: Read the sentence. Circle the word that makes sense. Use the picture clues to help you. Then, write the word.

I ride on a (bike) hike — bike

I ride on a (train) tree — train

I ride in a (car) can — car

I ride on a (bus) bug — bus

I ride in a jar (jet) — jet

I ride in a took (truck) — truck

78

Picture Clues

Directions: Read the sentence. Circle the word that makes sense. Use the picture clues to help you. Then, write the word.

I see the (bird) book — bird

I see the (fish) fork — fish

I see the (dogs) dig — dogs

I see the (cats) coat — cats

I see the (snake) snow — snake

I see the (rat) rake — rat

79

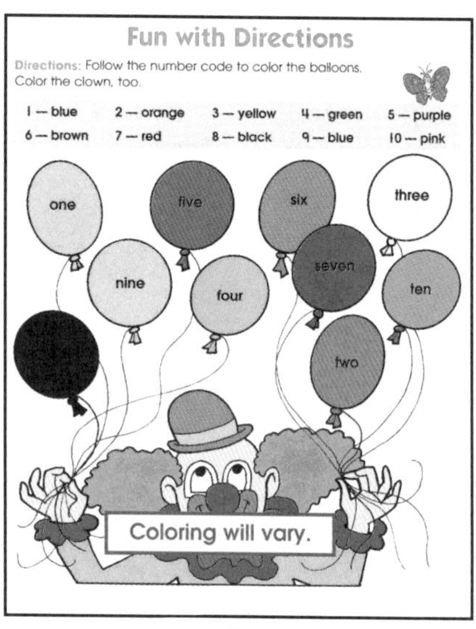

Fun with Directions

Directions: Follow the number code to color the balloons. Color the clown, too.

1 — blue	2 — orange	3 — yellow	4 — green	5 — purple
6 — brown	7 — red	8 — black	9 — blue	10 — pink

Coloring will vary.

80

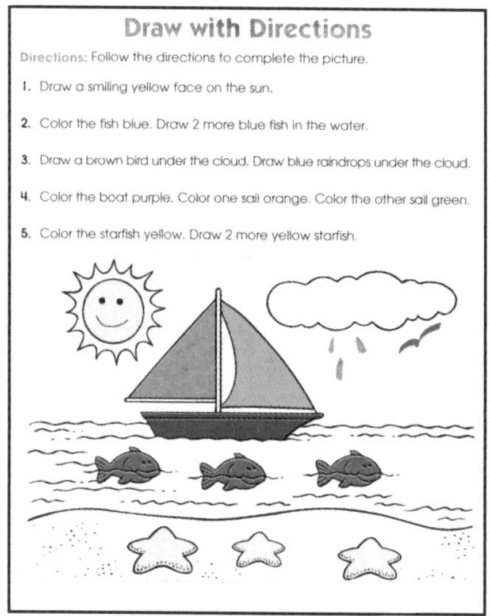

Draw with Directions

Directions: Follow the directions to complete the picture.

1. Draw a smiling yellow face on the sun.
2. Color the fish blue. Draw 2 more blue fish in the water.
3. Draw a brown bird under the cloud. Draw blue raindrops under the cloud.
4. Color the boat purple. Color one sail orange. Color the other sail green.
5. Color the starfish yellow. Draw 2 more yellow starfish.

81

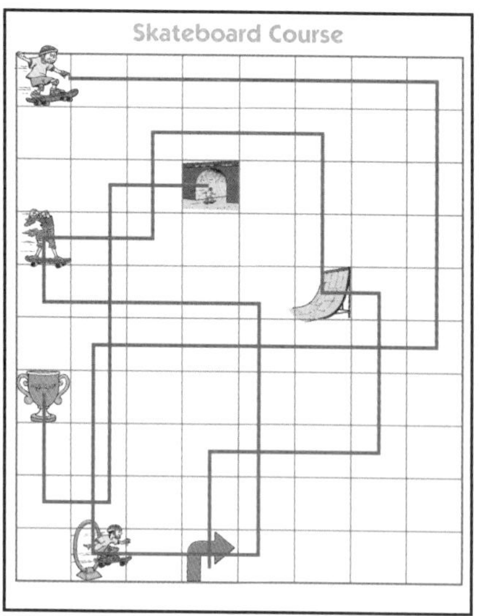

Skateboard Course

83

Directions for Decorating

Directions: Follow the directions to decorate the bedroom.

Draw a red [frame] between the two [hooks].

Draw a [chair] under the window. Color it green.

Draw three big [flowers] on the wall. Color them orange.

Draw a picture of something you would like to have in your bedroom.

84

Answer Key

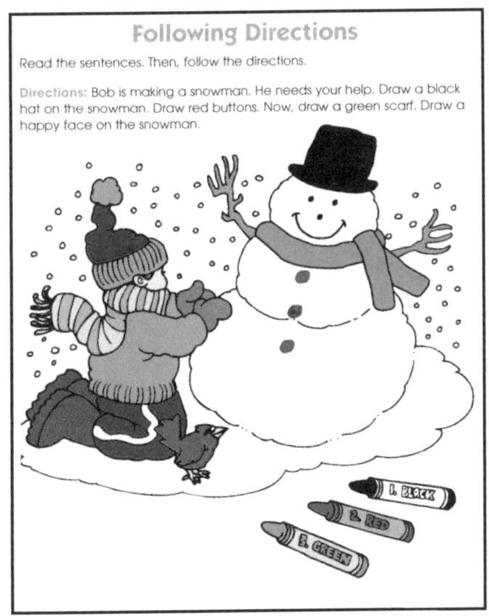

Following Directions

Read the sentences. Then, follow the directions.

Directions: Bob is making a snowman. He needs your help. Draw a black hat on the snowman. Draw red buttons. Now, draw a green scarf. Draw a happy face on the snowman.

85

Menu Mix-Up

Directions: Circle **names of drinks** in **red**.
Circle **names of vegetables** in **green**.
Circle **names of desserts** in **pink**.

Directions: Write each food word on the correct line.

Drinks	Vegetables	Desserts
milk	corn	pie
water	carrot	cookie
juice	peas	cake

86

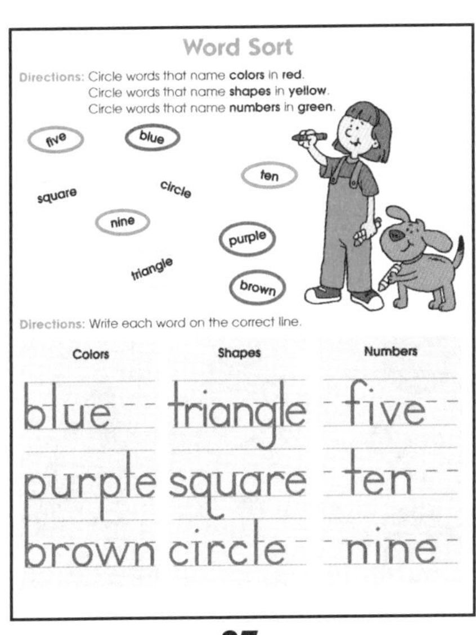

Word Sort

Directions: Circle words that name **colors** in **red**.
Circle words that name **shapes** in **yellow**.
Circle words that name **numbers** in **green**.

Directions: Write each word on the correct line.

Colors	Shapes	Numbers
blue	triangle	five
purple	square	ten
brown	circle	nine

87

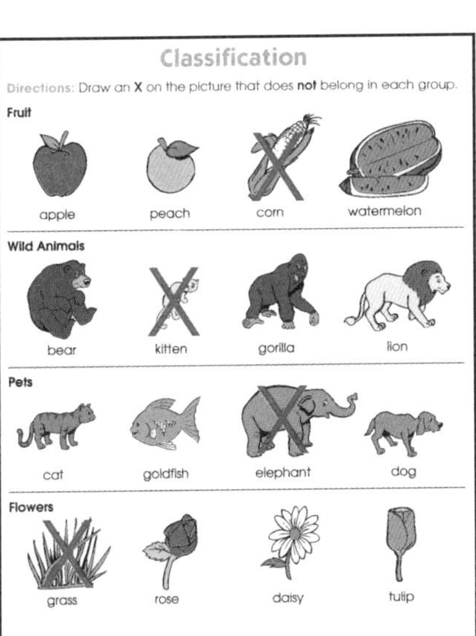

Classification

Directions: Draw an **X** on the picture that does **not** belong in each group.

Fruit

apple, peach, corn, watermelon

Wild Animals

bear, kitten, gorilla, lion

Pets

cat, goldfish, elephant, dog

Flowers

grass, rose, daisy, tulip

88

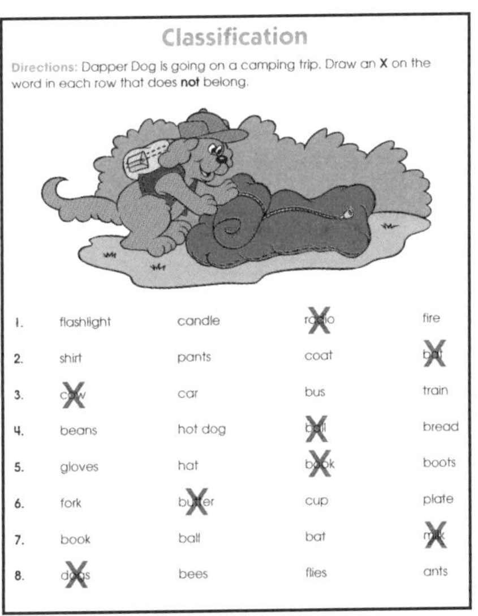

Classification

Directions: Dapper Dog is going on a camping trip. Draw an **X** on the word in each row that does **not** belong.

1.	flashlight	candle	radio	fire
2.	shirt	pants	coat	bat
3.	cow	car	bus	train
4.	beans	hot dog	bat	bread
5.	gloves	hat	book	boots
6.	fork	butter	cup	plate
7.	book	ball	bat	milk
8.	dogs	bees	flies	ants

89

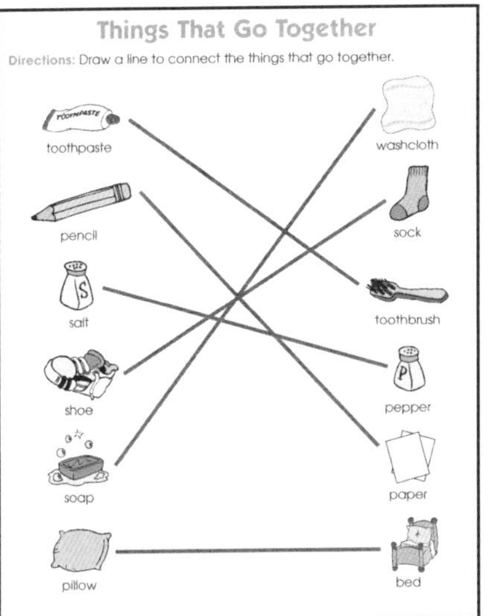

Things That Go Together

Directions: Draw a line to connect the things that go together.

90

Answer Key

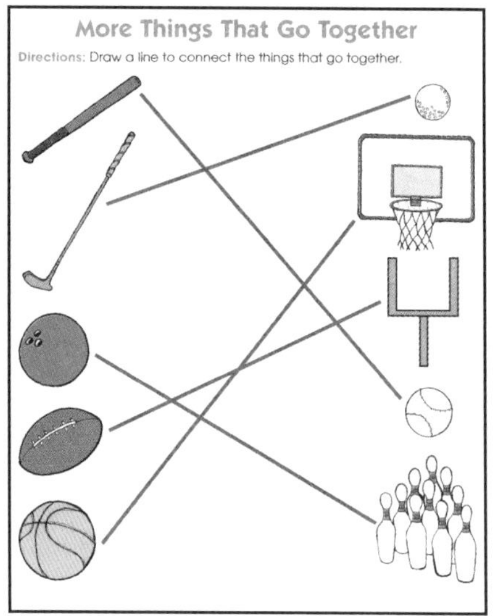

More Things That Go Together

Directions: Draw a line to connect the things that go together.

91

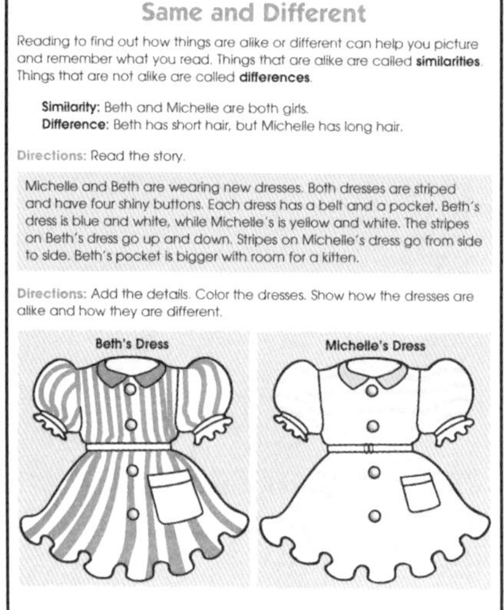

Same and Different

Reading to find out how things are alike or different can help you picture and remember what you read. Things that are alike are called **similarities**. Things that are not alike are called **differences**.

Similarity: Beth and Michelle are both girls.
Difference: Beth has short hair, but Michelle has long hair.

Directions: Read the story.

Michelle and Beth are wearing new dresses. Both dresses are striped and have four shiny buttons. Each dress has a belt and a pocket. Beth's dress is blue and white, while Michelle's is yellow and white. The stripes on Beth's dress go up and down. Stripes on Michelle's dress go from side to side. Beth's pocket is bigger with room for a kitten.

Directions: Add the details. Color the dresses. Show how the dresses are alike and how they are different.

Beth's Dress

Michelle's Dress

92

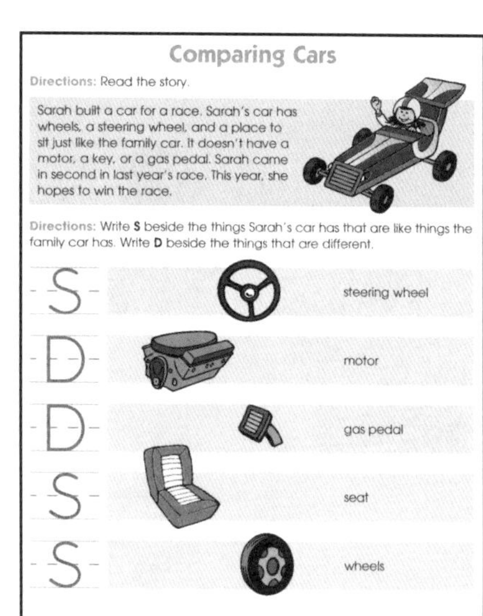

Comparing Cars

Directions: Read the story.

Sarah built a car for a race. Sarah's car has wheels, a steering wheel, and a place to sit just like the family car. It doesn't have a motor, a key, or a gas pedal. Sarah came in second in last year's race. This year, she hopes to win the race.

Directions: Write **S** beside the things Sarah's car has that are like things the family car has. Write **D** beside the things that are different.

S steering wheel
D motor
D gas pedal
S seat
S wheels

93

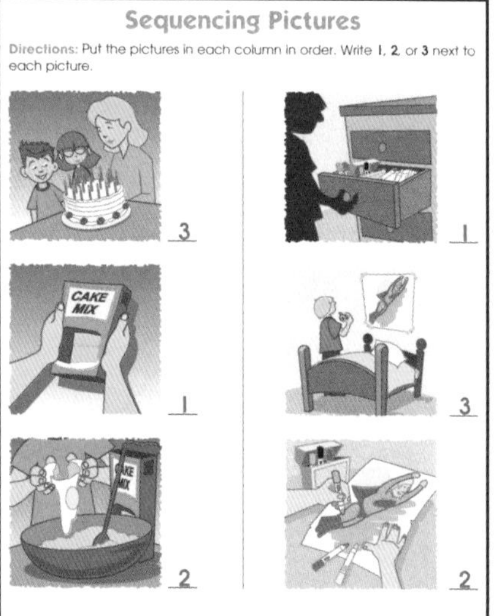

Sequencing Pictures

Directions: Put the pictures in each column in order. Write **1**, **2**, or **3** next to each picture.

3 1
1 3
2 2

94

Sequencing Riddles

Directions: To solve the riddles below, look at the letter underneath each line. Next, write the letter that comes **before** each letter.

How do you catch a squirrel?

CLIMB UP A TREE
D M J N C V Q B U S F F
AND ACT LIKE A NUT
B O E B D U M J L F B O V U

What has four wheels and flies?

A GARBAGE
B H B S C B H F
TRUCK
U S V D L

Why did the boy run around his bed?

TO CATCH UP ON
U P D B U D I V Q P O
HIS SLEEP
I J T T M F F Q

95

Story Time

Directions: Write each group of sentences in the correct order.

My cat was full and went to sleep. My cat was hungry.
I filled a bowl with cat food.

1. My cat was hungry.
2. I filled a bowl with cat food.
3. My cat was full and went to sleep.

Teacher

READ

I got a gold star. I studied for my spelling test.
My teacher gave us a list of spelling words.

1. My teacher gave us a list of spelling words.
2. I studied for my spelling test.
3. I got a gold star.

96

Answer Key

Sequencing

Tom and Tess are making a snack. They are fixing nacho chips and cheese.

Directions: Look at the picture. Then, look at the steps that Tom and Tess use. Put numbers beside each sentence to tell the correct order.

5 Tom and Tess cook the chips in the microwave oven for 2 minutes.
2 They get out a plate to cook on.
1 Tom and Tess get out the nacho chips and cheese.
6 Tom and Tess eat the food.
3 They put the chips on a plate.
4 They put cheese on the chips.

97

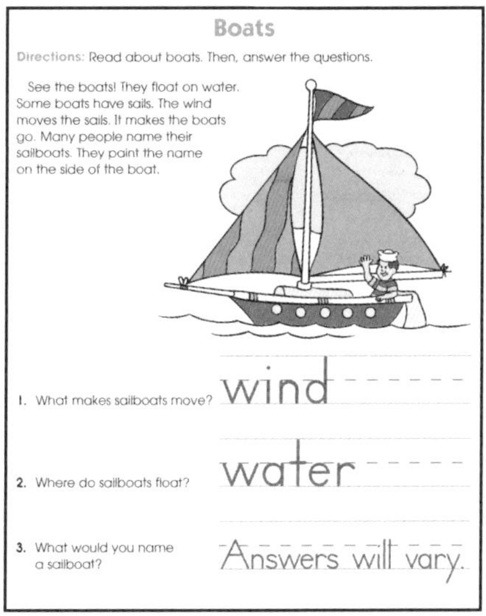

Boats

Directions: Read about boats. Then, answer the questions.

See the boats! They float on water. Some boats have sails. The wind moves the sails. It makes the boats go. Many people name their sailboats. They paint the name on the side of the boat.

1. What makes sailboats move? wind
2. Where do sailboats float? water
3. What would you name a sailboat? Answers will vary.

98

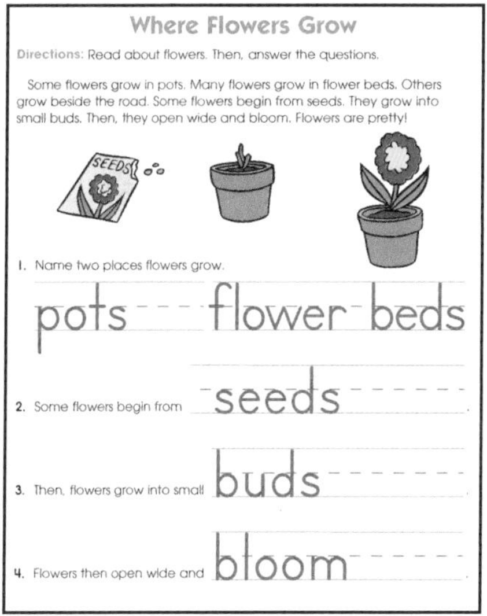

Where Flowers Grow

Directions: Read about flowers. Then, answer the questions.

Some flowers grow in pots. Many flowers grow in flower beds. Others grow beside the road. Some flowers begin from seeds. They grow into small buds. Then, they open wide and bloom. Flowers are pretty!

1. Name two places flowers grow. pots flower beds
2. Some flowers begin from seeds.
3. Then, flowers grow into small buds.
4. Flowers then open wide and bloom.

99

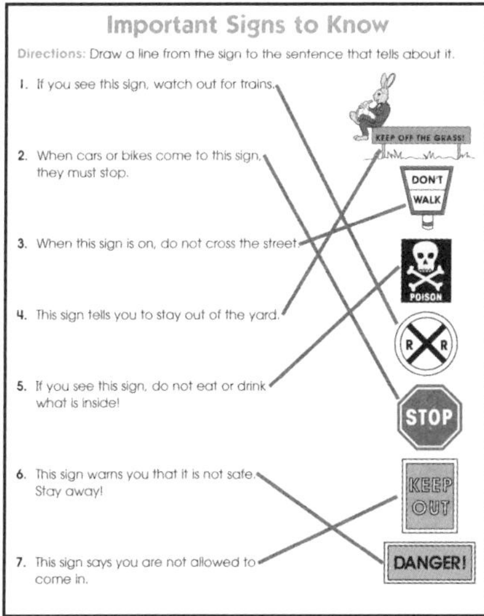

Important Signs to Know

Directions: Draw a line from the sign to the sentence that tells about it.

1. If you see this sign, watch out for trains.
2. When cars or bikes come to this sign, they must stop.
3. When this sign is on, do not cross the street.
4. This sign tells you to stay out of the yard.
5. If you see this sign, do not eat or drink what is inside!
6. This sign warns you that it is not safe. Stay away!
7. This sign says you are not allowed to come in.

100

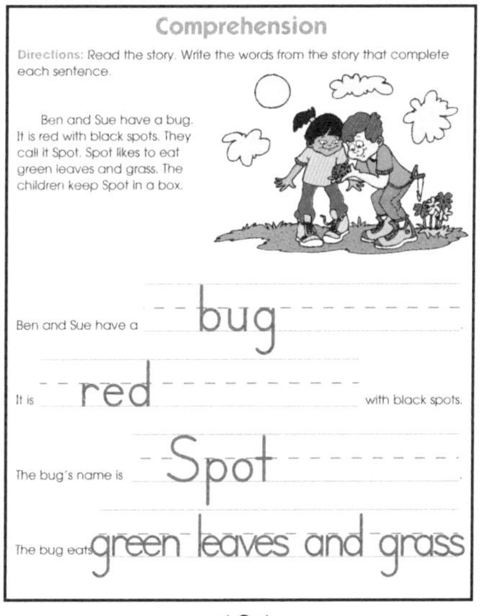

Comprehension

Directions: Read the story. Write the words from the story that complete each sentence.

Ben and Sue have a bug. It is red with black spots. They call it Spot. Spot likes to eat green leaves and grass. The children keep Spot in a box.

Ben and Sue have a bug.
It is red with black spots.
The bug's name is Spot.
The bug eats green leaves and grass

101

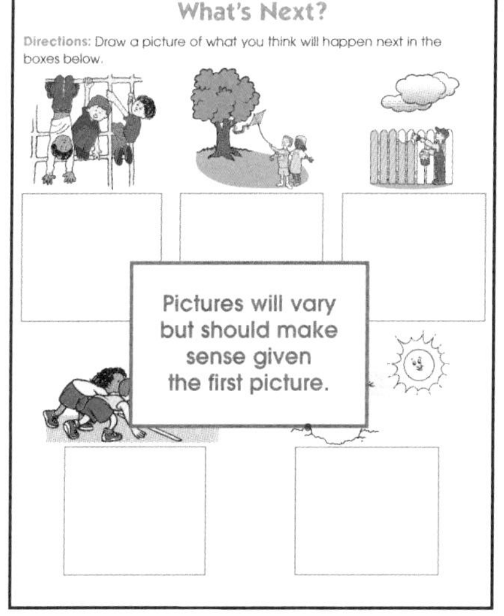

What's Next?

Directions: Draw a picture of what you think will happen next in the boxes below.

Pictures will vary but should make sense given the first picture.

102

Answer Key

What Happens Next?

Directions: Read the story. Predict what will happen and circle your answer choice.

David and Fran go the park. The friendly ice-cream man is there selling ice-cream cones. "Hi kids, would you two like an ice-cream cone?" he asks.

Fran and David reach into their pockets, which are empty. "We don't have any money," says Fran. The ice-cream man smiles at them and reaches into his freezer. Then, he says...

1. Ice cream is bad for children.
2. Today it is my treat. Free ice cream for both of you!
3. I am sorry, maybe next time.

Directions: Draw a picture of what you think will happen.

Pictures will vary.

103

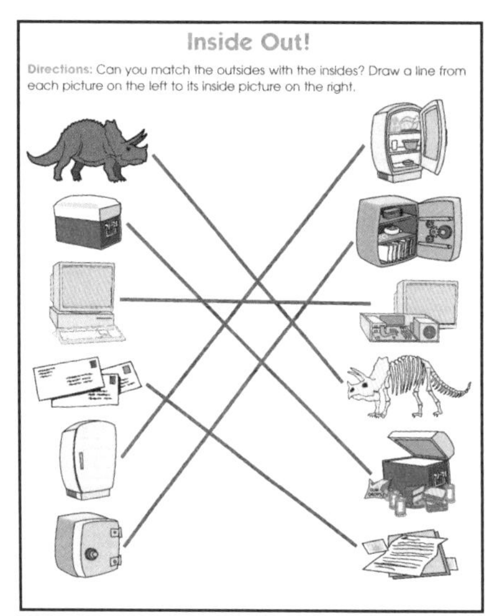

Inside Out!

Directions: Can you match the outsides with the insides? Draw a line from each picture on the left to its inside picture on the right.

104

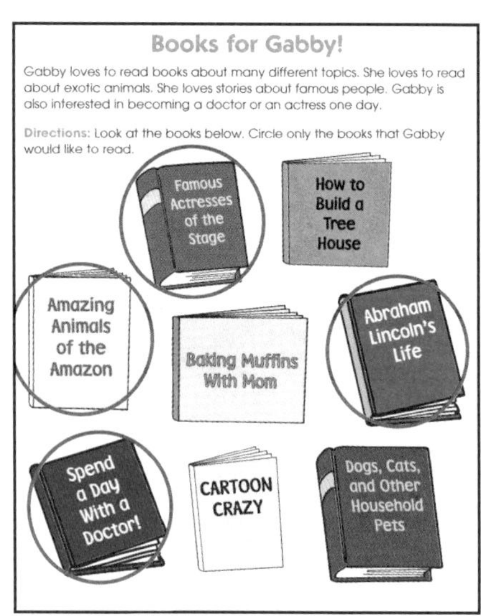

Books for Gabby!

Gabby loves to read books about many different topics. She loves to read about exotic animals. She loves stories about famous people. Gabby is also interested in becoming a doctor or an actress one day.

Directions: Look at the books below. Circle only the books that Gabby would like to read.

105

Use Your Head!

Directions: Read each sentence below. Then, read each statement that follows it. Using the information in the first sentence, decide which word best completes each statement. Then, write that word on the line.

"Please put on your heavy winter coat before you go sledding," said my mom.

My mom wanted me to keep warm. cool warm

I put on my coat before

I went sledding. before after

"Don't forget to bring your glasses, Tom! It will be hard to see the chalkboard if you don't wear them," reminded his dad.

Tom has poor eyesight.

good poor

Tom is forgetful.

forgetful aware

Tom is going to school.

school basketball practice

106

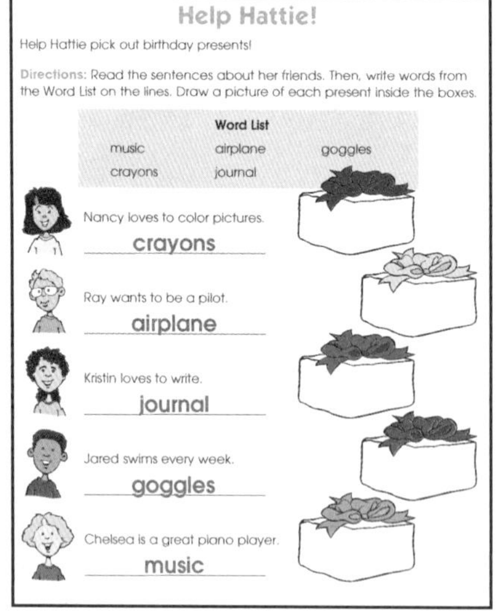

Help Hattie!

Help Hattie pick out birthday presents!

Directions: Read the sentences about her friends. Then, write words from the Word List on the lines. Draw a picture of each present inside the boxes.

Word List		
music	airplane	goggles
crayons	journal	

Nancy loves to color pictures. crayons

Ray wants to be a pilot. airplane

Kristin loves to write. journal

Jared swims every week. goggles

Chelsea is a great piano player. music

107

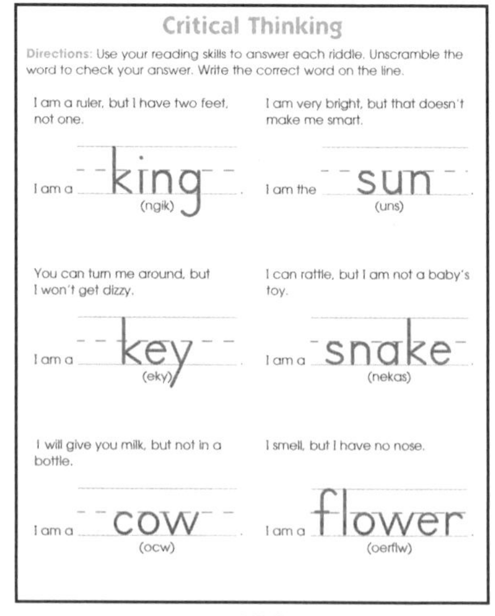

Critical Thinking

Directions: Use your reading skills to answer each riddle. Unscramble the word to check your answer. Write the correct word on the line.

I am a ruler, but I have two feet, not one.

I am a king (ngik)

I am very bright, but that doesn't make me smart.

I am the sun (uns)

You can turn me around, but I won't get dizzy.

I am a key (eky)

I can rattle, but I am not a baby's toy.

I am a snake (nekas)

I will give you milk, but not in a bottle.

I am a cow (ocw)

I smell, but I have no nose.

I am a flower (oerflw)

108

Answer Key

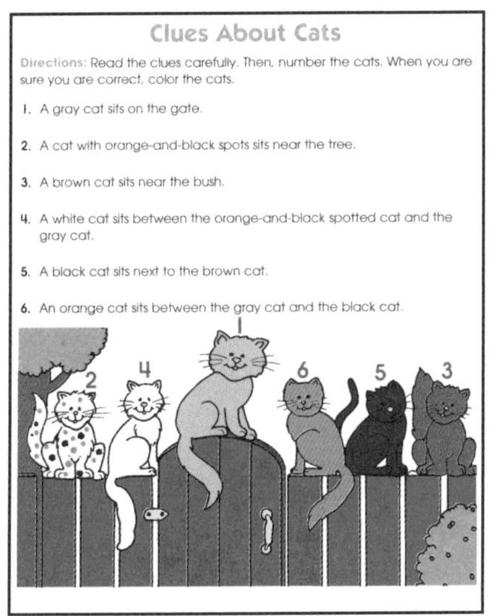

Clues About Cats

Directions: Read the clues carefully. Then, number the cats. When you are sure you are correct, color the cats.

1. A gray cat sits on the gate.
2. A cat with orange-and-black spots sits near the tree.
3. A brown cat sits near the bush.
4. A white cat sits between the orange-and-black spotted cat and the gray cat.
5. A black cat sits next to the brown cat.
6. An orange cat sits between the gray cat and the black cat.

109

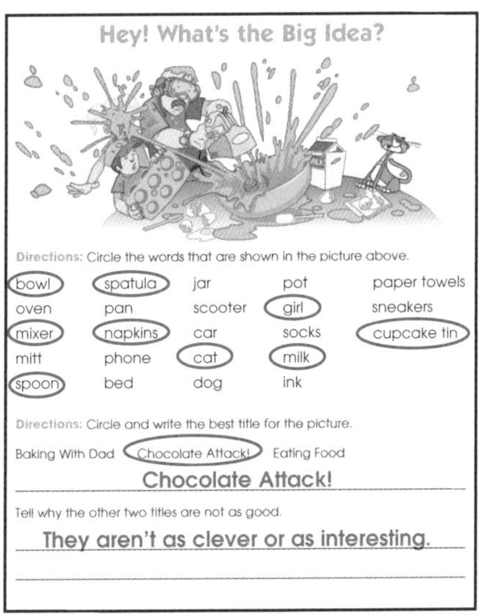

Hey! What's the Big Idea?

Directions: Circle the words that are shown in the picture above.

(bowl)	(spatula)	jar	pot	paper towels
oven	pan	scooter	(girl)	sneakers
(mixer)	(napkins)	car	socks	(cupcake tin)
mitt	phone	(cat)	(milk)	
(spoon)	bed	dog	ink	

Directions: Circle and write the best title for the picture.

Baking With Dad (Chocolate Attack!) Eating Food

Chocolate Attack!

Tell why the other two titles are not as good.

They aren't as clever or as interesting.

110

What's the Main Idea?

The **main idea** tells about the **whole picture**.

Directions: Does the sentence tell the main idea of the picture? Circle **yes** or **no**. Then, write the sentence that best states the main idea for each picture.

The cat wants to play. yes (no)

The cat takes a nap. (yes) no

Sentences will vary.

The brothers play together. (yes) no

The brothers are smart. yes (no)

The dog is hungry. (yes) no

The dog is playful. yes (no)

111

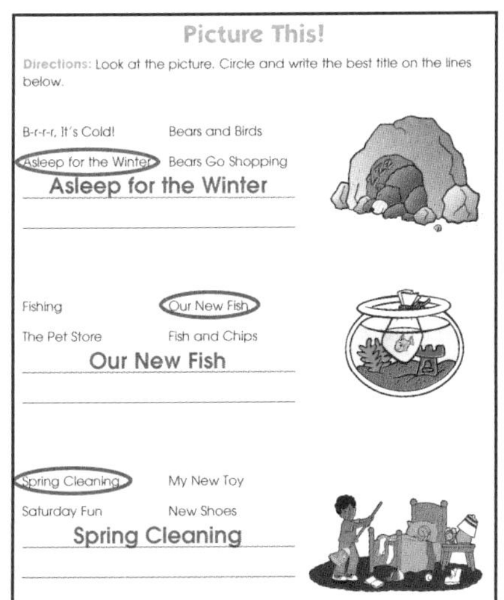

Picture This!

Directions: Look at the picture. Circle and write the best title on the lines below.

B-r-r-r, It's Cold! Bears and Birds

(Asleep for the Winter) Bears Go Shopping

Asleep for the Winter

Fishing (Our New Fish)

The Pet Store Fish and Chips

Our New Fish

(Spring Cleaning) My New Toy

Saturday Fun New Shoes

Spring Cleaning

112

Story Time

The **main idea** tells about the **whole story**.

Read the story below.

"Mom, can we build a fort in the dining room?" John asked.

"Sure, honey," said John's mom. Then, John's mom covered the dining room table with a giant sheet. "Do you want to eat lunch in our fort?" asked John's mom.

"Yes!" said John. Then, John's mom brought two peanut butter sandwiches on paper plates and sat under the table, too!

"Mom, making a fort with you is so much fun!" said John, smiling.

Directions: Does the sentence tell the main idea? Write **yes** or **no**.

1. Then, John's mom covered the dining room table with a giant sheet. no
2. "Do you want to eat lunch in our fort?" asked John's mom. no
3. "Mom, making a fort with you is so much fun!" no
4. Write a sentence that tells the main idea: John and his mother made a fort.

113

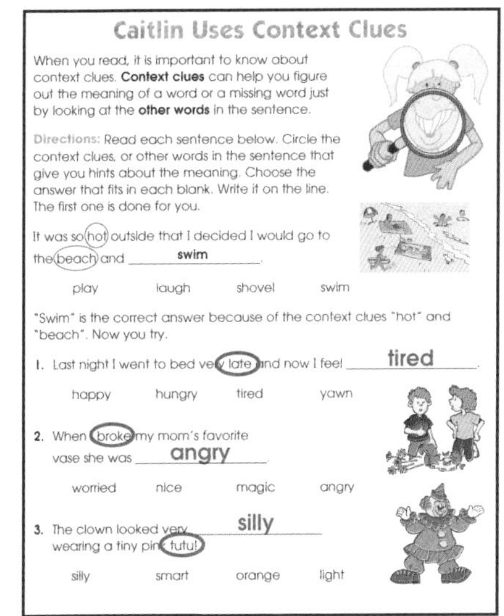

Caitlin Uses Context Clues

When you read, it is important to know about context clues. **Context clues** can help you figure out the meaning of a word or a missing word just by looking at the **other words** in the sentence.

Directions: Read each sentence below. Circle the context clues, or other words in the sentence that give you hints about the meaning. Choose the answer that fits in each blank. Write it on the line. The first one is done for you.

It was so (hot) outside that I decided I would go to the (beach) and swim.

play laugh shovel swim

"Swim" is the correct answer because of the context clues "hot" and "beach". Now you try.

1. Last night I went to bed very (late) and now I feel tired.

   happy hungry tired yawn

2. When I (broke) my mom's favorite vase she was angry.

   worried nice magic angry

3. The clown looked very silly wearing a tiny pink (tutu).

   silly smart orange light

114

Answer Key

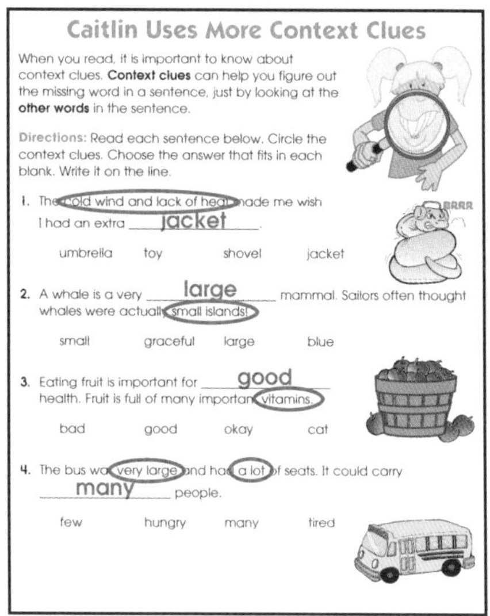

Caitlin Uses More Context Clues

When you read, it is important to know about context clues. **Context clues** can help you figure out the missing word in a sentence, just by looking at the **other words** in the sentence.

Directions: Read each sentence below. Circle the context clues. Choose the answer that fits in each blank. Write it on the line.

1. The cold wind and lack of heat made me wish I had an extra jacket.
   umbrella toy shovel jacket
2. A whale is a very large mammal. Sailors often thought whales were actually small islands.
   small graceful large blue
3. Eating fruit is important for good health. Fruit is full of many important vitamins.
   bad good okay cat
4. The bus was very large and had a lot of seats. It could carry many people.
   few hungry many tired

115

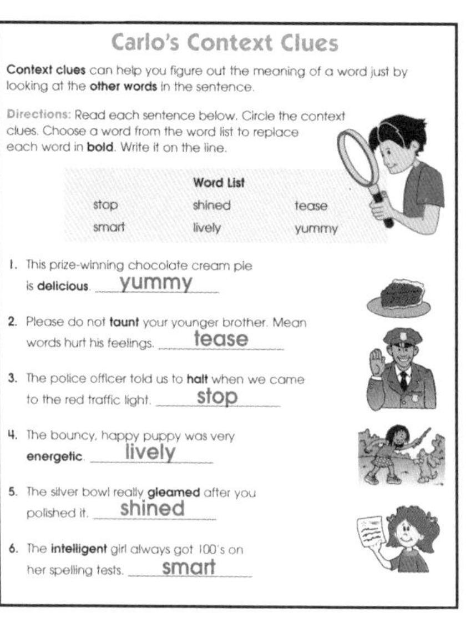

Carlo's Context Clues

Context clues can help you figure out the meaning of a word just by looking at the **other words** in the sentence.

Directions: Read each sentence below. Circle the context clues. Choose a word from the word list to replace each word in **bold**. Write it on the line.

Word List

stop	shined	tease
smart	lively	yummy

1. This prize-winning chocolate cream pie is **delicious**. yummy
2. Please do not **taunt** your younger brother. Mean words hurt his feelings. tease
3. The police officer told us to **halt** when we came to the red traffic light. stop
4. The bouncy, happy puppy was very **energetic**. lively
5. The silver bowl really **gleamed** after you polished it. shined
6. The **intelligent** girl always got 100's on her spelling tests. smart

116

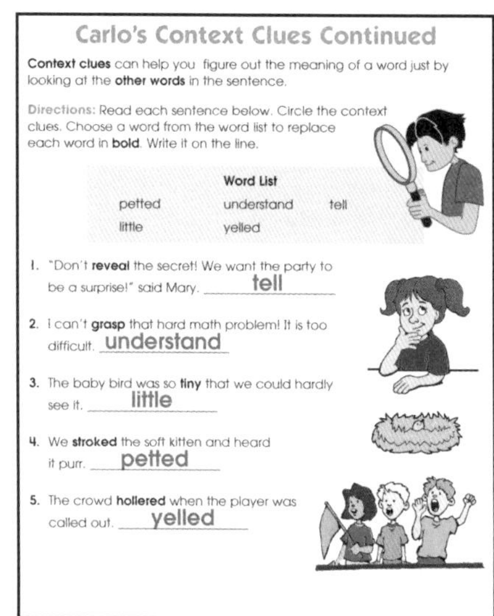

Carlo's Context Clues Continued

Context clues can help you figure out the meaning of a word just by looking at the **other words** in the sentence.

Directions: Read each sentence below. Circle the context clues. Choose a word from the word list to replace each word in **bold**. Write it on the line.

Word List

petted	understand	tell
little	yelled	

1. "Don't **reveal** the secret! We want the party to be a surprise!" said Mary. tell
2. I can't **grasp** that hard math problem! It is too difficult. understand
3. The baby bird was so **tiny** that we could hardly see it. little
4. We **stroked** the soft kitten and heard it purr. petted
5. The crowd **hollered** when the player was called out. yelled

117

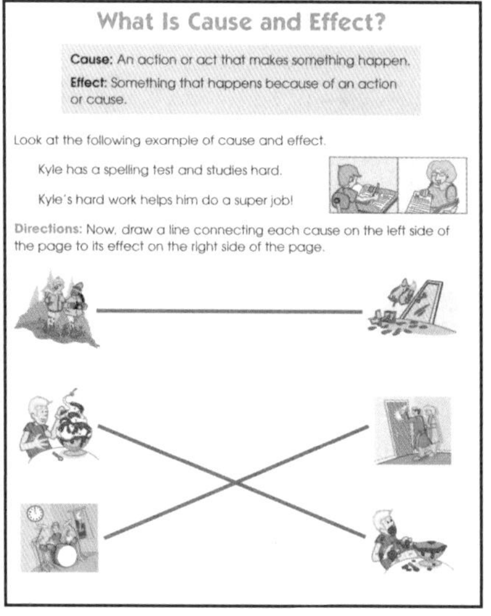

What Is Cause and Effect?

Cause: An action or act that makes something happen.
Effect: Something that happens because of an action or cause.

Look at the following example of cause and effect.

Kyle has a spelling test and studies hard.

Kyle's hard work helps him do a super job!

Directions: Now, draw a line connecting each cause on the left side of the page to its effect on the right side of the page.

118

We Go Together!

Directions: Draw a line connecting the pictures that go together. Then, figure out which picture is the cause and which is the effect. Write **C** for **cause** or **E** for **effect** under each picture.

C E
C E
C E

119

Realistic Story or Fantasy?

Many stories are made-up stories. A made-up story about things that could really happen is a **realistic story**. Some made-up stories, such as fairy tales, tell about things that could never really happen. Those stories are **fantasies**.

Realistic story: A girl hits a home run and wins the game for her team.

Fantasy: A girl hits the ball. It sprouts wings and flies away on an adventure.

Directions: Read the book reviews. Fill in the circle to show whether each story is a realistic story or a fantasy.

The Flying Hippo is about a hippo that flies through the sky. He lands at a busy airport and wanders through New York City.
○ Realistic story ● Fantasy

A Goose Learns to Fly is about a family who saves an injured baby goose. Later, they teach it to fly on its own.
● Realistic story ○ Fantasy

The First Airplane is about the Wright Brothers and the airplane they invented.
● Realistic story ○ Fantasy

The Magic Airplane is about a toy airplane that flies to the planet Mars.
○ Realistic story ● Fantasy

120

Answer Key

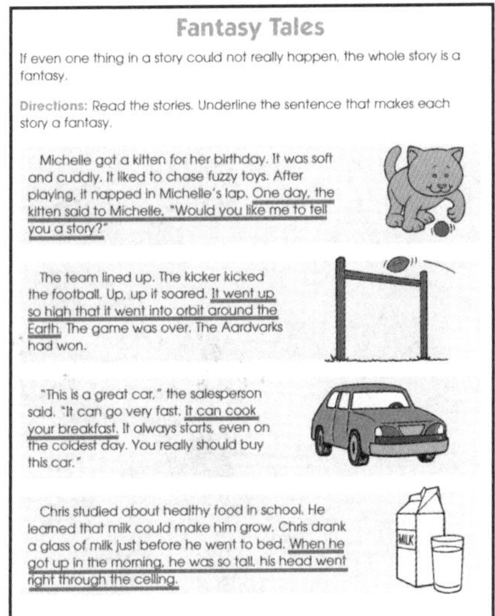

Fantasy Tales

If even one thing in a story could not really happen, the whole story is a fantasy.

Directions: Read the stories. Underline the sentence that makes each story a fantasy.

Michelle got a kitten for her birthday. It was soft and cuddly. It liked to chase fuzzy toys. After playing, it napped in Michelle's lap. One day, the kitten said to Michelle, "Would you like me to tell you a story?"

The team lined up. The kicker kicked the football. Up, up it soared. It went up so high that it went into orbit around the Earth. The game was over. The Aardvarks had won.

"This is a great car," the salesperson said. "It can go very fast. It can cook your breakfast. It always starts, even on the coldest day. You really should buy this car."

Chris studied about healthy food in school. He learned that milk could make him grow. Chris drank a glass of milk just before he went to bed. When he got up in the morning, he was so tall, his head went right through the ceiling.

121

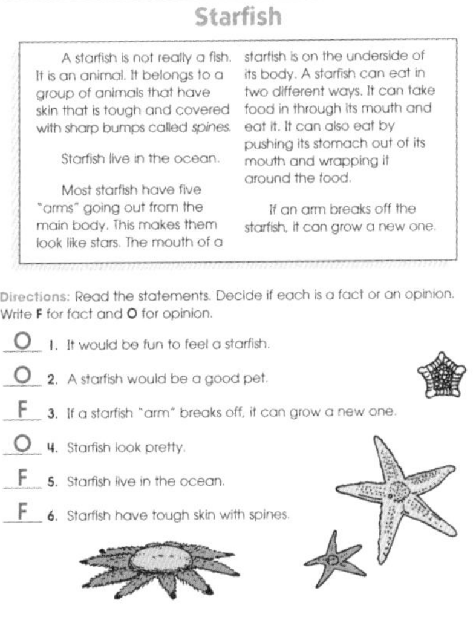

Starfish

A starfish is not really a fish. It is an animal. It belongs to a group of animals that have skin that is tough and covered with sharp bumps called spines.

Starfish live in the ocean.

Most starfish have five "arms" going out from the main body. This makes them look like stars. The mouth of a starfish is on the underside of its body. A starfish can eat in two different ways. It can take food in through its mouth and eat it. It can also eat by pushing its stomach out of its mouth and wrapping it around the food.

If an arm breaks off the starfish, it can grow a new one.

Directions: Read the statements. Decide if each is a fact or an opinion. Write **F** for fact and **O** for opinion.

O 1. It would be fun to feel a starfish.
O 2. A starfish would be a good pet.
F 3. If a starfish "arm" breaks off, it can grow a new one.
O 4. Starfish look pretty.
F 5. Starfish live in the ocean.
F 6. Starfish have tough skin with spines.

122

Figs

Fig is the name of a fruit and of the plant the fruit grows on. The plant can look like a bush or like a tree. Fig plants grow where it is warm all year long.

The fig fruit grows in bunches on the stems of fig plants. Some figs can be picked two times each year. They can be picked from old branches in June or July. They can be picked from new branches in August or September.

Many people like to eat figs. They can be eaten in fig cookies or in fig bars. They can be canned or eaten fresh. Sometimes figs are dried.

Directions: Color the fig **red** if the sentence is a **fact**. Color the fig **blue** if the sentence is an **opinion**.

1. A fig is a plant and a fruit.
2. The fig tree is very pretty.
3. Fig plants do not grow where it is very cold.
4. Figs grow in a bunch.
5. You can pick figs two times each year.
6. Figs taste very good.
7. You can eat figs in many ways.
8. The best way to eat a fig is in a fig cookie.

123

What's My Name?

Different words have different jobs. A **naming word** names a person, place, or thing. Naming words are also called **nouns**.

Example: person — nurse
place — store
thing — drum

Directions: In the word box below, circle only the words that name a person, place, or thing. Then, use the nouns you circled to name each picture.

(teacher)	up	(dog)	the	(library)
runs	is	(cowhand)	(cap)	(zoo)

dog library teacher

cap cowboy zoo

124

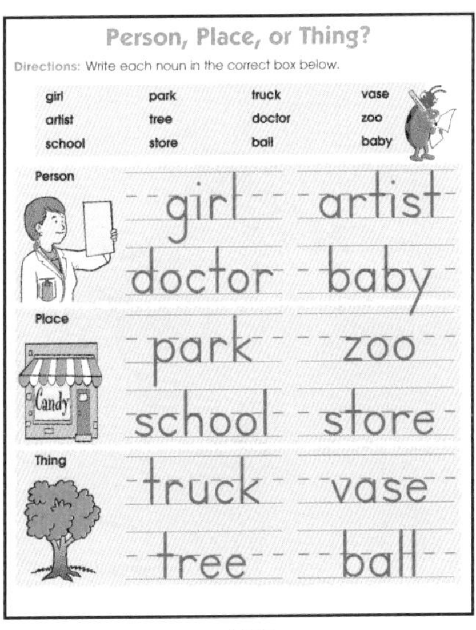

Person, Place, or Thing?

Directions: Write each noun in the correct box below.

girl	park	truck	vase
artist	tree	doctor	zoo
school	store	ball	baby

Person: girl, artist, doctor, baby

Place: park, zoo, school, store

Thing: truck, vase, tree, ball

125

Finding Nouns

A **noun** names a person, place, or thing.

Directions: Circle two nouns in each sentence below. The first one is done for you.

The (pig) has a curly (tail).
The (hen) is sitting on her (nest).
A (horse) is in the (barn).
The (goat) has (horns).
The (cow) has a (calf).
The (farmer) is painting the (fence).

126

Answer Key

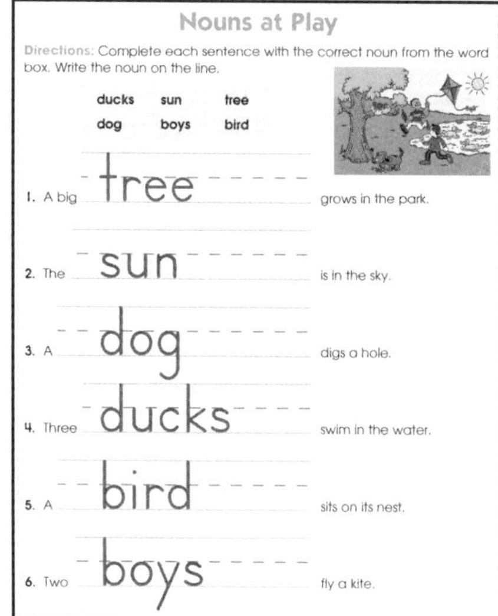

Nouns at Play

Directions: Complete each sentence with the correct noun from the word box. Write the noun on the line.

ducks sun tree
dog boys bird

1. A big tree grows in the park.
2. The sun is in the sky.
3. A dog digs a hole.
4. Three ducks swim in the water.
5. A bird sits on its nest.
6. Two boys fly a kite.

127

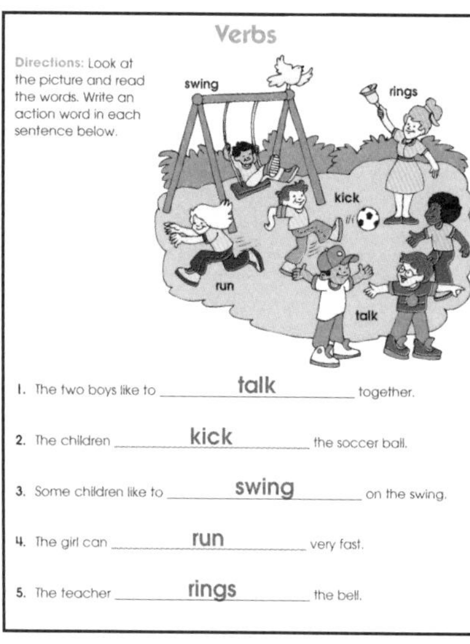

Verbs

Directions: Look at the picture and read the words. Write an action word in each sentence below.

1. The two boys like to talk together.
2. The children kick the soccer ball.
3. Some children like to swing on the swing.
4. The girl can run very fast.
5. The teacher rings the bell.

128

Ready, Set, Go!

An **action word** tells what a person or thing can do.

Example: Fred **kicks** the ball.

Directions: Read the words below. Circle words that tell what the children are doing.

129

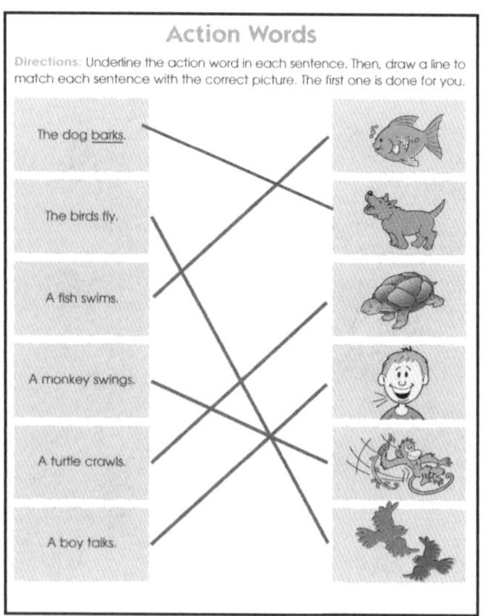

Action Words

Directions: Underline the action word in each sentence. Then, draw a line to match each sentence with the correct picture. The first one is done for you.

The dog barks.

The birds fly.

A fish swims.

A monkey swings.

A turtle crawls.

A boy talks.

130

What Is a Verb?

A **verb** is an action word. A verb tells what a person or thing does.

Example: Jane **reads** a book.

Directions: Circle the verb in each sentence below.

Two tiny dogs dance.

The bear climbs a ladder.

The clown falls down.

A tiger jumps through a ring.

A boy eats popcorn.

A woman swings on a trapeze.

131

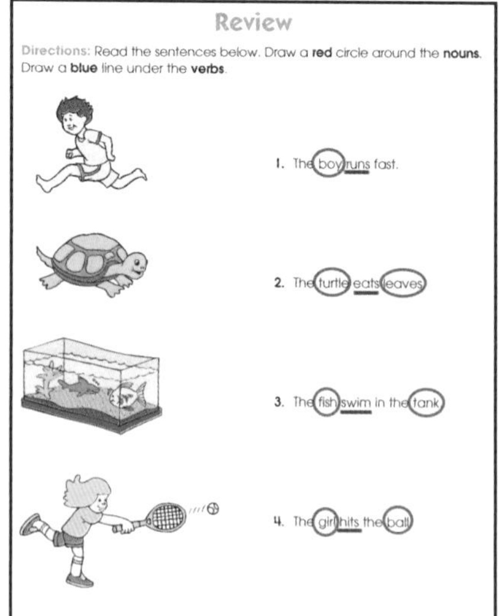

Review

Directions: Read the sentences below. Draw a **red** circle around the **nouns**. Draw a **blue** line under the **verbs**.

1. The boy runs fast.
2. The turtle eats leaves.
3. The fish swim in the tank.
4. The girl hits the ball.

132

Answer Key

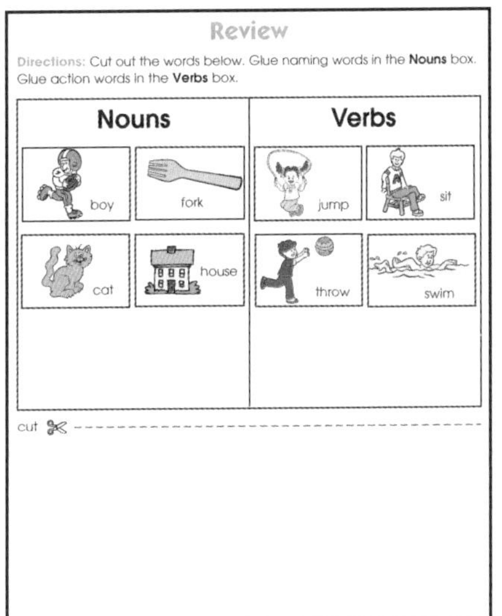

Review

Directions: Cut out the words below. Glue naming words in the **Nouns** box. Glue action words in the **Verbs** box.

Nouns	Verbs
boy, fork, cat, house	jump, sit, throw, swim

cut ✂ - - - - - - - - - -

133

Words That Describe

Directions: Read the words in the box. Choose the word that describes, or tells about, the picture. Write it next to the picture.

wet round funny soft sad tall

soft | tall

funny | sad

round | wet

135

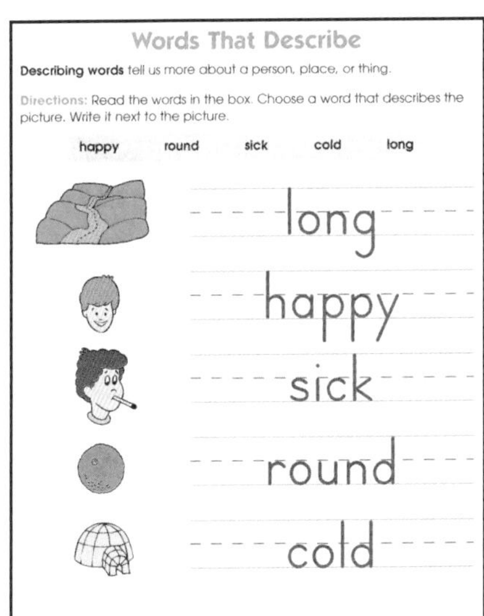

Words That Describe

Describing words tell us more about a person, place, or thing.

Directions: Read the words in the box. Choose a word that describes the picture. Write it next to the picture.

happy round sick cold long

long

happy

sick

round

cold

136

Adjectives

Describing words are also called **adjectives**.

Directions: Circle the describing words in the sentences.

1. The (juicy) apple is on the plate.
2. The (furry) dog is eating a bone.
3. It was a (sunny) day.
4. The kitten drinks (warm) milk.
5. The baby has a (loud) cry.

137

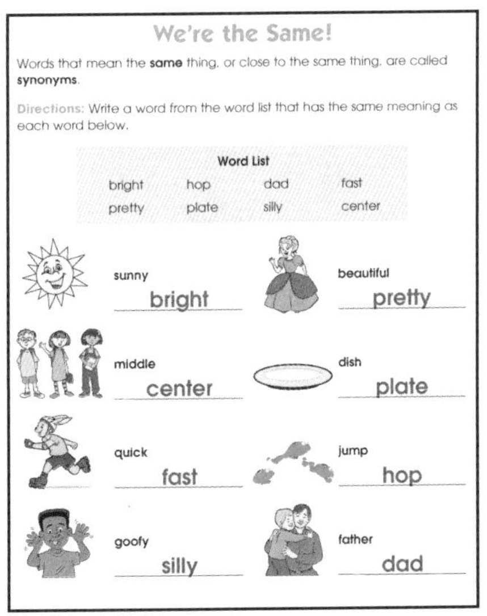

We're the Same!

Words that mean the **same** thing, or close to the same thing, are called **synonyms**.

Directions: Write a word from the word list that has the same meaning as each word below.

Word List			
bright	hop	dad	fast
pretty	plate	silly	center

sunny bright | beautiful pretty

middle center | dish plate

quick fast | jump hop

goofy silly | father dad

138

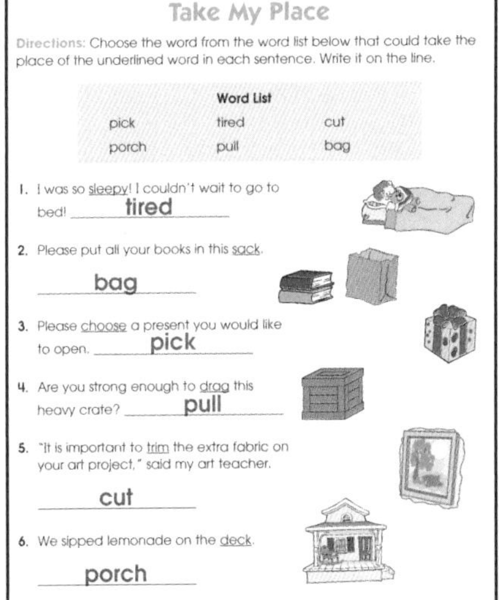

Take My Place

Directions: Choose the word from the word list below that could take the place of the underlined word in each sentence. Write it on the line.

Word List		
pick	tired	cut
porch	pull	bag

1. I was so sleepy! I couldn't wait to go to bed! tired
2. Please put all your books in this sack. bag
3. Please choose a present you would like to open. pick
4. Are you strong enough to drag this heavy crate? pull
5. "It is important to trim the extra fabric on your art project," said my art teacher. cut
6. We sipped lemonade on the deck. porch

139

Answer Key

Antonym Artists!

Antonyms are words that have **opposite** meanings. Abby and Abe are Antonym Artists! They like to draw opposite pictures.

Directions: Help Abe draw the opposite of Abby's pictures.

Pictures will vary but should portray the opposite of the first picture.

140

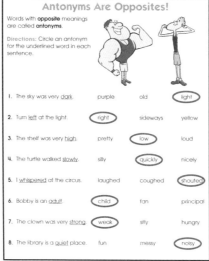

Antonyms Are Opposites!

Words with **opposite** meanings are called **antonyms**.

Directions: Circle an antonym for the underlined word in each sentence.

1. The sky was very dark. purple old (light)
2. Turn left at the light. (right) sideways yellow
3. The shelf was very high. pretty (low) loud
4. The turtle walked slowly. silly (quickly) nicely
5. I whispered at the circus. laughed coughed (shouted)
6. Bobby is an adult. (child) fan principal
7. The clown was very strong. (weak) silly hungry
8. The library is a quiet place. fun messy (noisy)

141

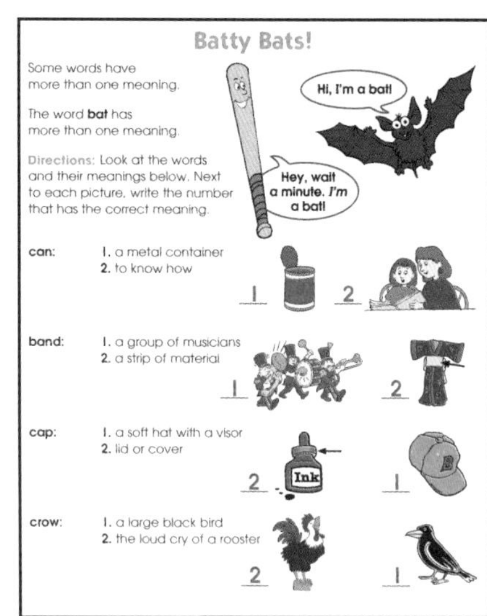
Batty Bats!

Some words have more than one meaning.

The word **bat** has more than one meaning.

Directions: Look at the words and their meanings below. Next to each picture, write the number that has the correct meaning.

can: 1. a metal container 2. to know how — 1, 2

band: 1. a group of musicians 2. a strip of material — 1, 2

cap: 1. a soft hat with a visor 2. lid or cover — 2, 1

crow: 1. a large black bird 2. the loud cry of a rooster — 2, 1

142

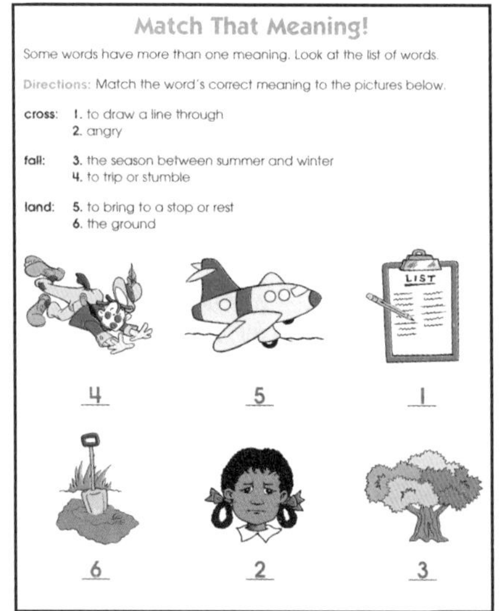
Match That Meaning!

Some words have more than one meaning. Look at the list of words.

Directions: Match the word's correct meaning to the pictures below.

cross: 1. to draw a line through 2. angry

fall: 3. the season between summer and winter 4. to trip or stumble

land: 5. to bring to a stop or rest 6. the ground

4 5 1

6 2 3

143

Homonyms

Homonyms are words that sound the same, but are spelled differently and have different meanings. For example, **sun** and **son** are homonyms.

Directions: Look at the word. Circle the picture that goes with the word.

1. sun
2. hi
3. ate
4. four
5. buy
6. hear

144

Homonyms

Directions: Look at each picture. Circle the homonym that is spelled the correct way.

(deer) dear

blue (blew)

to (two)

hi (high)

by (bye)

(new) knew

ate (eight)

red (read)

145

Answer Key

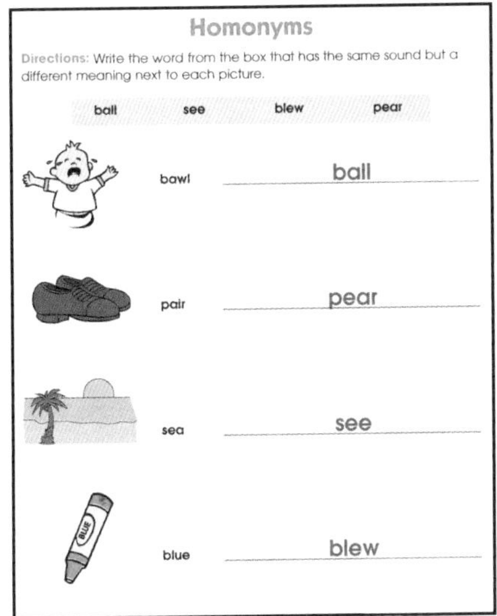

Homonyms

Directions: Write the word from the box that has the same sound but a different meaning next to each picture.

ball see blew pear

bowl	ball
pair	pear
sea	see
blue	blew

146

Homonyms

Directions: Jane is having a birthday party. Complete each sentence with a homonym from the box. Then, write the word in the puzzle.

blew	son
blue	two
too	to
sun	write
right	bee
be	knew
new	

Puzzle: 1. BLEW, 2. WRITE, 1. BLUE, 3. SON, 4. BEE, 5. TWO

Across:
1. Jane ______ out the candles.
4. Two days ago, she was stung by a ______.
5. But after ______ days, she felt better.

Down:
1. She has on a ______ dress for her party.
2. She will ______ a letter to her grandma.
3. Jane is a girl, so she is not a ______.

147

Make Compound Words

Some short words can be put together to make one new word. The new word is called a **compound word**.

cow + hand = cowhand

Directions: Look at each pair of pictures and words below. Join the two words to make a compound word. Write it on the line.

rain + coat = raincoat
door + bell = doorbell
dog + house = doghouse
pan + cake = pancake
horse + shoe = horseshoe

148

Two Words in One

Directions: Write the two words that make up each compound word.

snowball	snow	ball
raincoat	rain	coat
airplane	air	plane
watermelon	water	melon
haircut	hair	cut
football	foot	ball
sunshine	sun	shine

149

Compound Word Riddles

Directions: Underline the two words in each sentence that can make a compound word. Write the compound word on the line to complete the sentence.

A kind of bird that is black is a blackbird
A horse that can race is a racehorse
A cloth that covers a table is a tablecloth
A room with a bed is a bedroom
A book with a story is a storybook
A bowl that holds fish is a fishbowl

150

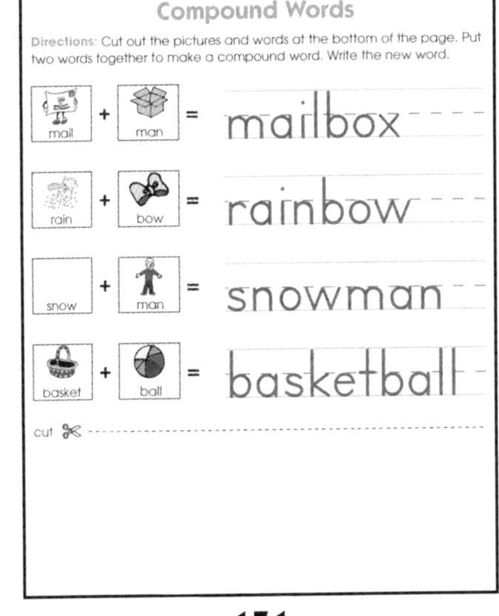

Compound Words

Directions: Cut out the pictures and words at the bottom of the page. Put two words together to make a compound word. Write the new word.

mail + man = mailbox
rain + bow = rainbow
snow + man = snowman
basket + ball = basketball

cut

151

Answer Key

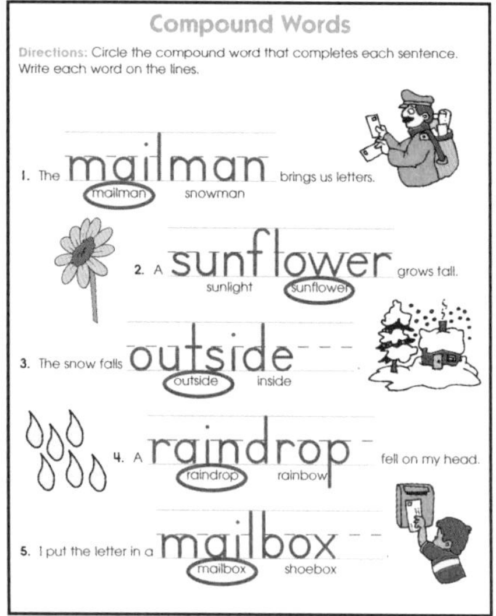

Compound Words

Directions: Circle the compound word that completes each sentence. Write each word on the lines.

1. The mailman brings us letters.
mailman snowman

2. A sunflower grows tall.
sunlight sunflower

3. The snow falls outside
outside inside

4. A raindrop fell on my head.
raindrop rainbow

5. I put the letter in a mailbox
mailbox shoebox

153

One or More Than One?

Directions: Circle the correct word under each picture. The first one is done for you.

hat hats

car cars

frog frogs

shirt shirts

cloud clouds

wheel wheels

dish dishes

glass glasses

fox foxes

154

How Many Toys?

Directions: Read the nouns under the pictures. Write each noun under **One** or **More Than One**.

One	More Than One
boat	yo-yos
jet	cars
doll	blocks
drum	balls

155

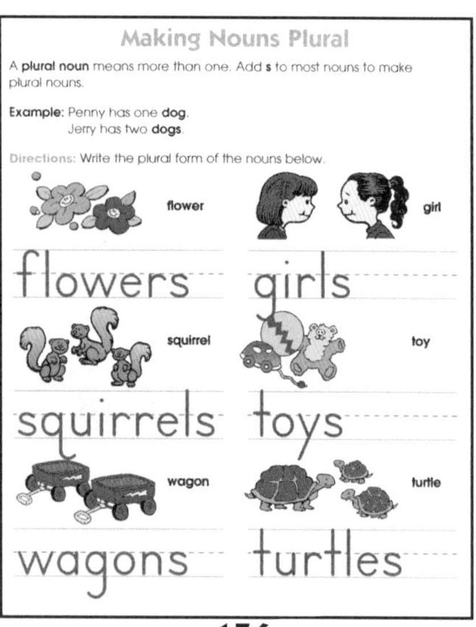

Making Nouns Plural

A **plural noun** means more than one. Add **s** to most nouns to make plural nouns.

Example: Penny has one **dog**.
Jerry has two **dogs**.

Directions: Write the plural form of the nouns below.

flower — flowers

girl — girls

squirrel — squirrels

toy — toys

wagon — wagons

turtle — turtles

156

More Than One

Some nouns name more than one person, place, or thing.

Directions: Add **s** to make the words tell about the picture.

frog s

pan s

boy s

egg s

horn s

girl s

157

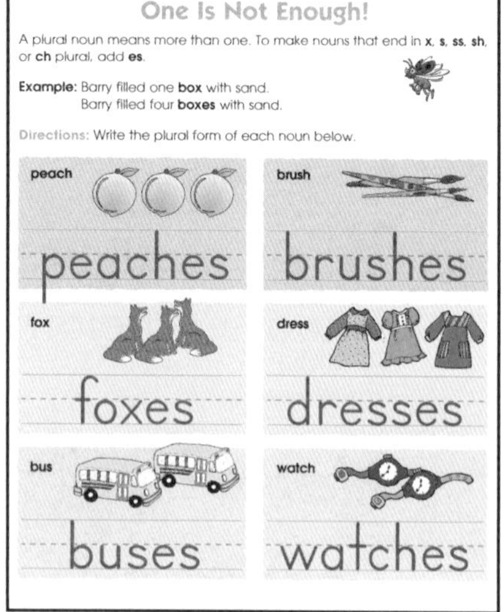

One Is Not Enough!

A plural noun means more than one. To make nouns that end in **x**, **s**, **ss**, **sh**, or **ch** plural, add **es**.

Example: Barry filled one **box** with sand.
Barry filled four **boxes** with sand.

Directions: Write the plural form of each noun below.

peach — peaches

brush — brushes

fox — foxes

dress — dresses

bus — buses

watch — watches

158

Answer Key

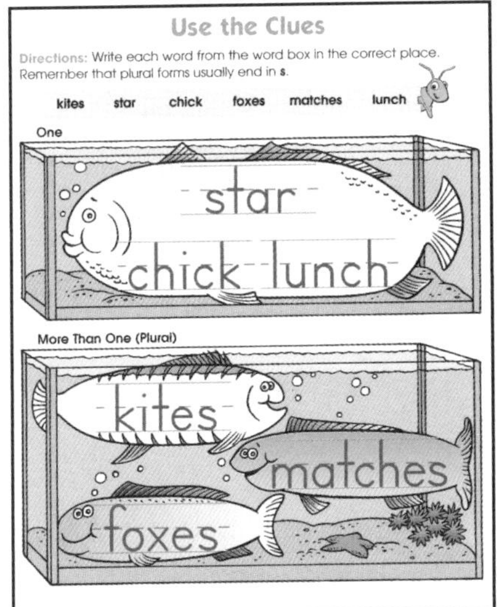

Use the Clues

Directions: Write each word from the word box in the correct place. Remember that plural forms usually end in **s**.

kites star chick foxes matches lunch

One

star

chick lunch

More Than One (Plural)

kites

matches

foxes

159

Sentences That Tell

Some sentences tell something. Every **telling sentence** ends with a **period**.

Example: The bird sings.

Directions: Circle only the sentences that tell something.

1. Two turtles sat on a log.
2. One turtle fell off.
3. Did you see her?
4. She swam away.
5. The water is cold.
6. Can you swim?

160

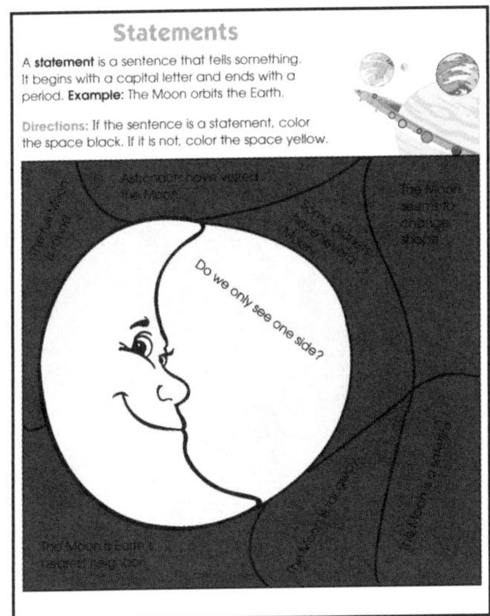

Statements

A **statement** is a sentence that tells something. It begins with a capital letter and ends with a period. **Example:** The Moon orbits the Earth.

Directions: If the sentence is a statement, color the space black. If it is not, color the space yellow.

161

Sentences

Sentences begin with capital letters.

Directions: Read the sentences and write them below. Begin each sentence with a capital letter.

Example: the cat is fat.

The cat is fat.

my dog is big.

My dog is big.

the boy is sad.

The boy is sad.

bikes are fun!

Bikes are fun!

dad can bake.

Dad can bake.

162

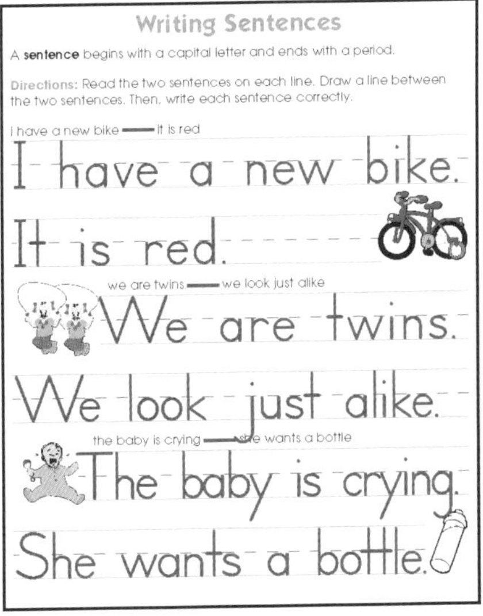

Writing Sentences

A **sentence** begins with a capital letter and ends with a period.

Directions: Read the two sentences on each line. Draw a line between the two sentences. Then, write each sentence correctly.

I have a new bike it is red

I have a new bike.

It is red.

we are twins we look just alike

We are twins.

We look just alike.

the baby is crying she wants a bottle

The baby is crying.

She wants a bottle.

163

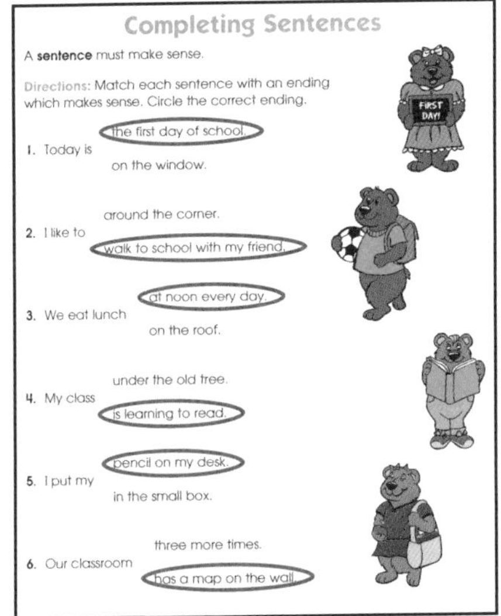

Completing Sentences

A **sentence** must make sense.

Directions: Match each sentence with an ending which makes sense. Circle the correct ending.

1. Today is — the first day of school. / on the window.
2. I like to — around the corner. / walk to school with my friend.
3. We eat lunch — at noon every day. / on the roof.
4. My class — under the old tree. / is learning to read.
5. I put my — pencil on my desk. / in the small box.
6. Our classroom — three more times. / has a map on the wall.

164

Answer Key

Making Sentences

A **sentence** tells a whole idea.

Directions: Cut out and glue each picture and group of words together to make a sentence.

Six candles	are on the cake.
The rabbit	has four carrots.
The apple	is on a dish.
A little spider	makes a web.

165

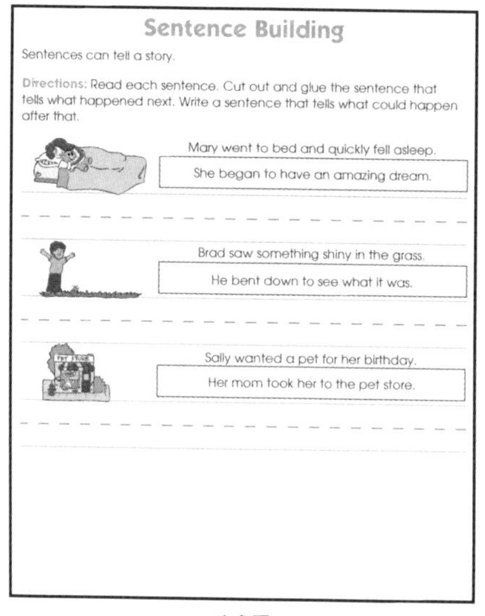

Sentence Building

Sentences can tell a story.

Directions: Read each sentence. Cut out and glue the sentence that tells what happened next. Write a sentence that tells what could happen after that.

Mary went to bed and quickly fell asleep.
She began to have an amazing dream.

Brad saw something shiny in the grass.
He bent down to see what it was.

Sally wanted a pet for her birthday.
Her mom took her to the pet store.

167

Subjects of Sentences

The **subject** of a sentence tells who or what does something.

Examples: Polar bears love cold weather.
The bear's coat is thick.

Directions: Circle the subject of each sentence.

1. Polar bears live in the Arctic.
2. The Arctic is very cold.
3. The polar bear's coat is white.
4. The fur coat keeps the bear warm.
5. The bear has a layer of fat under its skin.
6. The fat is called *blubber*.
7. Blubber keeps the bear warm, too.
8. Polar bears eat seals.
9. A polar bear can sneak up on a seal.
10. The bear's white coat makes it hard to see.

169

Predicates of Sentences

The **predicate** of a sentence tells what the subject is or does.

Examples: Parrots **are not all alike**.
Some parrots **can learn tricks**.

Directions: Circle the predicate of each sentence.

1. Parrots live in hot places.
2. Some macaws are three-feet long.
3. Macaws live in rainforests.
4. Other parrots build nests in desert cactuses.
5. Most parrots have long beaks.
6. They use their beaks for cracking nuts.
7. Some parrots cannot crack nuts.
8. They eat seeds and fruits instead.
9. Parrots are colorful birds.
10. These birds have loud voices.

170

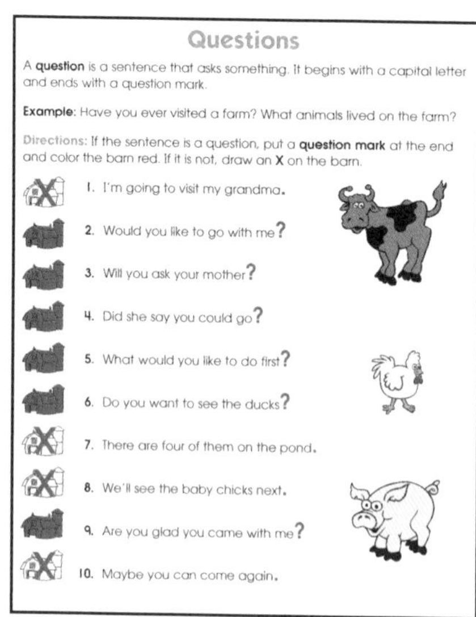

Questions

A **question** is a sentence that asks something. It begins with a capital letter and ends with a question mark.

Example: Have you ever visited a farm? What animals lived on the farm?

Directions: If the sentence is a question, put a **question mark** at the end and color the barn red. If it is not, draw an **X** on the barn.

1. I'm going to visit my grandma.
2. Would you like to go with me?
3. Will you ask your mother?
4. Did she say you could go?
5. What would you like to do first?
6. Do you want to see the ducks?
7. There are four of them on the pond.
8. We'll see the baby chicks next.
9. Are you glad you came with me?
10. Maybe you can come again.

171

More Questions

Directions: A **question** begins with a capital letter and ends with a question mark. Look at each picture of Panda. Ask Panda a question to go with each picture.

Sample questions:

Is it Panda's birthday?

What kind of cookies did he bake?

What is the name of the book?

Did Panda make a snowman?

172

Answer Key

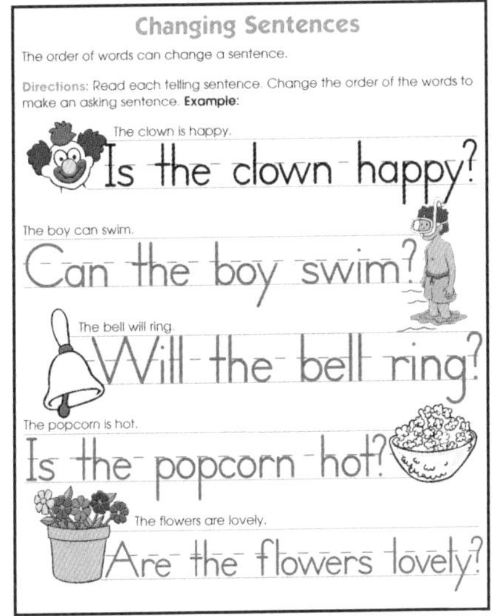

Changing Sentences

The order of words can change a sentence.

Directions: Read each telling sentence. Change the order of the words to make an asking sentence. **Example:**

The clown is happy.

Is the clown happy?

The boy can swim.

Can the boy swim?

The bell will ring.

Will the bell ring?

The popcorn is hot.

Is the popcorn hot?

The flowers are lovely.

Are the flowers lovely?

173

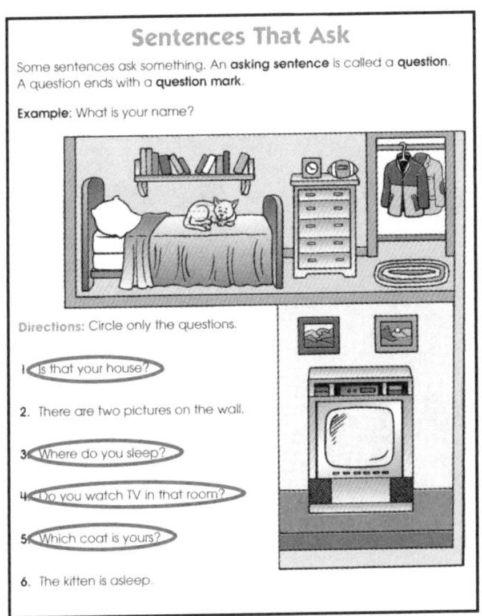

Sentences That Ask

Some sentences ask something. An **asking sentence** is called a **question**. A question ends with a **question mark**.

Example: What is your name?

Directions: Circle only the questions.

1. Is that your house?
2. There are two pictures on the wall.
3. Where do you sleep?
4. Do you watch TV in that room?
5. Which coat is yours?
6. The kitten is asleep.

174

Questions, Questions

A **question** begins with a capital letter and ends with a question mark.

Directions: Write each question correctly on the line.

is our class going to the Science Museum

Is our class going to the Science Museum?

will we see dinosaur bones

Will we see dinosaur bones?

does the museum have a mummy

Does the museum have a mummy?

175

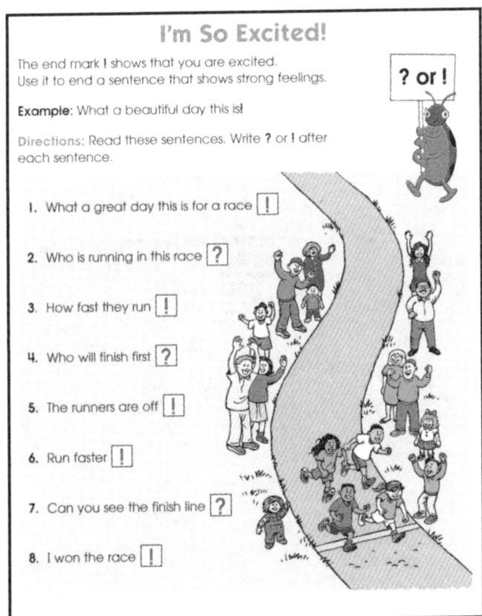

I'm So Excited!

The end mark ! shows that you are excited. Use it to end a sentence that shows strong feelings.

Example: What a beautiful day this is!

Directions: Read these sentences. Write ? or ! after each sentence.

1. What a great day this is for a race !
2. Who is running in this race ?
3. How fast they run !
4. Who will finish first ?
5. The runners are off !
6. Run faster !
7. Can you see the finish line ?
8. I won the race !

176

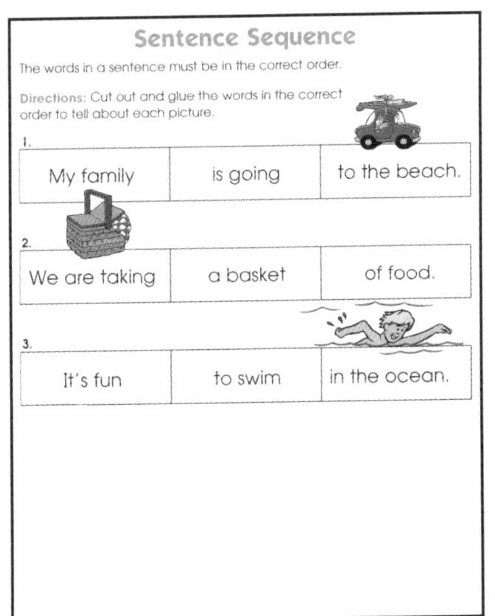

Sentence Sequence

The words in a sentence must be in the correct order.

Directions: Cut out and glue the words in the correct order to tell about each picture.

1.

My family	is going	to the beach.

2.

We are taking	a basket	of food.

3.

It's fun	to swim	in the ocean.

177

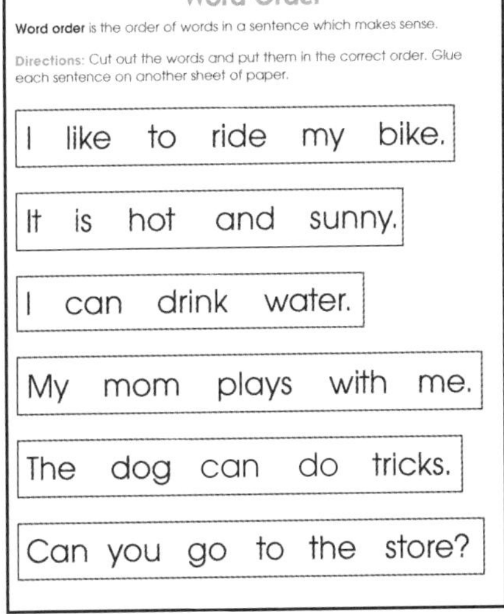

Word Order

Word order is the order of words in a sentence which makes sense.

Directions: Cut out the words and put them in the correct order. Glue each sentence on another sheet of paper.

I like to ride my bike.

It is hot and sunny.

I can drink water.

My mom plays with me.

The dog can do tricks.

Can you go to the store?

179

Answer Key

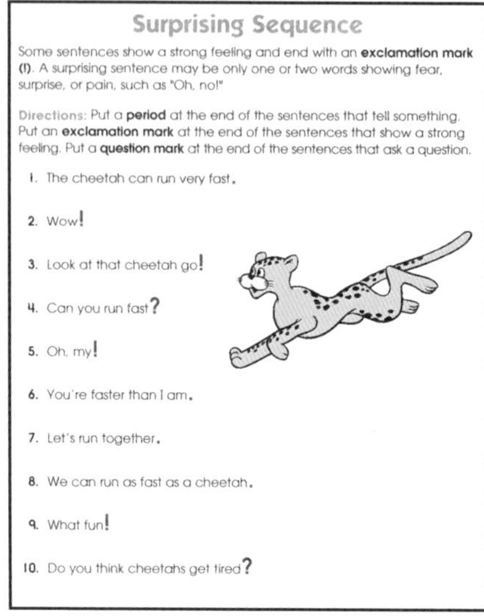

Surprising Sequence

Some sentences show a strong feeling and end with an **exclamation mark (!)**. A surprising sentence may be only one or two words showing fear, surprise, or pain, such as "Oh, no!"

Directions: Put a **period** at the end of the sentences that tell something. Put an **exclamation mark** at the end of the sentences that show a strong feeling. Put a **question mark** at the end of the sentences that ask a question.

1. The cheetah can run very fast.
2. Wow!
3. Look at that cheetah go!
4. Can you run fast?
5. Oh, my!
6. You're faster than I am.
7. Let's run together.
8. We can run as fast as a cheetah.
9. What fun!
10. Do you think cheetahs get tired?

181

ABC Order

Sometimes, words are put in **ABC order**. That means that if a word starts with **a**, it comes first. If it starts with **b**, it comes next, and so on in the order of the alphabet.

Directions: Circle the first letter of each word below. Then, put the words in ABC order. The first one is done for you.

car bird | moon two | nest fan

bird | moon | fan

car | two | nest

card dog | pig bike | sun pie

card | bike | pie

dog | pig | sun

182

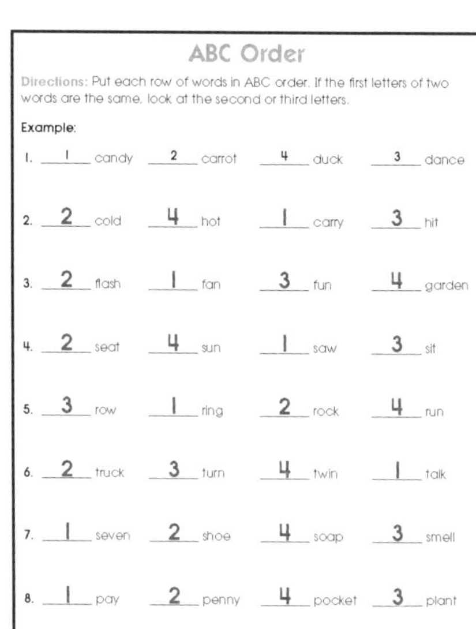

ABC Order

Directions: Put each row of words in ABC order. If the first letters of two words are the same, look at the second or third letters.

Example:

1. 1 candy 2 carrot 4 duck 3 dance
2. 2 cold 4 hot 1 carry 3 hit
3. 2 flash 1 fan 3 fun 4 garden
4. 2 seat 4 sun 1 saw 3 sit
5. 3 row 1 ring 2 rock 4 run
6. 2 truck 3 turn 4 twin 1 talk
7. 1 seven 2 shoe 4 soap 3 smell
8. 1 pay 2 penny 4 pocket 3 plant

183

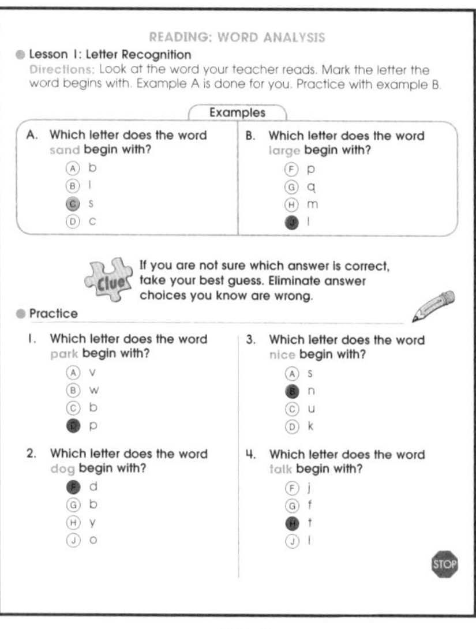

READING: WORD ANALYSIS

Lesson 1: Letter Recognition

Directions: Look at the word your teacher reads. Mark the letter the word begins with. Example A is done for you. Practice with example B.

Examples

A. Which letter does the word sand begin with?
Ⓐ b Ⓑ l ● s Ⓓ c

B. Which letter does the word large begin with?
Ⓕ p Ⓖ q Ⓗ m ● l

Clue: If you are not sure which answer is correct, take your best guess. Eliminate answer choices you know are wrong.

Practice

1. Which letter does the word park begin with?
Ⓐ v Ⓑ w Ⓒ b ● p

2. Which letter does the word dog begin with?
● d Ⓖ b Ⓗ y Ⓙ o

3. Which letter does the word nice begin with?
Ⓐ s ● n Ⓒ u Ⓓ k

4. Which letter does the word talk begin with?
Ⓕ j Ⓖ f ● t Ⓙ l

STOP

186

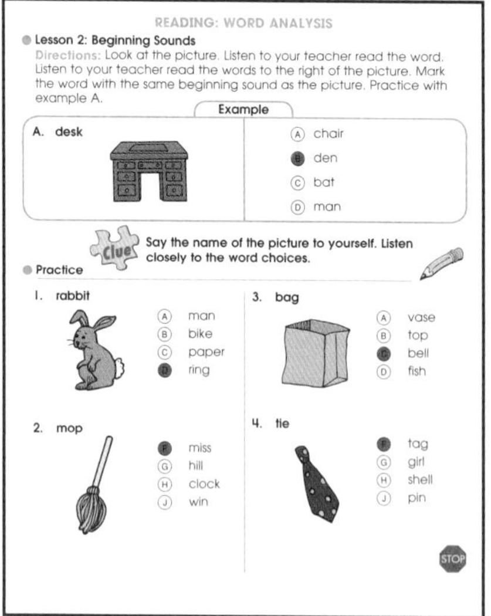

READING: WORD ANALYSIS

Lesson 2: Beginning Sounds

Directions: Look at the picture. Listen to your teacher read the word. Listen to your teacher read the words to the right of the picture. Mark the word with the same beginning sound as the picture. Practice with example A.

Example

A. desk
Ⓐ chair ● den Ⓒ bat Ⓓ man

Clue: Say the name of the picture to yourself. Listen closely to the word choices.

Practice

1. rabbit
Ⓐ man Ⓑ bike Ⓒ paper ● ring

2. mop
● miss Ⓖ hill Ⓗ clock Ⓙ win

3. bag
Ⓐ vase Ⓑ top ● bell Ⓓ fish

4. tie
● tag Ⓖ girl Ⓗ shell Ⓙ pin

STOP

187

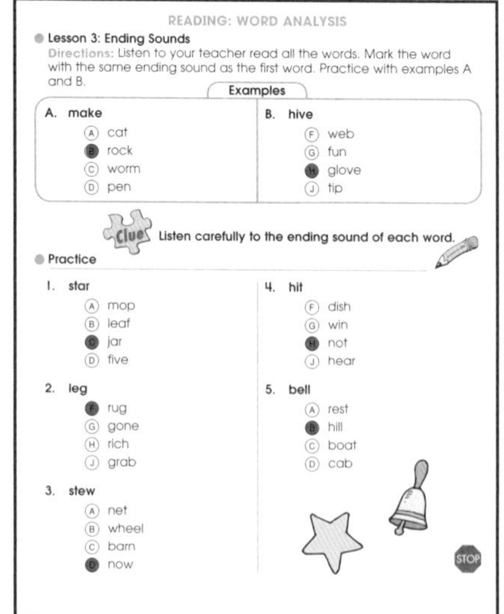

READING: WORD ANALYSIS

Lesson 3: Ending Sounds

Directions: Listen to your teacher read all the words. Mark the word with the same ending sound as the first word. Practice with examples A and B.

Examples

A. make
Ⓐ cat ● rock Ⓒ worm Ⓓ pen

B. hive
Ⓕ web Ⓖ fun ● glove Ⓙ tip

Clue: Listen carefully to the ending sound of each word.

Practice

1. star
Ⓐ mop Ⓑ leaf ● jar Ⓓ five

2. leg
● rug Ⓖ gone Ⓗ rich Ⓙ grab

3. stew
Ⓐ net Ⓑ wheel Ⓒ barn ● now

4. hit
Ⓕ dish Ⓖ win ● not Ⓙ hear

5. bell
Ⓐ rest ● hill Ⓒ boat Ⓓ cab

STOP

188

Answer Key

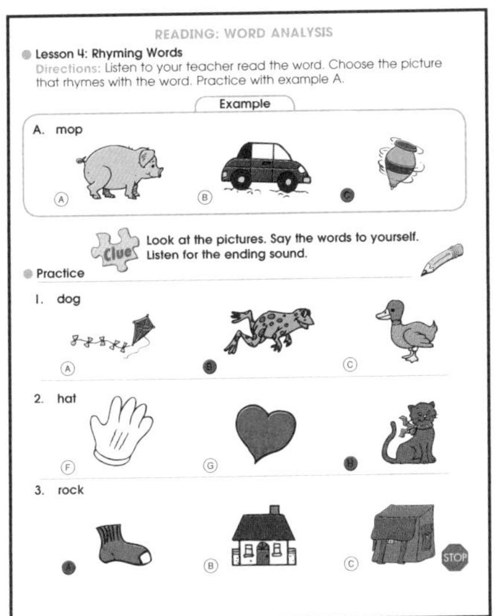

READING: WORD ANALYSIS

Lesson 4: Rhyming Words

Directions: Listen to your teacher read the word. Choose the picture that rhymes with the word. Practice with example A.

Example

A. mop (A) (B) (C)

Clue: Look at the pictures. Say the words to yourself. Listen for the ending sound.

Practice

1. dog (A) (B) (C)
2. hat (F) (G) (H)
3. rock (A) (B) (C)

STOP

189

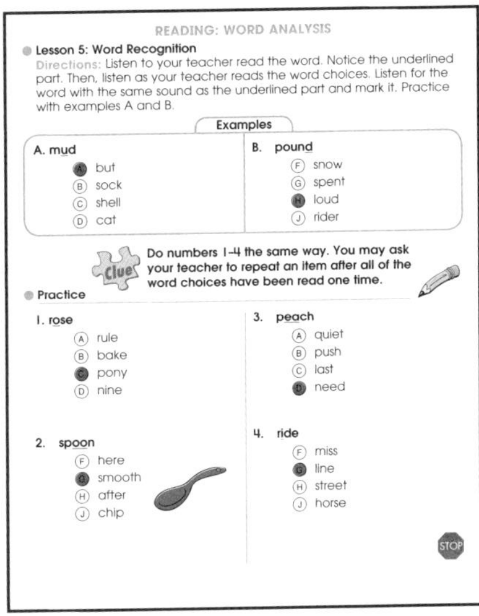

READING: WORD ANALYSIS

Lesson 5: Word Recognition

Directions: Listen to your teacher read the word. Notice the underlined part. Then, listen as your teacher reads the word choices. Listen for the word with the same sound as the underlined part and mark it. Practice with examples A and B.

Examples

A. mud
(A) but
(B) sock
(C) shell
(D) cat

B. pound
(F) snow
(G) spent
(H) loud
(J) rider

Clue: Do numbers 1–4 the same way. You may ask your teacher to repeat an item after all of the word choices have been read one time.

Practice

1. rose
(A) rule
(B) bake
(C) pony
(D) nine

2. spoon
(F) here
(G) smooth
(H) after
(J) chip

3. peach
(A) quiet
(B) push
(C) last
(D) need

4. ride
(F) miss
(G) line
(H) street
(J) horse

STOP

190

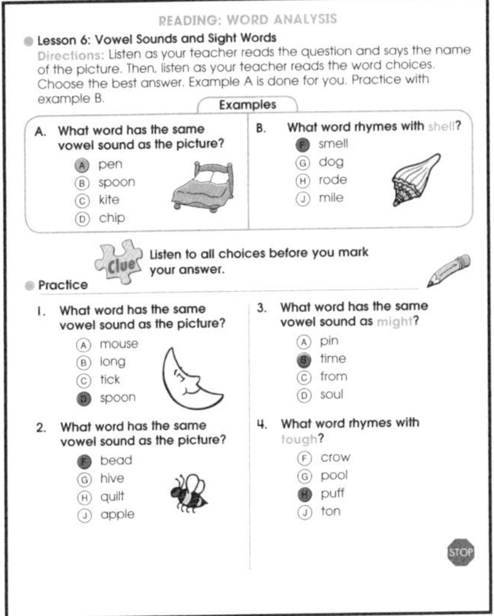

READING: WORD ANALYSIS

Lesson 6: Vowel Sounds and Sight Words

Directions: Listen as your teacher reads the question and says the name of the picture. Then, listen as your teacher reads the word choices. Choose the best answer. Example A is done for you. Practice with example B.

Examples

A. What word has the same vowel sound as the picture?
(A) pen
(B) spoon
(C) kite
(D) chip

B. What word rhymes with shell?
(F) smell
(G) dog
(H) rode
(J) mile

Clue: Listen to all choices before you mark your answer.

Practice

1. What word has the same vowel sound as the picture?
(A) mouse
(B) long
(C) tick
(D) spoon

2. What word has the same vowel sound as the picture?
(F) bead
(G) hive
(H) quilt
(J) apple

3. What word has the same vowel sound as might?
(A) pin
(B) time
(C) from
(D) soul

4. What word rhymes with tough?
(F) crow
(G) pool
(H) puff
(J) ton

STOP

191

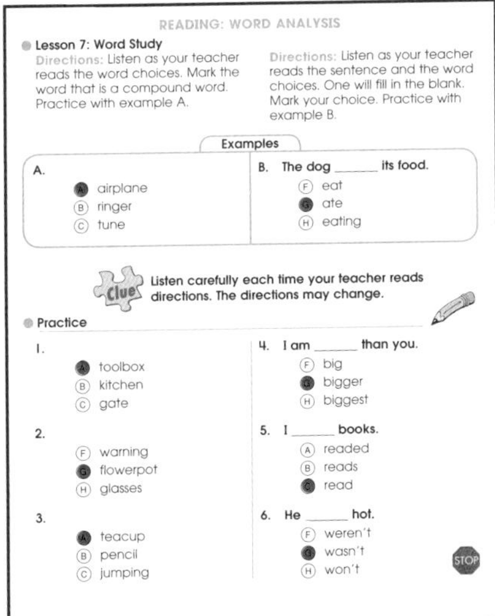

READING: WORD ANALYSIS

Lesson 7: Word Study

Directions: Listen as your teacher reads the word choices. Mark the word that is a compound word. Practice with example A.

Directions: Listen as your teacher reads the sentence and the word choices. One will fill in the blank. Mark your choice. Practice with example B.

Examples

A.
(A) airplane
(B) ringer
(C) tune

B. The dog ______ its food.
(F) eat
(G) ate
(H) eating

Clue: Listen carefully each time your teacher reads directions. The directions may change.

Practice

1.
(A) toolbox
(B) kitchen
(C) gate

2.
(F) warning
(G) flowerpot
(H) glasses

3.
(A) teacup
(B) pencil
(C) jumping

4. I am ______ than you.
(F) big
(G) bigger
(H) biggest

5. I ______ books.
(A) readed
(B) reads
(C) read

6. He ______ hot.
(F) weren't
(G) wasn't
(H) won't

STOP

192

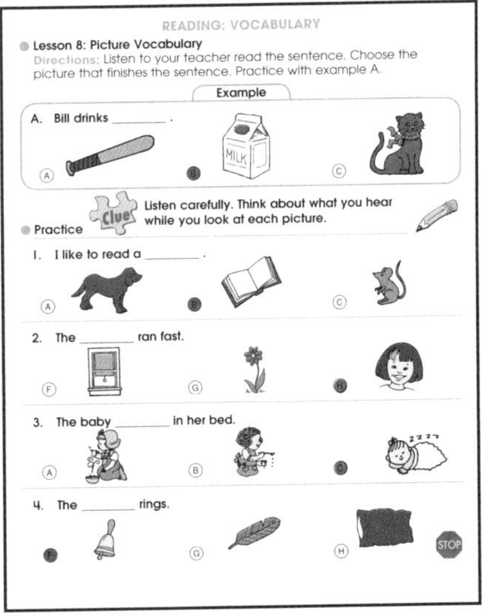

READING: VOCABULARY

Lesson 8: Picture Vocabulary

Directions: Listen to your teacher read the sentence. Choose the picture that finishes the sentence. Practice with example A.

Example

A. Bill drinks ______. (A) (B) (C)

Clue: Listen carefully. Think about what you hear while you look at each picture.

Practice

1. I like to read a ______. (A) (B) (C)
2. The ______ ran fast. (F) (G) (H)
3. The baby ______ in her bed. (A) (B) (C)
4. The ______ rings. (F) (G) (H)

STOP

193

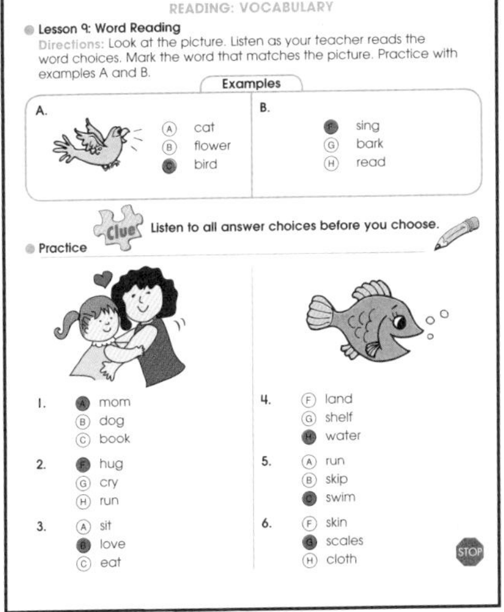

READING: VOCABULARY

Lesson 9: Word Reading

Directions: Look at the picture. Listen as your teacher reads the word choices. Mark the word that matches the picture. Practice with examples A and B.

Examples

A.
(A) cat
(B) flower
(C) bird

B.
(F) sing
(G) bark
(H) read

Clue: Listen to all answer choices before you choose.

Practice

1.
(A) mom
(B) dog
(C) book

2.
(F) hug
(G) cry
(H) run

3.
(A) sit
(B) love
(C) eat

4.
(F) land
(G) shelf
(H) water

5.
(A) run
(B) skip
(C) swim

6.
(F) skin
(G) scales
(H) cloth

STOP

194

Answer Key

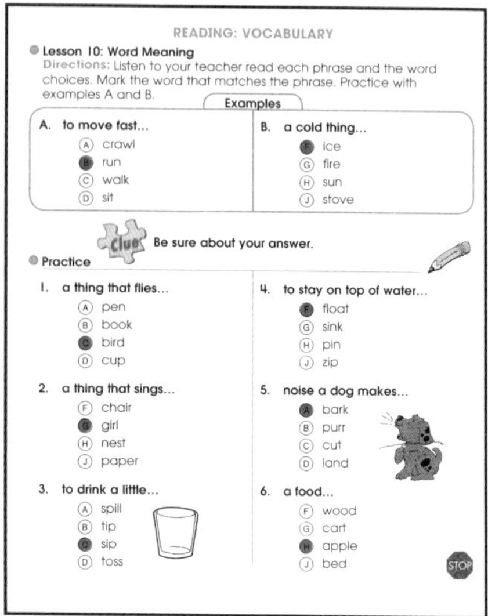

READING: VOCABULARY

Lesson 10: Word Meaning

Directions: Listen to your teacher read each phrase and the word choices. Mark the word that matches the phrase. Practice with examples A and B.

Examples

A. to move fast... (A) crawl ● run (C) walk (D) sit

B. a cold thing... ● ice (G) fire (H) sun (J) stove

Clue: Be sure about your answer.

Practice

1. a thing that flies... (A) pen (B) book ● bird (D) cup
2. a thing that sings... (F) chair ● girl (H) nest (J) paper
3. to drink a little... (A) spill (B) tip ● sip (D) toss
4. to stay on top of water... ● float (G) sink (H) pin (J) zip
5. noise a dog makes... ● bark (B) purr (C) cut (D) land
6. a food... (F) wood (G) cart ● apple (J) bed

STOP

195

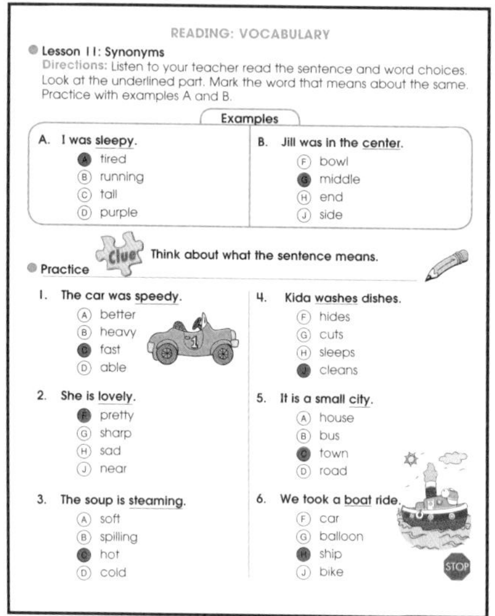

READING: VOCABULARY

Lesson 11: Synonyms

Directions: Listen to your teacher read the sentence and word choices. Look at the underlined part. Mark the word that means about the same. Practice with examples A and B.

Examples

A. I was sleepy. ● tired (B) running (C) tall (D) purple

B. Jill was in the center. (F) bowl ● middle (H) end (J) side

Clue: Think about what the sentence means.

Practice

1. The car was speedy. (A) better (B) heavy ● fast (D) able
2. She is lovely. ● pretty (G) sharp (H) sad (J) near
3. The soup is steaming. (A) soft (B) spilling ● hot (D) cold
4. Kida washes dishes. (F) hides (G) cuts (H) sleeps ● cleans
5. It is a small city. (A) house (B) bus ● town (D) road
6. We took a boat ride. (F) car (G) balloon ● ship (J) bike

STOP

196

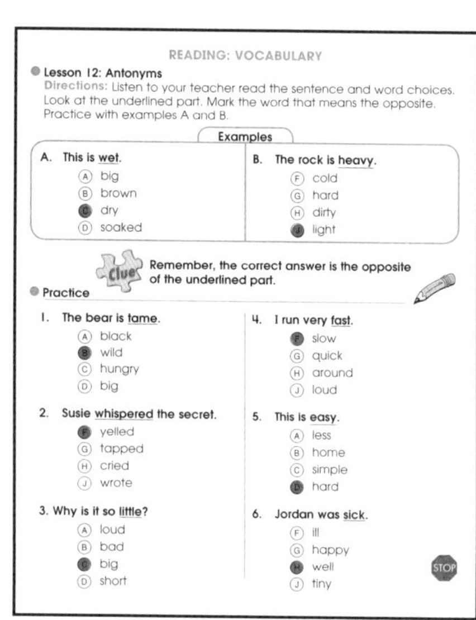

READING: VOCABULARY

Lesson 12: Antonyms

Directions: Listen to your teacher read the sentence and word choices. Look at the underlined part. Mark the word that means the opposite. Practice with examples A and B.

Examples

A. This is wet. (A) big (B) brown ● dry (D) soaked

B. The rock is heavy. (F) cold (G) hard (H) dirty ● light

Clue: Remember, the correct answer is the opposite of the underlined part.

Practice

1. The bear is tame. (A) black ● wild (C) hungry (D) big
2. Susie whispered the secret. ● yelled (G) tapped (H) cried (J) wrote
3. Why is it so little? (A) loud (B) bad ● big (D) short
4. I run very fast. ● slow (G) quick (H) around (J) loud
5. This is easy. (A) less (B) home (C) simple ● hard
6. Jordan was sick. (F) ill (G) happy ● well (J) tiny

STOP

197

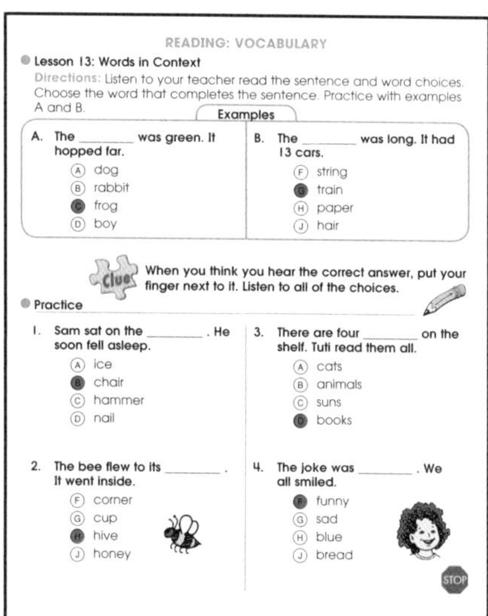

READING: VOCABULARY

Lesson 13: Words in Context

Directions: Listen to your teacher read the sentence and word choices. Choose the word that completes the sentence. Practice with examples A and B.

Examples

A. The ________ was green. It hopped far. (A) dog (B) rabbit ● frog (D) boy

B. The ________ was long. It had 13 cars. (F) string ● train (H) paper (J) hair

Clue: When you think you hear the correct answer, put your finger next to it. Listen to all of the choices.

Practice

1. Sam sat on the ________. He soon fell asleep. (A) ice ● chair (C) hammer (D) nail
2. The bee flew to its ________. It went inside. (F) corner (G) cup ● hive (J) honey
3. There are four ________ on the shelf. Tuti read them all. (A) cats (B) animals (C) suns ● books
4. The joke was ________. We all smiled. ● funny (G) sad (H) blue (J) bread

STOP

198

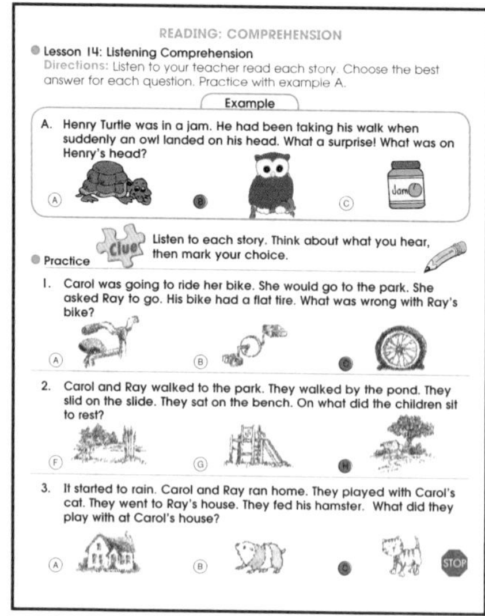

READING: COMPREHENSION

Lesson 14: Listening Comprehension

Directions: Listen to your teacher read each story. Choose the best answer for each question. Practice with example A.

Example

A. Henry Turtle was in a jam. He had been taking his walk when suddenly an owl landed on his head. What a surprise! What was on Henry's head? (A) ● (C)

Clue: Listen to each story. Think about what you hear, then mark your choice.

Practice

1. Carol was going to ride her bike. She would go to the park. She asked Ray to go. His bike had a flat tire. What was wrong with Ray's bike? (A) (B) ●
2. Carol and Ray walked to the park. They walked by the pond. They slid on the slide. They sat on the bench. On what did the children sit to rest? (F) (G) ●
3. It started to rain. Carol and Ray ran home. They played with Carol's cat. They went to Ray's house. They fed his hamster. What did they play with at Carol's house? (A) (B) ●

STOP

199

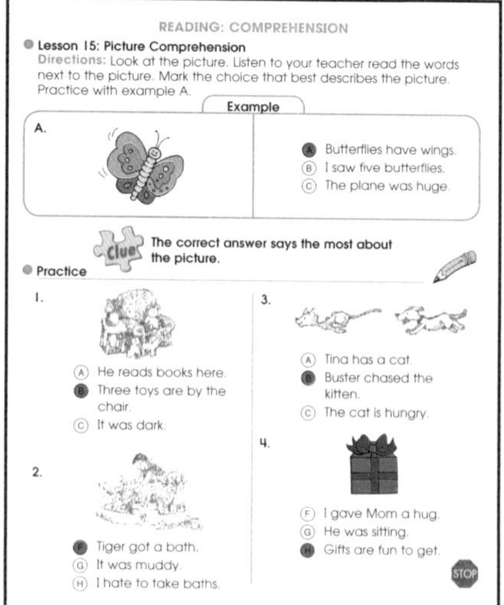

READING: COMPREHENSION

Lesson 15: Picture Comprehension

Directions: Look at the picture. Listen to your teacher read the words next to the picture. Mark the choice that best describes the picture. Practice with example A.

Example

A. ● Butterflies have wings. (B) I saw five butterflies. (C) The plane was huge.

Clue: The correct answer says the most about the picture.

Practice

1. (A) He reads books here. ● Three toys are by the chair. (C) It was dark.
2. ● Tiger got a bath. (G) It was muddy. (H) I hate to take baths.
3. (A) Tina has a cat. ● Buster chased the kitten. (C) The cat is hungry.
4. (F) I gave Mom a hug. (G) He was sitting. ● Gifts are fun to get.

STOP

200

Answer Key

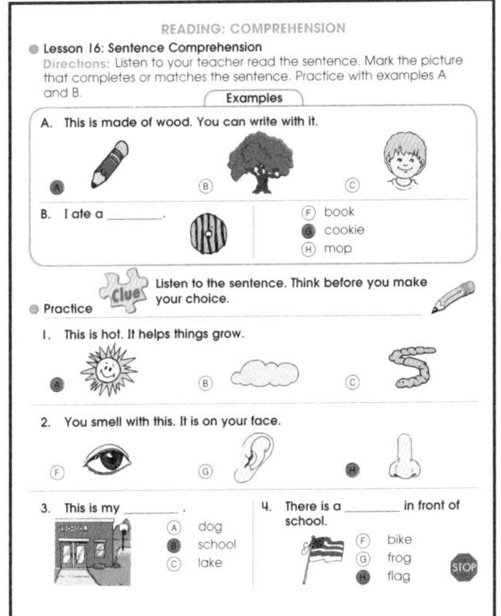

READING: COMPREHENSION

Lesson 16: Sentence Comprehension

Directions: Listen to your teacher read the sentence. Mark the picture that completes or matches the sentence. Practice with examples A and B.

Examples

A. This is made of wood. You can write with it.

● (B) (C)

B. I ate a ______.

(F) book
● cookie
(H) mop

Clue: Listen to the sentence. Think before you make your choice.

Practice

1. This is hot. It helps things grow.

● (B) (C)

2. You smell with this. It is on your face.

(F) (G) ●

3. This is my ______.

(A) dog
● school
(C) lake

4. There is a ______ in front of school.

(F) bike
(G) frog
● flag

STOP

201

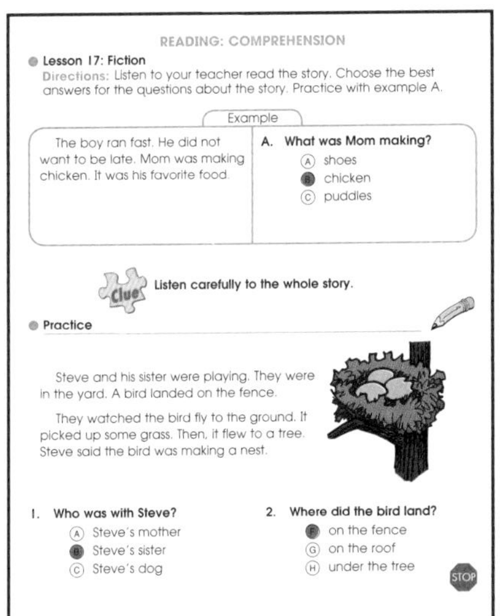

READING: COMPREHENSION

Lesson 17: Fiction

Directions: Listen to your teacher read the story. Choose the best answers for the questions about the story. Practice with example A.

Example

The boy ran fast. He did not want to be late. Mom was making chicken. It was his favorite food.

A. What was Mom making?

(A) shoes
● chicken
(C) puddles

Clue: Listen carefully to the whole story.

Practice

Steve and his sister were playing. They were in the yard. A bird landed on the fence.

They watched the bird fly to the ground. It picked up some grass. Then, it flew to a tree. Steve said the bird was making a nest.

1. Who was with Steve?

(A) Steve's mother
● Steve's sister
(C) Steve's dog

2. Where did the bird land?

● on the fence
(G) on the roof
(H) under the tree

STOP

202

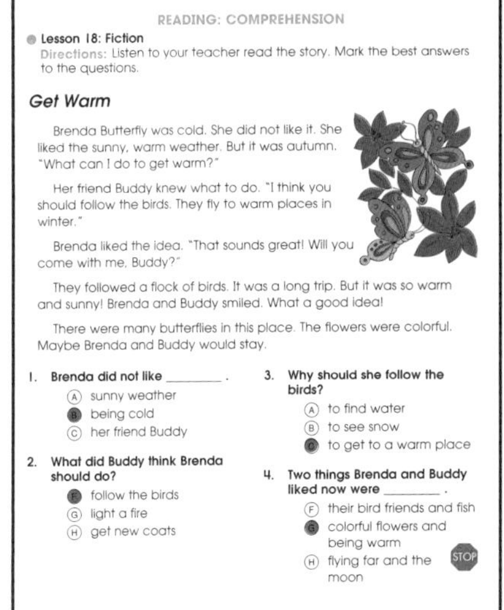

READING: COMPREHENSION

Lesson 18: Fiction

Directions: Listen to your teacher read the story. Mark the best answers to the questions.

Get Warm

Brenda Butterfly was cold. She did not like it. She liked the sunny, warm weather. But it was autumn. "What can I do to get warm?"

Her friend Buddy knew what to do. "I think you should follow the birds. They fly to warm places in winter."

Brenda liked the idea. "That sounds great! Will you come with me, Buddy?"

They followed a flock of birds. It was a long trip. But it was so warm and sunny! Brenda and Buddy smiled. What a good idea!

There were many butterflies in this place. The flowers were colorful. Maybe Brenda and Buddy would stay.

1. Brenda did not like ______.

(A) sunny weather
● being cold
(C) her friend Buddy

2. What did Buddy think Brenda should do?

● follow the birds
(G) light a fire
(H) get new coats

3. Why should she follow the birds?

(A) to find water
(B) to see snow
● to get to a warm place

4. Two things Brenda and Buddy liked now were ______.

(F) their bird friends and fish
● colorful flowers and being warm
(H) flying far and the moon

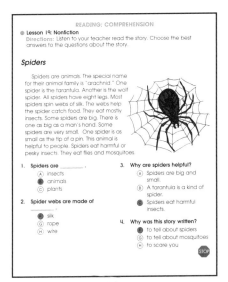

STOP

203

READING: COMPREHENSION

Lesson 19: Nonfiction

Directions: Listen to your teacher read the story. Choose the best answers to the questions about the story.

Spiders

Spiders are animals. The special name for their animal family is "arachnid." One spider is the tarantula. Another is the wolf spider. All spiders have eight legs. Most spiders spin webs of silk. The webs help the spider catch food. They eat mostly insects. Some spiders are big. There is one as big as a man's hand. Some spiders are very small. One spider is as small as the tip of a pin. This animal is helpful to people. Spiders eat harmful or pesky insects. They eat flies and mosquitoes.

1. Spiders are ______.

(A) insects
● animals
(C) plants

2. Spider webs are made of ______.

● silk
(G) rope
(H) wire

3. Why are spiders helpful?

(A) Spiders are big and small.
(B) A tarantula is a kind of spider.
● Spiders eat harmful insects.

4. Why was this story written?

● to tell about spiders
(G) to tell about mosquitoes
(H) to scare you

STOP

204

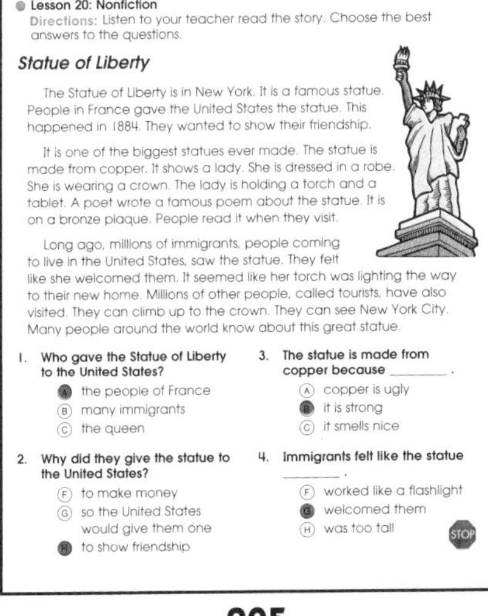

READING: COMPREHENSION

Lesson 20: Nonfiction

Directions: Listen to your teacher read the story. Choose the best answers to the questions.

Statue of Liberty

The Statue of Liberty is in New York. It is a famous statue. People in France gave the United States the statue. This happened in 1884. They wanted to show their friendship.

It is one of the biggest statues ever made. The statue is made from copper. It shows a lady. She is dressed in a robe. She is wearing a crown. The lady is holding a torch and a tablet. A poet wrote a famous poem about the statue. It is on a bronze plaque. People read it when they visit.

Long ago, millions of immigrants, people coming to live in the United States, saw the statue. They felt like she welcomed them. It seemed like her torch was lighting the way to their new home. Millions of other people, called tourists, have also visited. They can climb up to the crown. They can see New York City. Many people around the world know about this great statue.

1. Who gave the Statue of Liberty to the United States?

● the people of France
(B) many immigrants
(C) the queen

2. Why did they give the statue to the United States?

(F) to make money
(G) so the United States would give them one
● to show friendship

3. The statue is made from copper because ______.

(A) copper is ugly
● it is strong
(C) it smells nice

4. Immigrants felt like the statue ______.

(F) worked like a flashlight
● welcomed them
(H) was too tall

STOP

205

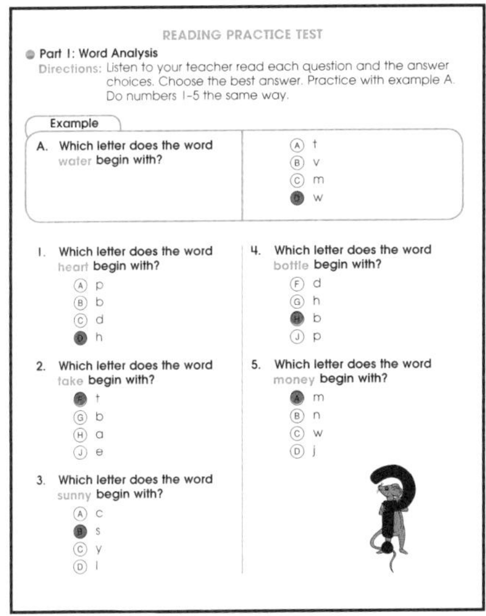

READING PRACTICE TEST

Part 1: Word Analysis

Directions: Listen to your teacher read each question and the answer choices. Choose the best answer. Practice with example A. Do numbers 1–5 the same way.

Example

A. Which letter does the word water begin with?

(A) t
(B) v
(C) m
● w

1. Which letter does the word heart begin with?

(A) p
(B) b
(C) d
● h

2. Which letter does the word take begin with?

● t
(G) b
(H) a
(J) e

3. Which letter does the word sunny begin with?

(A) c
● s
(C) y
(D) i

4. Which letter does the word bottle begin with?

(F) d
(G) h
● b
(J) p

5. Which letter does the word money begin with?

● m
(B) n
(C) w
(D) j

207

Answer Key

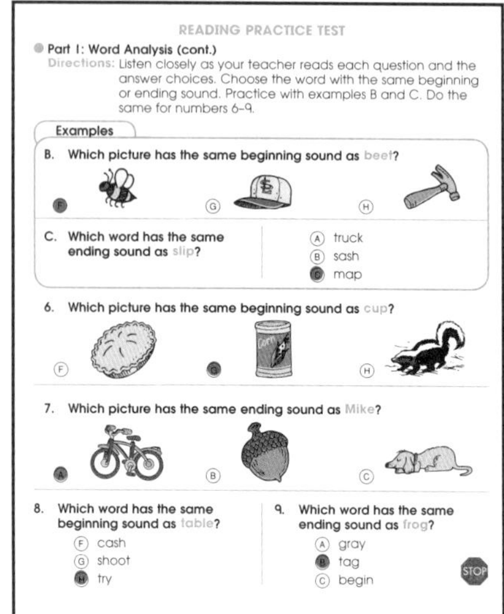
READING PRACTICE TEST

Part 1: Word Analysis (cont.)

Directions: Listen closely as your teacher reads each question and the answer choices. Choose the word with the same beginning or ending sound. Practice with examples B and C. Do the same for numbers 6–9.

Examples

B. Which picture has the same beginning sound as beet?
Ⓕ Ⓖ Ⓗ

C. Which word has the same ending sound as slip?
Ⓐ truck
Ⓑ sash
Ⓒ map

6. Which picture has the same beginning sound as cup?
Ⓕ Ⓖ Ⓗ

7. Which picture has the same ending sound as Mike?
Ⓐ Ⓑ Ⓒ

8. Which word has the same beginning sound as table?
Ⓕ cash
Ⓖ shoot
Ⓗ try

9. Which word has the same ending sound as frog?
Ⓐ gray
Ⓑ tag
Ⓒ begin

STOP

208

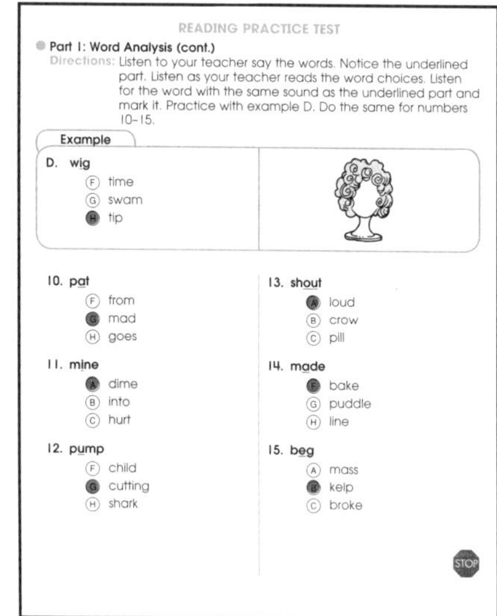
READING PRACTICE TEST

Part 1: Word Analysis (cont.)

Directions: Listen to your teacher say the words. Notice the underlined part. Listen as your teacher reads the word choices. Listen for the word with the same sound as the underlined part and mark it. Practice with example D. Do the same for numbers 10–15.

Example

D. wig
Ⓕ time
Ⓖ swam
Ⓗ tip

10. pat
Ⓕ from
Ⓖ mad
Ⓗ goes

11. mine
Ⓐ dime
Ⓑ into
Ⓒ hurt

12. pump
Ⓕ child
Ⓖ cutting
Ⓗ shark

13. shout
Ⓐ loud
Ⓑ crow
Ⓒ pill

14. made
Ⓕ bake
Ⓖ puddle
Ⓗ line

15. beg
Ⓐ mass
Ⓑ kelp
Ⓒ broke

STOP

209

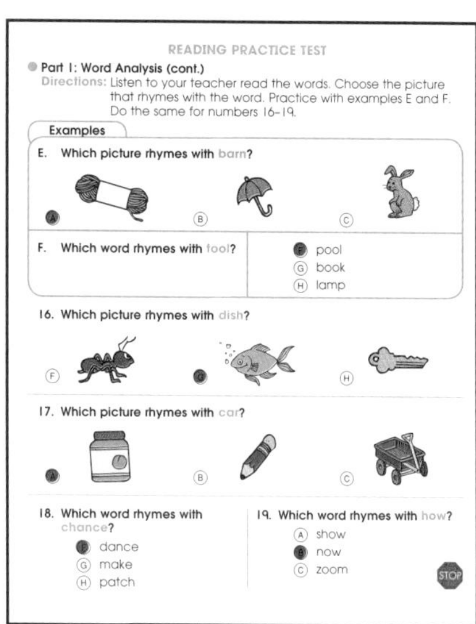
READING PRACTICE TEST

Part 1: Word Analysis (cont.)

Directions: Listen to your teacher read the words. Choose the picture that rhymes with the word. Practice with examples E and F. Do the same for numbers 16–19.

Examples

E. Which picture rhymes with barn?
Ⓐ Ⓑ Ⓒ

F. Which word rhymes with tool?
Ⓕ pool
Ⓖ book
Ⓗ lamp

16. Which picture rhymes with dish?
Ⓕ Ⓖ Ⓗ

17. Which picture rhymes with car?
Ⓐ Ⓑ Ⓒ

18. Which word rhymes with chance?
Ⓕ dance
Ⓖ make
Ⓗ patch

19. Which word rhymes with how?
Ⓐ show
Ⓑ now
Ⓒ zoom

STOP

210

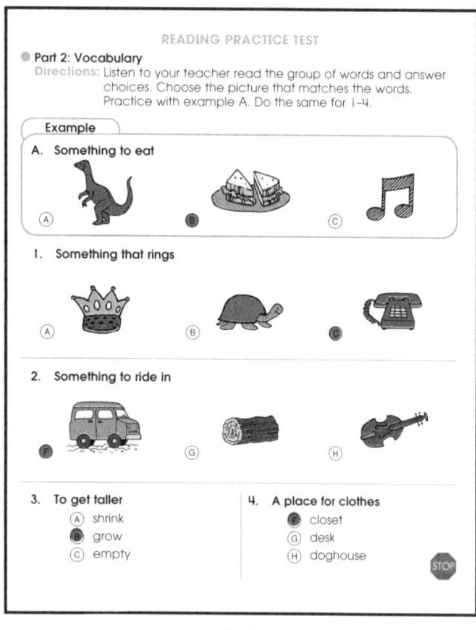
READING PRACTICE TEST

Part 2: Vocabulary

Directions: Listen to your teacher read the group of words and answer choices. Choose the picture that matches the words. Practice with example A. Do the same for 1–4.

Example

A. Something to eat
Ⓐ Ⓑ Ⓒ

1. Something that rings
Ⓐ Ⓑ Ⓒ

2. Something to ride in
Ⓕ Ⓖ Ⓗ

3. To get taller
Ⓐ shrink
Ⓑ grow
Ⓒ empty

4. A place for clothes
Ⓕ closet
Ⓖ desk
Ⓗ doghouse

STOP

211

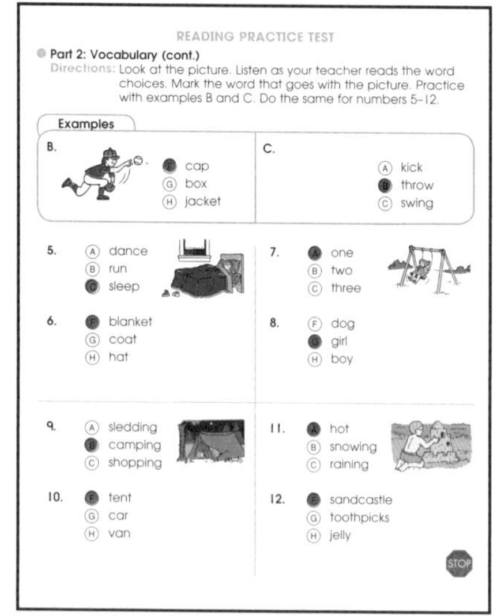
READING PRACTICE TEST

Part 2: Vocabulary (cont.)

Directions: Look at the picture. Listen as your teacher reads the word choices. Mark the word that goes with the picture. Practice with examples B and C. Do the same for numbers 5–12.

Examples

B.
Ⓕ cap
Ⓖ box
Ⓗ jacket

C.
Ⓐ kick
Ⓑ throw
Ⓒ swing

5.
Ⓐ dance
Ⓑ run
Ⓒ sleep

6.
Ⓕ blanket
Ⓖ coat
Ⓗ hat

7.
Ⓐ one
Ⓑ two
Ⓒ three

8.
Ⓕ dog
Ⓖ girl
Ⓗ boy

9.
Ⓐ sledding
Ⓑ camping
Ⓒ shopping

10.
Ⓕ tent
Ⓖ car
Ⓗ van

11.
Ⓐ hot
Ⓑ snowing
Ⓒ raining

12.
Ⓕ sandcastle
Ⓖ toothpicks
Ⓗ jelly

STOP

212

Answer Key

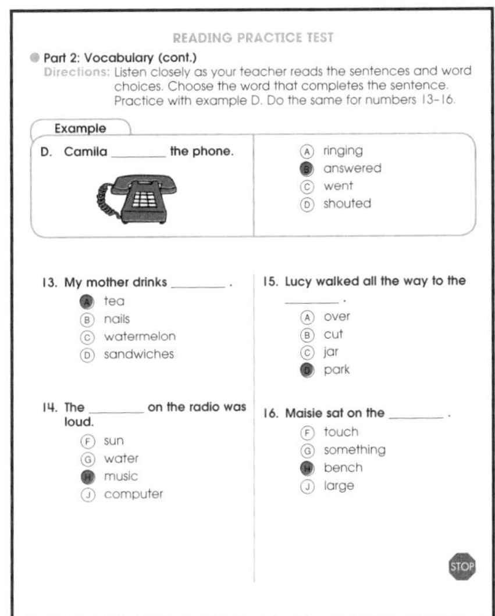

READING PRACTICE TEST

Part 2: Vocabulary (cont.)

Directions: Listen closely as your teacher reads the sentences and word choices. Choose the word that completes the sentence. Practice with example D. Do the same for numbers 13–16.

Example

D. Camila ________ the phone.
- Ⓐ ringing
- Ⓑ answered
- Ⓒ went
- Ⓓ shouted

13. My mother drinks ________ .
- Ⓐ tea
- Ⓑ nails
- Ⓒ watermelon
- Ⓓ sandwiches

14. The ________ on the radio was loud.
- Ⓕ sun
- Ⓖ water
- Ⓗ music
- Ⓙ computer

15. Lucy walked all the way to the ________ .
- Ⓐ over
- Ⓑ cut
- Ⓒ jar
- Ⓓ park

16. Maisie sat on the ________ .
- Ⓕ touch
- Ⓖ something
- Ⓗ bench
- Ⓙ large

STOP

213

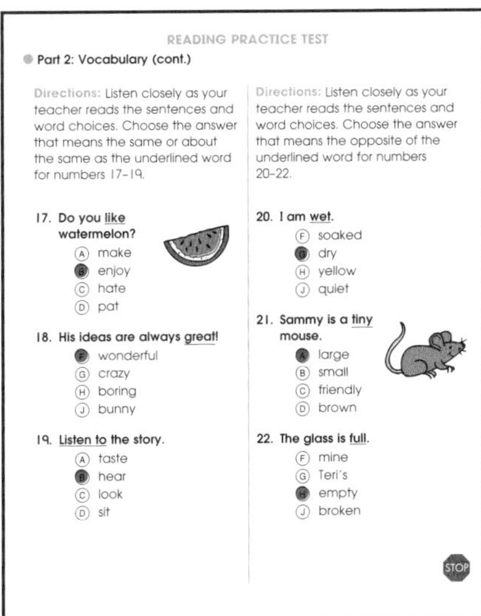

READING PRACTICE TEST

Part 2: Vocabulary (cont.)

Directions: Listen closely as your teacher reads the sentences and word choices. Choose the answer that means the same or about the same as the underlined word for numbers 17–19.

17. Do you like watermelon?
- Ⓐ make
- Ⓑ enjoy
- Ⓒ hate
- Ⓓ pat

18. His ideas are always great!
- Ⓕ wonderful
- Ⓖ crazy
- Ⓗ boring
- Ⓙ bunny

19. Listen to the story.
- Ⓐ taste
- Ⓑ hear
- Ⓒ look
- Ⓓ sit

Directions: Listen closely as your teacher reads the sentences and word choices. Choose the answer that means the opposite of the underlined word for numbers 20-22.

20. I am wet.
- Ⓕ soaked
- Ⓖ dry
- Ⓗ yellow
- Ⓙ quiet

21. Sammy is a tiny mouse.
- Ⓐ large
- Ⓑ small
- Ⓒ friendly
- Ⓓ brown

22. The glass is full.
- Ⓕ mine
- Ⓖ Teri's
- Ⓗ empty
- Ⓙ broken

STOP

214

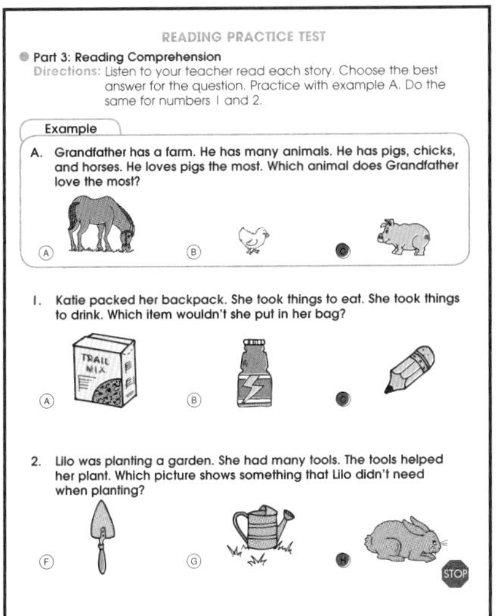

READING PRACTICE TEST

Part 3: Reading Comprehension

Directions: Listen to your teacher read each story. Choose the best answer for the question. Practice with example A. Do the same for numbers 1 and 2.

Example

A. Grandfather has a farm. He has many animals. He has pigs, chicks, and horses. He loves pigs the most. Which animal does Grandfather love the most?

Ⓐ Ⓑ Ⓒ

1. Katie packed her backpack. She took things to eat. She took things to drink. Which item wouldn't she put in her bag?

Ⓐ Ⓑ Ⓒ

2. Lilo was planting a garden. She had many tools. The tools helped her plant. Which picture shows something that Lilo didn't need when planting?

Ⓕ Ⓖ Ⓗ

STOP

215

READING PRACTICE TEST

Part 3: Reading Comprehension (cont.)

Directions: Listen to your teacher read the sentences. Look at the pictures. Choose the sentence that matches the picture. Practice with example B. Do 3–6 the same way.

Example

B.
- Ⓕ Todd ate cereal.
- Ⓖ I love my horse.
- Ⓗ The weather is nice.

3.
- Ⓐ The boat sunk.
- Ⓑ My pen does not work.
- Ⓒ Tanika swims every day.

4.
- Ⓕ Lee gave him a car.
- Ⓖ My dad has a new watch.
- Ⓗ I see the clock.

5.
- Ⓐ We read together.
- Ⓑ I ran away from my brother.
- Ⓒ He plays the flute.

6.
- Ⓕ It was snowing.
- Ⓖ Parker was singing.
- Ⓗ I go to the library.

STOP

216

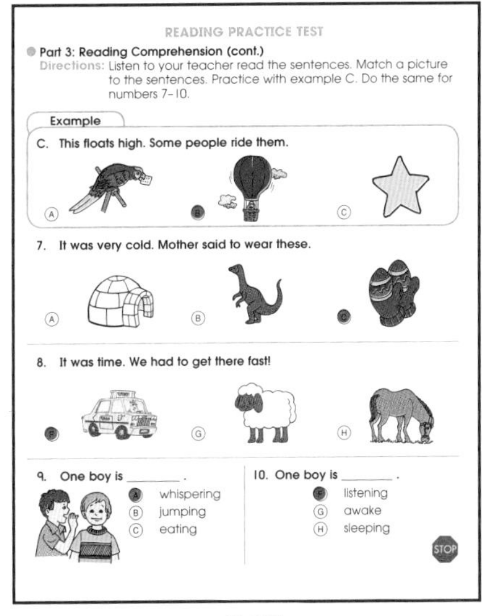

READING PRACTICE TEST

Part 3: Reading Comprehension (cont.)

Directions: Listen to your teacher read the sentences. Match a picture to the sentences. Practice with example C. Do the same for numbers 7–10.

Example

C. This floats high. Some people ride them.

Ⓐ Ⓑ Ⓒ

7. It was very cold. Mother said to wear these.

Ⓐ Ⓑ Ⓒ

8. It was time. We had to get there fast!

Ⓕ Ⓖ Ⓗ

9. One boy is ________ .
- Ⓐ whispering
- Ⓑ jumping
- Ⓒ eating

10. One boy is ________ .
- Ⓕ listening
- Ⓖ awake
- Ⓗ sleeping

STOP

217

Answer Key

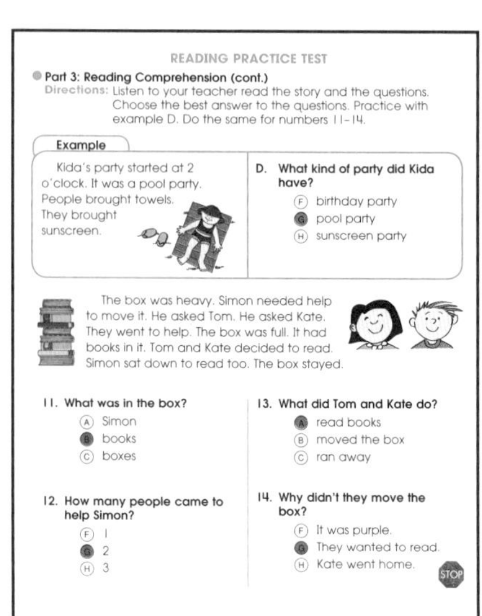

READING PRACTICE TEST

Part 3: Reading Comprehension (cont.)

Directions: Listen to your teacher read the story and the questions. Choose the best answer to the questions. Practice with example D. Do the same for numbers 11–14.

Example

Kida's party started at 2 o'clock. It was a pool party. People brought towels. They brought sunscreen.

D. What kind of party did Kida have?
- (F) birthday party
- (G) pool party
- (H) sunscreen party

The box was heavy. Simon needed help to move it. He asked Tom. He asked Kate. They went to help. The box was full. It had books in it. Tom and Kate decided to read. Simon sat down to read too. The box stayed.

11. What was in the box?
- (A) Simon
- (B) books
- (C) boxes

12. How many people came to help Simon?
- (F) 1
- (G) 2
- (H) 3

13. What did Tom and Kate do?
- (A) read books
- (B) moved the box
- (C) ran away

14. Why didn't they move the box?
- (F) It was purple.
- (G) They wanted to read.
- (H) Kate went home.

STOP

218

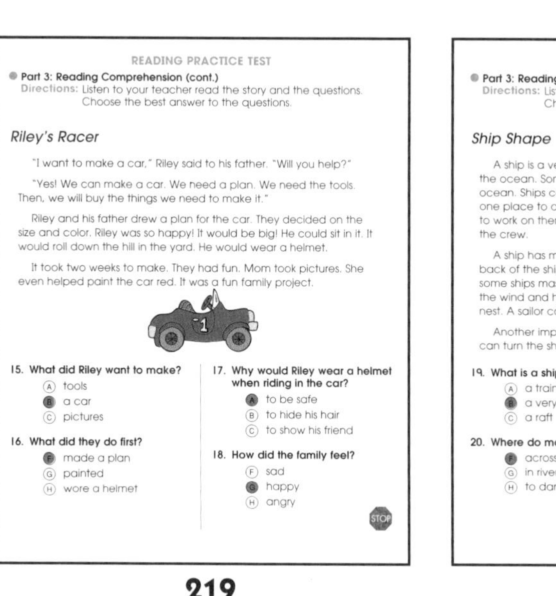

READING PRACTICE TEST

Part 3: Reading Comprehension (cont.)

Directions: Listen to your teacher read the story and the questions. Choose the best answer to the questions.

Riley's Racer

"I want to make a car," Riley said to his father. "Will you help?"

"Yes! We can make a car. We need a plan. We need the tools. Then, we will buy the things we need to make it."

Riley and his father drew a plan for the car. They decided on the size and color. Riley was so happy! It would be big! He could sit in it. It would roll down the hill in the yard. He would wear a helmet.

It took two weeks to make. They had fun. Mom took pictures. She even helped paint the car red. It was a fun family project.

15. What did Riley want to make?
- (A) tools
- (B) a car
- (C) pictures

16. What did they do first?
- (F) made a plan
- (G) painted
- (H) wore a helmet

17. Why would Riley wear a helmet when riding in the car?
- (A) to be safe
- (B) to hide his hair
- (C) to show his friend

18. How did the family feel?
- (F) sad
- (G) happy
- (H) angry

STOP

219

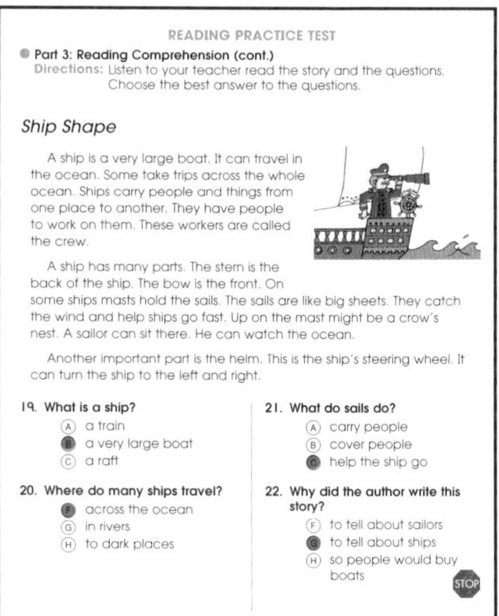

READING PRACTICE TEST

Part 3: Reading Comprehension (cont.)

Directions: Listen to your teacher read the story and the questions. Choose the best answer to the questions.

Ship Shape

A ship is a very large boat. It can travel in the ocean. Some take trips across the whole ocean. Ships carry people and things from one place to another. They have people to work on them. These workers are called the crew.

A ship has many parts. The stern is the back of the ship. The bow is the front. On some ships masts hold the sails. The sails are like big sheets. They catch the wind and help ships go fast. Up on the mast might be a crow's nest. A sailor can sit there. He can watch the ocean.

Another important part is the helm. This is the ship's steering wheel. It can turn the ship to the left and right.

19. What is a ship?
- (A) a train
- (B) a very large boat
- (C) a raft

20. Where do many ships travel?
- (F) across the ocean
- (G) in rivers
- (H) to dark places

21. What do sails do?
- (A) carry people
- (B) cover people
- (C) help the ship go

22. Why did the author write this story?
- (F) to tell about sailors
- (G) to tell about ships
- (H) so people would buy boats

STOP

220

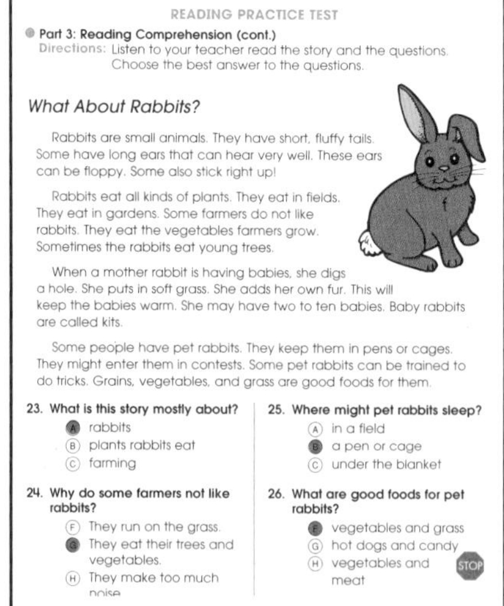

READING PRACTICE TEST

Part 3: Reading Comprehension (cont.)

Directions: Listen to your teacher read the story and the questions. Choose the best answer to the questions.

What About Rabbits?

Rabbits are small animals. They have short, fluffy tails. Some have long ears that can hear very well. These ears can be floppy. Some also stick right up!

Rabbits eat all kinds of plants. They eat in fields. They eat in gardens. Some farmers do not like rabbits. They eat the vegetables farmers grow. Sometimes the rabbits eat young trees.

When a mother rabbit is having babies, she digs a hole. She puts in soft grass. She adds her own fur. This will keep the babies warm. She may have two to ten babies. Baby rabbits are called kits.

Some people have pet rabbits. They keep them in pens or cages. They might enter them in contests. Some pet rabbits can be trained to do tricks. Grains, vegetables, and grass are good foods for them.

23. What is this story mostly about?
- (A) rabbits
- (B) plants rabbits eat
- (C) farming

24. Why do some farmers not like rabbits?
- (F) They run on the grass.
- (G) They eat their trees and vegetables.
- (H) They make too much noise.

25. Where might pet rabbits sleep?
- (A) in a field
- (B) a pen or cage
- (C) under the blanket

26. What are good foods for pet rabbits?
- (F) vegetables and grass
- (G) hot dogs and candy
- (H) vegetables and meat

STOP

221